THE PLIGHT OF THE TROPICAL RAINFOREST

VANISHING EDEN

With a Foreword by Olivia Newton-John

Editor North American Edition: Edward G. Atkins, PhD

BARRON'S

Preface

Preserving Eden

When I was asked to introduce this beautiful book, I was very flattered and at the same time concerned. How could I, a nonscientist, a nonexpert, write anything of interest prefacing this incredible book. I saw the photos and was greatly moved by their beauty, their clarity, their incredible captivation of life in the rainforest. The text of the first edition is in German, and having a smattering of knowledge of the language (my father was a professor of German, my mother German-born), I could work out a few words here and there. My parents never taught my brother, my sister, or me the language because it was their way of communicating privately in front of us. Fortunately, one doesn't need to be bilingual nor a genius to understand what these pictures are telling us—the danger this delicate ecosystem is in and the graveness of the situation. The best way I feel I can contribute is to share some of my feelings and my personal experiences of the rainforest.

Although I now live in America, I was raised in Australia and have a farm there that borders a rainforest. One of the joys of going home is to wander through the giant Morton Bay fig trees that have stood for hundreds of years and to hear the sounds of the many varieties of wildlife that live there. Sadly, this rainforest is very small, most of it having been cut down many years ago for farms such as mine.

In 1989, I was very fortunate to have acted as a reporter for a news program that was doing a piece on the Brazilian rainforest. My husband, Matt, and I flew to Manaus. We arrived at night, and I always will remember the feeling of excitement and anticipation at being there—the humidity, the new sounds, and the smells. The dawn brought with it the sounds of the jungle that bordered our hotel. On our first day, we flew over the rainforest canopy in a helicopter and it was absolutely awe inspiring—as far as our eyes could see, green and thick, lush forest, but dotted everywhere with the smoke and flames from the burning.

The second day we went to the Rio Negro River in a small boat, and this is when I felt overwhelmingly that I had to do all I could to help the world to see that we have to preserve this wondrous, irreplaceable, and beautiful place. I can't begin to explain the feeling of looking into the water and seeing thousands of tiny fish feeding, or of disturbing hundreds of birds from the trees as our boat puttered along the river, or of viewing the numerous species of plants on the banks that were so lush and varied, that it took my breath away. Look through the photographs in *Vanishing Eden* to begin to get some sense of what I experienced.

Over the course of the week that we were there, we witnessed much. We spoke with the local farmers—the ones we hear so much about in the American papers, the ones who slash and burn the forest to grow crops. From them we heard the other side of the problem. These poor farmers, whose only way of survival is off the land, were given land as a promise of a better life, only to find that the burnt rainforest cannot support them for long. After the canopy is removed, the fragile soil is too thin and unprotected for long-term farming; so the farmers move on and start the same process all over again. These people, of course, are a small problem compared to the ranchers who cut and burn thousands of acres to graze cattle only to find that after approximately ten years the same problems apply.

The governments really have to find ways of encouraging the planting of crops that will not require deforestation, and the farming of self-replenishing crops such as rubber and Brazil nuts. It is the largest and most overwhelming problem, for the life-giving force of the rainforest not only supports its own system, but is interconnected to much of the world's climate It is feared that destruction of the rainforest will cause global warming, the loss of indigenous peoples, the loss of untold medical cures from plants that may be destroyed before they are even discovered, as well as the obvious loss of animal species, many of which have even yet to be found and identified.

I am not a politician nor a scientist. My connection to these environmental issues is as a concerned citizen and as a goodwill ambassador for the United Nations Environment Programme—a position I accepted with great honor. I feel that my way of helping is by letting people know that we all have influence preserving the rainforest with our daily choices. Our purchase power for instance. By buying Brazil nuts, latex products, and so on, we encourage the farming of these products. And by avoiding such rainforest woods as teak and mahogany, we'll stop the demand for them. I don't mean to oversimplify the enormity of the problems that face the world in the preservation of the tropical forests. It's going to take worldwide cooperation of the industrialized nations to help the third world countries solve these complex, but ultimately solvable problems.

I believe that mankind can and will find solutions to help resolve the deforestation of the rainforests of the world. I know many people feel totally helpless in the face of our environmental problems, and I understand this feeling. But we must all believe that we can turn things around and educate mankind, that the greed and short-sightedness must end, that we can find the answers.

When I became a mother, I made the promise to my daughter that I would fight for her to have a healthy planet...and this promise, I intend to keep.

Olivia Newton-John
Goodwill Ambassador for the
United Nations Environment Programme

THE PLIGHT OF THE TROPICAL RAINFOREST

VANISHING EDEN

BARRON'S

Contents

Thomas Wassmann

The Discovery of Endless Forests: First Accounts Five Hundred Years Ago

Five hundred years ago, adventurers and navigators brought back to Europe the first accounts of tropical rainforests, but it was only recently that scientists began to unlock the secrets of a world whose wealth of creativity goes beyond anything the human mind has yet imagined.

Christopher Columbus, who discovered the tropical world of the Caribbean in 1492, told about the "profusion of nature everywhere" in the rainforest. Three hundred years later the young Alexander von Humboldt described it in similarly ecstatic terms.

Nature in its pristine state

This oil painting produced by Ferdinand Bellermann in 1866 makes the inaccessibility and impenetrability of this river scene in the middle reaches of the Orinoco River look almost too romantic, but the primordial extravagance of the rainforest vegetation is observed in accurate detail and reproduced with masterly skill.

Artistic exploration of new lands

Christopher Columbus (1451–1506) (top) discovered the New World for Europe. His travel accounts show him to have been deeply impressed by the tropical vegetation, even though

he became familiar only with plants near the coasts of some Caribbean islands. Engraving of Columbus by Theodro de Bry (1590). The utter strangeness of the newly discovered lands was perplexing to discerning observers and gave rise to reactions in which the very foreignness of a scene was often deliberately emphasized—as in this lithograph of a Brazilian family of Botokudo (bottom) or in this luminous, rain-washed view of a tropical rainforest (right page).

The planet Earth is often called the blue planet. The first astronauts assigned it that color during their early space flights because, from the icy distance of space, it looked like a shimmering sapphire against a background of black velvet. A closer look reveals a planet clothed in green; no other heavenly body of our solar system displays this color. The color green has a special significance; it is the most reliable indicator of life and consequently sends a message: Our Earth is a special case, the result of a unique set of conditions, as well as chemical, physical, and historical contingencies. Earth is not subject to the extremes of other planets, but represents a happy coincidence of favorable conditions for life.

Green plants, like much of life, developed over the course of billions of years, and most of their history took place in the water. Plant life first ventured onto land only about 400 million years ago. As soon as plant life had spread across the continents, it proceeded to create the most diverse of all plant-based ecological communities: the forests of the equatorial latitudes. In these regions, luxuriant green vegetation has remained the special mark of forests. It was in the tropical climates that the evolution of flowering plants started about 125 million years ago, in the Cretaceous period, and until the present day the tropics have remained the real center of diversity for most plant life. One is tempted to say that vegetation can be seen in its full magnificence only in the tropics. By comparison, all other plant communities found in regions outside the tropics appear impoverished, the results of the adaptation and specialization made necessary by different ecological conditions.

About half the earth's forests lie in the equatorial belt between the Tropic of Cancer and the Tropic of Capricorn. Only parts of these broad-leaved evergreen forests are rain or cloud forests, no doubt the most magnificent and abundantly diversified ecosystem in the world. With almost constant temperatures above 68°F (20°C) and a rainfall of at least 70 inches (1,800 mm) distributed more or less evenly throughout the year, rainforests evolved almost independently of each other on different continents. Rainforests are found in South America in the Amazon and Orinoco basins, in Central America, in central Africa and Madagascar, in South East Asia, and throughout the entire Malay Archipelago. Smaller areas of rainforest exist even in northeastern Australia. Almost half of Earth's rainforest is found in South America; Africa and Asia each claim about one fifth; and the rest is located in Central America and Australia. In 1492, only five days after landing in what is now San Salvador, Christopher Columbus reported seeing strange trees with different kinds of branches seemingly growing from the same trunk. This is the first authentic account of a rainforest in the New World. At the time, Columbus could not know that he was describing a tree in an evergreen tropical forest, a tree covered with hanging air plants, or epiphytes, ranging in size from small plants to shrubs. There is a vast difference between a tropical forest and the forests Columbus would have seen in central and southern Europe, and his amazement is easy to understand.

Gonzalo Fernandez de Oviedo, an early New World explorer, wrote in 1526: "I would say that the trees are so numerous and stand so close together that it is impossible to see the sky from the ground. This world could really be compared to a huge, dark sea, only some of which is visible, while by far the greater part is impenetrable to our eyes."

The tropical rainforest is a phenomenon that reveals itself only slowly to our senses and our understanding. Even today, the sight of a rainforest evokes respect and amazement. How much more amazing it must have appeared to the first European discoverers!

The world of the Phoenicians, Greeks, and Romans was centered around the Mediterranean Sea, including the Near East, neighboring North Africa, and those parts of Europe that had been explored in military campaigns. Whether these seafaring peoples ventured outside the relatively surveyable Mediterranean world in the first millennium before Christ and possibly discovered parts of the New World remains a controversial question in the absence of written sources and archaeological evidence. Wherever references to regions lying outside the Mediterranean realm are found in ancient sources, there is no clear line dividing realistic accounts from myth.

In early recorded history, it is generally only the military exploits that are described with great geographical exactness. Thus we have relatively detailed information about Alexander the Great's campaign into India, and the accounts of these exploits—which prove that as early as the fourth century B.C. the mental horizon of the Greeks had begun to extend beyond the limits of the Mediterranean world—including some remarkable observations on the landscape traversed. The Indian campaign was probably also the first occasion on which citizens of classical Greece encountered the very different natural world of the tropics and its creatures.

As a result of these travels, the Greeks became acquainted with a wild form of our modern cultivated banana and with rice, sugar cane, and a number of aromatic plants. Around 300 B.C. Theophrastus of Eresus, a philosopher and naturalist, described and commented on the new botanical discoveries. In his writings there is an interesting passage describing a mangrove forest in which trees—as Theophrastus says—"grow in the sea." This is the first scientific mention of a tropical forest, and a rather unusual kind at that.

From the great age of discovery

The history of global discovery during the fifteenth century centers around relatively few names. Amerigo Vespucci (1451–1512) (top) is commemorated in the names of the American continents.

An anonymous colored copperplate engraving of his portrait appears to be a copy of a contemporary painting. Vasco da Gama (1460–1524) (bottom) was surely one of most important seafarers and discoverers of that time.

Theophrastus was probably referring to stretches of mangrove forest along the Red Sea, the most northerly occurrence of this strange ecological community of trees that grow in the tidal zones. For centuries, explorers traveled mainly by ship, so mangroves were usually the first trees they saw in the newly discovered tropical regions.

In late antiquity and even more during the Middle Ages, reports from the earth's warmer regions were few and far between. In European monasteries, where the study, both theoretical and practical, of botany was carried on, monks kept busy with a close examination of plants from the world around them. The great discoveries of unknown and almost unimaginably far-away continents—discoveries that ushered in the beginning of modern civilization—allowed new and tremendous advances to be made in the knowledge of nature outside of Europe.

One of the most fateful ventures in modern history

began on August 3, 1492, when Christopher Columbus, sponsored by Ferdinand and Isabella of Spain, set out with three ships to find a sea passage westward to India. On October 12 of the same year, the flagship *Santa Maria,* along with the accompanying vessels *Pinta* and *Niña,* landed on the Bahamian island of San Salvador and, a little later, on what are now Cuba and Haiti. On this first voyage Columbus discovered parts of the Caribbean island world. By March 4, 1493, he was back in Lisbon with his

three caravels, and on March 15 he returned to Palos, Spain the port from which he had started.

Aboard ship on the way back to Europe, Columbus—under the impression that he had reached India—wrote a fairly lengthy travel account in the form of a letter. This is the famous "Letter Concerning Recently Discovered Islands," a Latin version of which appeared in print in Rome in April 1493. Columbus speaks with unbounded enthusiasm of the many material advantages his discoveries would unfold, of the

possibility of converting entire peoples to Christianity, and also of the incredibly lush island vegetation. His descriptions of nature are probably the first based on an actual encounter with a tropical rainforest.

That same year, Columbus—known in Spain as Cristóbal Colón—set out on his second sea voyage, this time with 17 ships. He discovered Jamaica, Puerto Rico, and the Lesser Antilles before returning in 1496. It was not until his third journey (1498–1500), undertaken with six

ships, that Columbus actually reached the South American mainland near the island of Trinidad and the mouth of the Orinoco River. The age of discovery was launched.

The voyages of Columbus had revealed new lands, but there was at first no clear awareness that these lands were of continental dimensions. Even the explorations of the northern and northeastern coast of South America undertaken by the Italian explorer Amerigo Vespucci, first in the service of

In the first Latin edition of Christopher Columbus's travel letters, the Indians are depicted as cannibals (left page). One of the first maps of the South American continent (right page) was published in Diego Homen's atlas, published around 1558. The Orinoco River was at that time known in its approximate dimensions, whereas the mouth of the Amazon River is shown on the map merely as an unusually large bay.

A scientist discovers new wonders of the world

Alexander von Humboldt (1769–1859) (below) was one of the foremost natural scientists of the nineteenth century. Together with the

Frenchman Aimé Bonpland, he traveled through the rainforest regions of Venezuela, Colombia, Ecuador, Peru, and Mexico. The wood engraving (1877) was made from a painting by Ferdinand Keller (right), which shows the explorer with some forest Indians in the middle reaches of the Orinoco. Humboldt tried to see and describe nature as a unified whole. The results of his research were published in more than 30 volumes. "I may go crazy if this series of miracles does not cease soon," he wrote in his travel journal.

Spain (1499–1500) and later of Portugal (1501–1502) initially brought no major revision of geography. However, Vespucci, unlike Columbus, was convinced that what he had found on the other side of the Atlantic was a new continent.

That is why German cosmographer Mathias Ringmann, in a broadside published in 1507, called Vespucci the true discoverer of the New World. Ringmann gave the new continent the name "America" and specifically instructed carto-grapher Martin Waldseemüller to enter this new name on a globe. Although Waldseemüller used the name America only to designate the regions newly described by Vespucci, the term quickly gained currency as the name of the entire hemisphere.

At approximately the time of Vespucci's discoveries, Pedro Álvares Cabral, a Portuguese navigator, sailed across the Atlantic to the southwest and, on April 22, 1500, discovered the coast of what is now the state of Bahia in Brazil. The Spaniards Vicente Yañez Pinzón and Diego Lepe are said to have landed on the Brazilian coast a few months before Cabral. These explorers, too, were at first uncertain whether they had found a continent or an unusually large island. The name they gave to the new land, "Tierra de Santa Cruz," remained in use well into the sixteenth century, when it was gradually replaced by the name "Brazil." This name was derived from "brasil," the Portuguese word for brazilwood, a red wood yielded by a certain tree (*Caesalpinia echinata*) native to South America. ("Brasil" comes from Spanish "brasa," meaning "live coal.") Cabral had discovered this tree—highly valued in his time for the dye its wood yielded—along the east coast of South America.

Although the sea voyages to Central and South America were not the only travels undertaken to find out more about a world still largely unknown—in 1498 Vasco da Gama, sailing under orders of the Portuguese crown, had found a sea passage to India around the Cape of Good Hope—the exploration of the South American continent is of particular interest as a demonstration of the motivations, successes, and consequences associated with the new discoveries. Rounding out knowledge of what the earth looked like was hardly the sole motive for these enterprises. The immediate purpose was almost always the search for new resources, the exploitation of natural materials, the subjugation of native peoples, and, wherever possible, their forced conversion to Christianity. Past historians have represented the movement to conquer new horizons, a movement initiated by the Spaniards and Portuguese at the turn of the sixteenth century, as a great

cultural achievement and have depicted it in needlessly glorious colors. It undoubtedly brought the mother countries untold riches, but modern critics also see it as the first step in the course that led to the disastrous economic and social situation in which most of the Latin American countries find themselves today.

As early as 1494, the Portuguese and the Spaniards had settled on a boundary to delineate their spheres of interest in South America. A meridian running 370 miles west of the Cape Verde Islands was established as the demarcation line. This meridian cut off the mouth of the Amazon and a large part of the coast jutting out eastward from

there and assigned the lands east of this line to Portugal. The huge interior, the dimensions of which no one had any idea, was claimed by Spain. Here, as later in North America, discovery of the Atlantic coast determined the division of the territory. By claiming a narrow strip of land along the sea, Portugal almost automatically acquired the entire huge country of Brazil, for at first only the coastal zone was of any importance. There were neither the monetary resources nor, for that matter, the settlers to open up the vast interior of the continent.

Systematic exploration of what the land was like—in particular, examination of the phenomena of vegetation that depended on

Circling the Earth

The Antis, or Campas is the title of this crayon lithograph (left), which focuses on the way of life of the rainforest dwellers of Peru and depicts typical animals of their environment. It was thanks to the Bavarian king

Maximilian Joseph I (1756–1825) (top) that the Munich scientists von Spix and von Martius were able to take part in an Austrian expedition to South America. The knowledge these scientists gained and published in book form afterward is still considered a brilliant accomplishment in systematic botany. Captain James Cook (1728–1779) (bottom) was the last of the great explorers who set out to discover unknown parts of the world by sailing across the oceans.

Impressions of exotic beauty

Maria Sybilla Merian (1647–1717) (below), the daughter of the well-known engraver Matthaus Merian, the Elder, inherited her father's artistic talent and was also an outstanding biologist. She was invited by the Dutch govern-

ment to work in Surinam in the years 1699 to 1701, and in 1705 she published a remarkable work about her findings, *Metamorphosis Insectorum Surinamensium*. The colored copperplate engraving *Pomegranate with Different Cicadas* (right) is from this book. The illustrations of the plant *Zomicarpa steigeriana* (right page), taken from a lavish work on botany published in 1879, are an example of the care natural scientists invested in books identifying plants.

the tropical climate and of an animal world shaped by unique historical and ecological factors—was a subject of no great interest in the sixteenth and seventeenth centuries. Territorial ownership was clearly foremost in everyone's mind. Only in exceptional cases was any mention made of the physical and biological nature of the tropical world in the reports and letters sent back to Europe. In the years after 1550, French traders came to what first seemed like an estuary but turned out to be the coastal bay of Rio de Janeiro and, with the tacit approval of the Portuguese, tried to establish a French colony (La France Antarctique) there. Among the colonists was a Franciscan monk by the name of André Thevet, who was interested in geography, collected flora and fauna, and captured many impressions of the new land in written accounts and descriptions. Georg Markgraf was

in the same tradition. Around 1630, he arrived in northern Brazil in the retinue of Count Johann Moritz of Nassau-Siegen, the Dutch governor of Recife. While his employer built a cultural center in the European baroque style in the midst of the tropics, Markgraf worked as an astronomer in the first observatory built in the southern hemisphere. At the same time, he directed a cartographic survey of the land and, like Thevet, started collections of plants and animals. Together with Willem Piso, Johann Moritz's personal physician, he published the first work on Brazil's natural history. The book, *Historia naturalis Brasiliae*, appeared in 1648, put out by an Amsterdam publishing house that still exists today and specializes in scientific works. The *Historia* includes extremely detailed reports on the fauna and flora, as well as the geography, meteorology, and ethnology of Brazil; it remained the standard

work on this tropical region until the beginning of the nineteenth century.

With the departure on June 5, 1799, of the frigate *Pizzaro* from the Spanish port of Coruña, one of the most exciting and significant scientific expeditions to South America was under way. Alexander von Humboldt, who had just turned thirty, and his friend, the French physician and botanist Aimé Bonpland, who was five years younger, had received permission from Charles IV to spend an unlimited period of time in the Spanish colonies of South America, regions that were ordinarily inaccessible to foreigners. At the death of his mother, Humboldt had inherited a considerable estate that enabled him to finance the ambitious travels he had long planned. On July 16, Humboldt and Bonpland arrived in Cumaná in what is today Venezuela. For four months, the two scientists explored the immediate sur-

6c   5   6a   7a   6b   7c   4

9a

7b

8

3a

12d

12e   12a

10b

12c   12b   2   9b   13a   10a

14a   14d   13b

1

3b   11a   14c   11b   14b   11c   3c

W. Liepoldt del. Ant. Heringer lith.   K.k.Hofchromolithografie & artist. Instit. v. Ant. Heringer & Sohn Wien.

Two worlds meet

In rainforest landscapes that are only thinly populated (right page), human beings live in harmony with nature. When catching fish or hunting, peoples took only what they needed to live. Systematic and unrestrained exploitation of the rainforest's resources did not begin until the arrival of the Europeans (wooden graving, ca. 1874, right). It resulted,

among other things, in a drastic decline in the numbers of colorful birds. In 1833, a monograph on South American toucans was published; it caused a considerable stir. The picture below is taken from this monograph.

roundings of this settlement, then they moved on to Carácas, and traveled across the llanos to the middle reaches of the Orinoco River. There they set out on their famous raft trip down the river, in the course of which they discovered that the huge river systems of the Amazon and the Orinoco basins were connected. The second part of the expedition took the explorers first to Cuba, then to Cartagena in Colombia, and from there, along the Andes to Quito, Ecuador and Lima, Peru. From Lima they traveled by ship to Mexico, where they spent over a year. Finally they returned to Europe by way of Cuba and Washington, D.C., landing in France on August 3, 1804.

Back in Berlin, Humboldt began the job of analyzing and organizing for publication the data gathered on his journey. Karl Ludwig Willdenow, then director of the Botanical Garden of Berlin, took over responsibility for preparing the sections on plants. In 1808 Humboldt moved to Paris because the institutes there offered him considerably better working conditions for his undertaking, and he stayed in the French capital for almost 20 years. By 1834, 23 volumes of his *Voyage de Humboldt et Bonpland aux Regions Equinoxiales du nouveau Continent, fait en 1799–1804* (English translation: *Personal Narrative of Travels to the Equatorial Regions of the New Continent During the Years 1799–1804*) had been published, an enterprise that exhausted almost all his private means. Botanical findings alone take up 14 volumes, including volumes VII to XIV, in which almost 3,600 previously unknown tropical plant species are described.

Humboldt's scientific work is not, however, limited to the classification of plants or to the field, created by him, of plant geography. It also includes almost all branches of natural science studied at the time. Humboldt combined genius and an encyclopedic mind with immense diligence and an unparalleled devotion to scientific inquiry. He was also aware of the problems caused by the Portuguese and Spanish colonists in South America and, far ahead of his time, spoke unequivocally in defense of human rights. Even though Humboldt did not actually travel in Brazil and the Amazon basin—he was refused entry into this area—his descriptions of the diverse natural world as seen in a large geographic region created an incomparable foundation for further study. The later understanding of tropical ecology was greatly stimulated by the scientific observations Humboldt made in his five-year expedition.

Humboldt was apparently deeply disappointed at being refused permission to travel in Brazil and suggested to Prince Maximilian zu Wied, who from 1815 on devoted himself primarily to ethnology, that he explore this huge area. The prince studied, among other things, the Indian dialects of aborigines who had had no prior contact with European civilization. Max zu Wied branched out into other areas, bringing back to Europe a sizable collection of specimens. He discovered about 80 species

Fascination of the unfamiliar

This aquatint of a raft on the Guayaquil River (right) is based on a sketch by Alexander von Humboldt. It appeared in a travel book

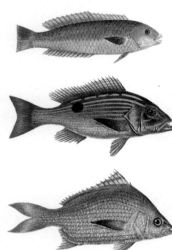

titled *Vue des Cordilleres.* Explorers and scientists continued to be amazed at and fascinated by the rich variety of species of tropical fauna, whether they were looking at bizarre birds of paradise from the Old World tropics (bottom) or fish species (top) first described by the zoologist von Spix in 1829. Tropical reptiles and amphibians (right page) exerted a strange fascination of their own.

of amphibians and reptiles, 468 different birds, and 82 new mammals during his years of travel, and later described them scientifically. His major work, *Travels to Brazil*, was published in Frankfurt in 1820–21 and is an outstanding example of nineteenth-century travel literature as well as an important standard work in the field of scientific research of tropical South America. Max zu Wied was still firmly convinced that tropical nature in its overwhelming prodigiousness was indestructible. "The animal world, the plant world, and even inanimate nature," he wrote in 1820, "are beyond the influence of Europeans and will retain their original vigor; their manifold riches will never be exhausted even if Brazil were to be mined for gold and precious stones to its very core." Only a few decades later, this view turned out to have been a disastrously erroneous underestimation of the

destructive potential of modern industrial civilization.

The matrimonial policies pursued by European ruling houses were to provide a boost for further exploration of the South American continent. The Austrian emperor Francis I decided, on the occasion of his daughter Leopoldina's marriage to the Brazilian heir to the throne, to send along with her a lavishly equipped scientific expedition. Because of the good relations between Francis I and the Bavarian royal family, Maximillian Joseph I was able to arrange for the scientists Johann Baptist von Spix and Karl Friedrich Philipp von Martius to participate in the expedition. The members of the expedition boarded three ships in Genoa and Leghorn in the early summer of 1817, and the *Austria,* with Spix and Martius on board, reached Rio de Janeiro on July 14, 1817. In December the two scientists set out on an inde-

pendent scientific expedition into the interior of Brazil, still largely terra incognita, and initiated a systematic exploration of the rainforests of the Amazon basin. In August 1819, the two scientists set out in a rowboat on a trip up the Amazon. On November 25, they reached the junction of the Amazon and the Japurá rivers and separated there in order to make more efficient use of their

time. Spix continued up the Amazon to the Peruvian border, while Martius opted to follow the Japurá. In early March of the next year, they met again in what is today Manaus, and on June 16 they left the New World. On December 8, 1820, they arrived back in Munich with all the booty their travels had yielded, including specimens of several hundred animals and over 6,000 plant species.

When Spix died suddenly in 1826, Martius assumed the job of analyzing and publishing the results of their journey. His

Tab. X.

Capturing the exotic

These beautifully colored engravings are from Charles Frederic Dubois' famous *Ornithological Gallery, or Portraits of All the Famous Birds,* published between 1834 and 1840. They depict the grenadier

bird (top), the short-tailed manakin (bottom), the striped, long-tailed, and thread-tailed manakins, the ornate diamond bird, and the red-headed manakin (right, from top left to bottom right).

nat. Gr.
Gestreifter Manakin.
Pipra strigilata.
Manakin rubis.

Langschwänziger Manakin.
Pipra longicauda.
Manakin à longue queue.

nat. Gr.
Fadenschwänziger Manakin.
Pipra filicauda.
Manakin à queue efilée

nat. Gr.
Gezierter Panthervogel.
Pardalotus ornatus.
Pardalote paré.

nat. Gr.
Rothköpfiger Manakin.
Pipra rubrocapilla.
Manakin à tête rouge.

The lithograph depicting various plant shapes found in tropical America (left) was published about 1830 in the work Johann Baptist von Spix and Karl Friedrich von Martius (top) produced collectively after their expedition to Brazil in the years 1817 to 1820. The exquisite picture of hummingbirds (bottom) is taken from John Gould's famous book, *A Monograph of the Trochilidae or Family of Hummingbirds*, published in 1861.

Travels in Brazil Undertaken in the Service of Maximilian Joseph I, King of Bavaria is a remarkable travel account, with striking descriptions of a world not yet in the least subjugated by man and still ecologically intact.

Of greater scientific import is the series *Flora Brasiliensis*, begun by Martius and carried on by the distinguished botanist August Wilhelm Eichler. Fifteen volumes were published in Munich and Leipzig between the years 1840 and 1906. This work describes and classifies the flora gathered by 145 collectors. The plants covered belong to 2,253 genera and 22,767 species, 5,689 of which were new. The *Flora Brasiliensis* is not only a mine of scientific data but also a work of art because of the unsurpassed quality of its plant illustrations. It is considered the greatest botanical work devoted to one geographic area.

The great expeditions of the seventeenth, eighteenth, and nineteenth centuries, not all of which were undertaken with the support of wealthy patrons, produced writings that gave a fairly complete picture of the proverbial profusion of nature found in tropical regions. The focus on South America, a focus clearly related to political factors, suggested quite early the exceptional wealth of plant and animal life on this continent, especially in Brazil, which is, after all, the biggest South American country.

However, exploratory and scientific expeditions were not restricted to South America. From 1768 to 1770, when James Cook, the last of the great explorers, sailed around the world for the first time, he investigated, among other places, the east coast of Australia and thus made a significant contribution to knowledge of that important part of the Old World. Among his companions was the ambitious young botanist Joseph Banks. Cook's expedition returned to London with more than 30,000 plant specimens belonging to about 3,600 different species. While aboard ship, the painter Sydney Parkinson painted approximately 900 pictures of plants belonging to the tropical flora of Australia.

In Africa, the famous missionary and explorer David Livingstone set out in 1840 on the first of his arduous expeditions into the interior of the Dark Continent. Having been believed dead, he was found in November 1871 on the eastern shore of Lake Tanganyika by the American journalist Henry Morton Stanley, who addressed him with these famous words: "Dr. Livingstone, I presume?" "Yes," the latter is said to have responded with a friendly smile, raising his hat in greeting. Stanley gave up his journalistic career soon after this encounter and also became a passionate explorer of Africa. In this capacity, he is remembered for his expeditions into the rainforests along the Congo River.

There are many other adventurers and restless wanderers, missionaries and scientists that should be mentioned if we were

Scenes from a faraway world

Here again, the great effort natural scientists made to capture and convey the beauty of nature is evident. The print of *Laborhamphus nobilis,* with its detailed depiction of the bird's gorgeous plumage (right) is taken from the work *Novitates Zoologicae,* published in 1903. John Gould's book about these birds is the source of the delicate picture of hummingbirds shown below.

Old scars are barely visible

The sites of earlier cultures (left) and their monuments have long since been reclaimed by the rainforest. Small surface wounds that humans inflict on the forest ecosystem close quickly. Large areas of devastation, however, will not recover because the potential for regeneration has been destroyed. Earlier settlers in the rainforest were unaware of this. Only the twentieth century has had to face this realization in its full, menacing implications.

to follow the exploration of the rainforests step by step. In each instance, dramatic life histories are associated with the journeys undertaken to penetrate into and understand this huge ecosystem. The data, observations, and accounts related to rainforests everywhere fill entire libraries.

This accumulation of material might imply that tropical rainforests are one of the best understood regions of the biosphere, but this is far from the truth. In view of the immense diversity that characterizes rainforests and in view of their evolutionary history, it is clear that the scientific investigation of rainforests has only just begun and may be coming too late. "Boredom is immoral," the American biologist Charles William Beebe

wrote. "All around us Nature does the most exciting things. All we have to do is look."

Hans-Joachim Fröhlich

An Ocean of Trees: Climbers, Stranglers, and Giants

The sea of rainforest trees is made up of a prodigious variety of species, but the populations of individual species are surprisingly small. As many as 100 different tree species have been counted on a single acre of forest, with hardly any of them occurring more than once. An order beyond our grasp dominates the apparent chaos of the jungle.

A stroke of genius on the part of creation: over 3,500 different tree species populate the tropical parts of the globe, turning their diversity into a strategy of survival.

A confusing wilderness on all levels

In the rainforest one seldom sees regular, constantly recurring shapes. Although the structure of the tree-tops and their foliage are variations of the same simple patterns, they create a spatial complexity that is bewildering at first glance. Everything is meshed and matted, apparently impossible to untangle, yet each section of the life community conforms to a highly structured order.

The rainforest as a spatial structure

The varying levels of treetops, the different shades and fine nuances of color, and the obvious variety of tree heights, foliage densities, and branching patterns convey an accurate impression of the mosaic-like species diversity of rainforests. Shades of red in the tree crowns do not always signal blossoming, but may be simply the color of newly unfolding leaves.

Structures striving toward the sky

Only those trees that grow taller than their neighbors are able to expose their foliage directly to the rays of the sun and get the full benefit of light. Anything lower down is shaded. Here, only plants that can get by on a fraction of full sunlight can grow. Mosses are one kind of plant that has specialized in adapting to such low levels of light. The rough bark of many trees offers a highly textured substrate on which they can grow.

Diverse in every respect

Rainforests are environments with highly complex spatial structures that bear practically no resemblance to other tree-based life communities. Many different levels exist between the forest floor and the canopy, and the coloring of the foliage also displays many gradations. Individual flowers or complex inflorescences diversify the picture even more and prevent any impression of monotony.

Conservative estimates suggest that before humans began to spread across the Earth, one third of the total land area, which amounts to 37 billion acres, was covered with a complex combination of vegetation that we designate as various types of forests. Another third was so dry that no tree growth of any significant density or height could develop. The remaining third was characterized—either because of the altitude of mountains or proximity to the poles—by climates too inhospitable for trees to grow. Needless to say, it is hard to assemble numbers that reflect the global situation. Often these numbers have to be based on estimates or, sometimes, mere conjecture. Even carefully conceived inventories, such as the surveys made by the Food and Agricultural Oganization (FAO) and the United Nations Environment Programme (UNEP), in the late 1970s using satellite images and modern computer analysis systems, can be marred by inaccuracies that are far from negligible in a regional context. We will have more accurate data in the 1990s, when a new inventory will become available.

Counting only the more or less closed forests (areas where shade from trees prevents grass from growing), which are estimated at between 7 and 10 billion square acres (3 to 4 billion hectares), the tropical forests in the equatorial belt between the Tropic of Cancer and the Tropic of Capricorn account for roughly half the Earth's total forested surface. According to an FAO study, the tropical zones of South America, Africa, and Asia contain 4.86 billion square acres (1.97 billion ha) of forest. In these areas, forests make up 40 percent of the land area, a very large proportion in comparison with the rest of the world. The geographical distribution of tropical forests is as follows:

In the tropical zones of South and Central America, 23 countries have rainforests. According to the FAO survey of 1982, these countries account for 1 billion 677 million acres (679 million ha) of primary, closed forest and 536 million acres (217 million ha) of open woodland, a total of about 2 billion 223 million acres (900 million ha), or almost half the primary forests in the tropical belt worldwide.

Except for Argentina, Chile, and Uruguay, all the countries of South America are in the tropics. This is where Amazonia, the largest continuous and probably the most interesting rainforest region of the world, is located. The Andes border it to the west, the smaller mountains of Guyana and Brazil to the north and south. Bolivia, Colombia, Ecuador, French Guiana, Peru, Surinam, and Venezuela also form part of Amazonia. The entire Amazon region is estimated to include about 2,500,000 square miles (6,500,000 km²). This forest region is so large that Texas, with its approximately 267,000 square miles, would fit into it over nine times. The seven Central American countries of Costa Rica, El Salvador, Guatemala, Honduras, Mexico, Nicaragua, and Panama, as well as the Caribbean islands, also lie within the tropical zone.

The tropical forest area of Africa consists of over 1.7 billion acres (703 million ha) of primary forests—536 million acres (217 million ha) of closed forest and 1.2 billion acres (486 million ha) of open woodland. This represents 32 percent of the Earth's tropical forests. Tropical rainforests in Africa are concentrated in the central part of the continent and on the island of Madagascar. Politically, this area is made up of 37 countries, of which the most important is Zaire. Zaire contains almost 10 percent of the global rainforest total, including large stretches of untouched forests. This ecologically positive assessment also applies to Gabon and the Congo, but a number of African countries, especially those on the west coast like Cameroon, the Ivory Coast, and Liberia, are decimating their natural vegetation. The only tropical forests in the east, on the island of Madagascar, are also suffering from human encroachment.

The tropical forest areas of Asia are heterogeneous both in geographical distribution and in species composition. Covering 7.5 percent of the land area and consisting primarily of closed forests—753 million acres (305 million ha) versus 77 million acres (31 million ha) of open woodland—the Asian rainforests are of preeminent importance. Southern Asia, including Bangladesh, Bhutan, India, Nepal, Pakistan, and Sri Lanka, has 164 million acres (66.5 million ha) of forest, which account for less than 15 percent of the land area. Continental Southeast Asia, including Myanmar (formerly Burma) and Thailand has a total of 118 million acres (47.6 million ha) of forests that take up 40 percent of the land area. Most of these forests are concentrated in southern Thailand and the lowlands of Myanmar. In the archipelago of Southeast Asia (Brunei, Indonesia, Malaysia, and the Philippines), conditions vary greatly. Although Brunei still has vast areas of untouched primeval forest and Indonesia boasts the largest rainforest in Asia, the forests on the Philippines have to a large extent lost their natural composition, primarily as a result of slash-and-burn agriculture.

The rainforests in the lowlands of Malaysia (36.5 million acres [147.7 million ha], accounting for 58 percent of the country) in large part have had to give way to palm and rubber tree plantations. The tropical regions of Central Asia (Cambodia, Laos, and Vietnam) are 48 percent wooded, accounting for 90 million acres (36.4 million ha) of forest. In many places the original composition of vegetation has been severely altered. Papua New Guinea in the South Pacific, a territory that is mostly hilly and in places very mountainous, still has large, original rainforests (94 million acres [38.2 million ha] of forest, accounting for 83 percent of the land area). Their inaccessibility has thus far

Everything tries to grow upwards

Light is the primary environmental factor that determines the structure of the canopy, and all light-hungry plants strive toward it. Not an inch of space in the rainforest goes unused. Tree trunks, festooned with multitudes of thin, rope-like liana stems or accompanied by probing roots of strangler figs seeking contact with the ground, stretch upward and lend support to one another. Somewhere between the forest floor and the canopy, lianas bear their flowers, either directly on the slender trunk (far right) or dangling on long strings (right)—whatever the method, the flowers are easily accessible to pollinating insects. Nothing would be more detrimental to the survival of these plants than to hide their blossoms and inflorescences, which are designed in shape and color to attract pollinators, among thick leaves or in a tangle of stems.

The silent battle between trees

The competition for light elicits amazing ingenuity in many trees and other woody plants, and they are anything but fastidious in their choice of strategies.

They clasp and burrow; they hang on like leeches or like clawed beasts, they twist and wind themselves around each other, penetrate each other, crawl on top of each other until they get—at any price—what they sought in all these tricky growth maneuvers: more light and more food. Some species plant roots in their "victims," roots that grow thicker and thicker and slowly but surely choke the host tree. Strangler figs keep growing new air roots from their branches, and the air roots gradually develop into strong pillars. These trees often reach colossal proportions, forming crowns with a diameter of several hundred yards. In many climbing plants, leaves or leaf stems, shoots or roots are modified into regular clasping organs.

Using these organs, lianas, for example, climb other plants. The so-called root climbers develop thin roots that they either sink into the cracks of the tree bark or wrap around the host tree's trunk.

These climbing plants make use of spreading shoots that they send forth into the branches of other plants, where, with the help of thorns and spines, they gain permanent support. No matter how crafty the method, the end—as always in nature— justifies the means.

The many faces of the rainforest

Many rainforest trees vary their multihued evergreen appearance with other colors, be it during the blossoming season or during the phase of new foliage growth. One spectacular example is the

flaming red of the appropriately named fire trees (right page). Strangely, the red pigments of these flowers are not stable and therefore not suitable for use in dyeing. An entirely different effect is created by the moss-draped tree trunks and branches characteristic of the forests in the Ruwenzori Mountains of East Africa, where rain pours down on the vegetation over 300 days per year, thus practically guaranteeing that every component of the forest is continually saturated with water.

prevented their exploitation. On these islands, perhaps more than in any other place, the populations still live in such harmony with nature that large forests remain intact.

Scientists have made many attempts to classify the huge variety of rainforest vegetation. They start with certain factors of climate that allow them to define different climatic environments. Several factors—temperature and precipitation, along with soil type—determine the types of vegetation and the species they represent. Many tropical life forms cannot live in regions that have frost in winter. Conversely, plants and animals that have evolved in the cooler parts of the world would suffer from the heat, experience metabolic imbalances, or fall prey to fungal or other diseases in the equatorial tropics.

Although some plants and animals seem to be able to get along without water, this element is crucial to all life. The truth of this is shown over and over again: The greater the amount of water and the more evenly it is available through precipitation, flowing streams, and soil moisture, the more various the life forms that exist. Where water is plentiful, much less specialization is needed for conserving or finding it. Indeed, where ample water and the right temperatures exist, nature manifests herself in lavish and almost playful variety. Soil, too, plays an important role, determining by its degree of fertility, its ability to hold water, its humus content, and its permeability to roots the combinations of species it can sustain. Another factor to remember is created by the living organisms themselves: The way different species compete with each other for survival also strongly affects the make-up of ecological communities. If, for instance, one kind of tree is able to make better use than another of a certain location and environment, it will prevail in the long run and eventually determine the type of climax vegetation that will evolve. As

agriculture is abandoned in the northern sections of the eastern United States, much of the land is growing back into woods. Oak, aspen, ash, and many other tree species are growing up in what once were fields. Maples ultimately will take over, because maple seedlings can tolerate shade and many others, such as oak, cannot. The maples push their way up through the other growth, and only then spread their crowns to crowd out competitors. Thus, the forest eventually becomes dominated by one or a limited number of species in the temperate zone, but not in the tropics.

Because of the tremendous variety of forest vegetation, any attempt at classification is problematic and bound to fall short of completeness; it should never be regarded as anything more than a device to help establish a mental frame of reference. In terms of global geography, forests, the most important type of vegetation, are classified as follows:

Tropical forests grow along the equator between the Tropic of Cancer and the Tropic of Capricorn and include evergreen and rain-green forests, both moist and dry, in the hot, moderate, and cool tropics. These forests are made up almost exclusively of broad-leaved trees. Many species are intermingled, and there are no seasonal changes.

Subtropical forests lie next to the tropical zone to the north and south. These are rain-green forests in subtropical dry and subtropical winter-rain regions.

In the northern hemisphere, from the 30th to 50th degrees of latitude, lie the forests of the temperate zone. The climate there is moderate but humid, with frost and precipitation periods of various durations throughout the year. The forests are a mixture of conifers and deciduous trees, species diversity is low, and composition of species varies greatly with location.

Boreal forests are found in their characteristic form primarily in the northern hemisphere near

the polar region and in the high mountains. The climate is relatively cold, with cool summers and long winters. The forests consist almost exclusively of conifers of stunted growth and twisted shape. There are a few deciduous species, such as birch, poplar, willow, and alder, that do not need much warmth. Toward the north, boreal forests give way to tundra.

This latitudinal system of classification has to be complemented by a system that defines vegetation in terms of altitude. Altitude affects vegetation dramatically and may make a redrawing of the lines of latitudinal mapping necessary. Thus, the plant growth and distribution of species in subtropical regions with montane altitudes can take on characteristics of the temperate zone.

Rainforests generally have constant, high temperatures and precipitation evenly distributed throughout the year. But this forest type is not determined solely by these two factors, or else all the rainforests on Earth would be practically identical. Many other elements—short or relatively long dry periods, elevation above sea level, soil type, and slope—produce variations. Whether there is flooding and what kind of flooding, the water quality, the presence of land and sea winds, geographical location, and much else affects the diversity of the forests. There has been a growing tendency to focus study on local variants and to call different forest types by the names of the regions where they occur. But if we keep in mind that in nature transitions are fluid—including the borders between the tropics and the subtropics and between the subtropics and the temperate zones—we realize how important it is to have a clear system of reference, one that will, most important, reveal ecological connections. The system proposed by Lamprecht (1986) seems to answer this need best:

1. **Evergreen moist forests**
   Precipitation distributed more or less

A forest without a glimpse of light

A rain or cloud forest is by no means an impenetrable jungle, but many are dense enough to keep one from seeing farther than a few yards into the surrounding

greenery. There are no long views or distant perspectives. A visitor to these forests is plunged into a sea of various leaf shapes and dripping foliage. Greens in every conceivable shade dominate the scene, but occasionally a beautiful flower exerts an optical attraction that inevitably catches the eye (above).

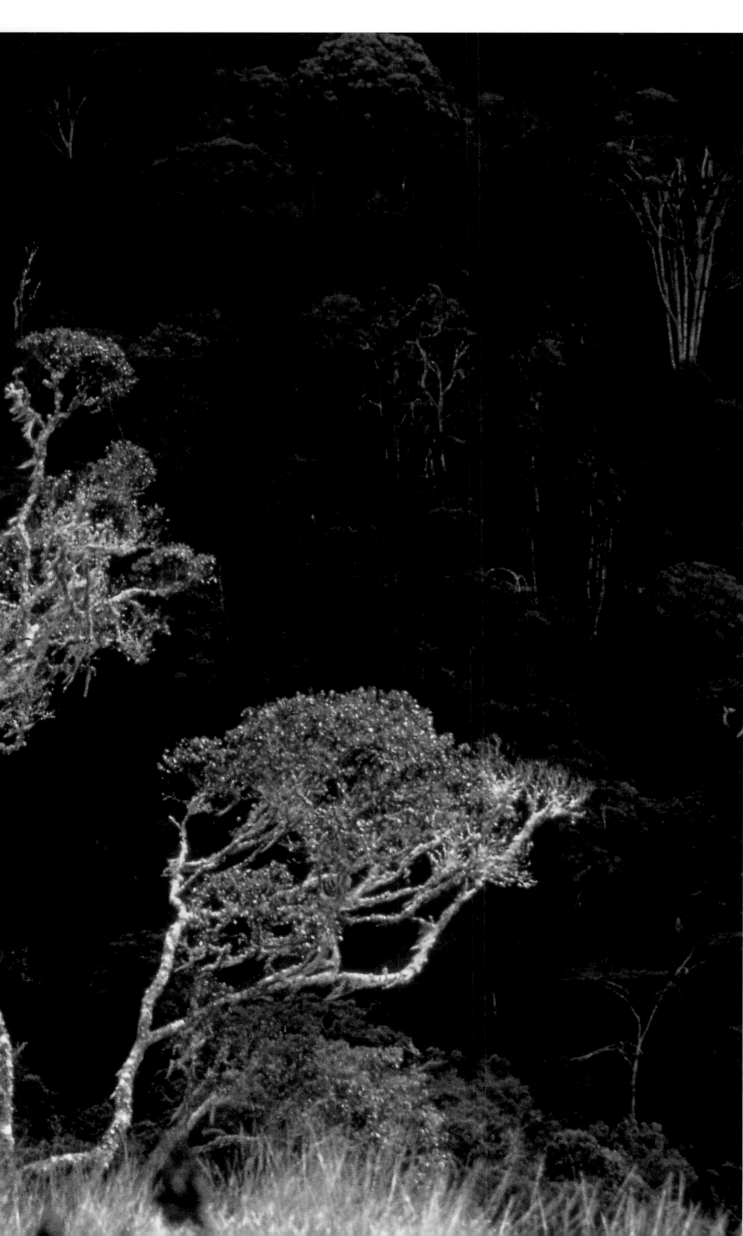

Brightly colored birds

The many-storied rainforests constitute an environment that reaches from the surface of the earth high into the air and contains great structural variety. This wealth of spatial structures is an important prerequisite for the presence of animals belonging to a great variety of different groups. Birds are one group of animals that profits from this three-dimensional aspect of forest ecosystems. The magnificently colored birds of paradise, most species of which live in New Guinea, are rainforest dwellers.

Beauties of the jungle

Only a few flowers grow on the poor soils of the forest floor and in the dim light conditions prevailing there. They are, almost without exception, small and inconspicuous. The real beauty of the tropical rainforests—high up, in the sun-drenched canopy, where orchids and other flowering plants abound—is, for the most part, hidden to the human observer. Sweet, pungent, intoxicating

scents waft down from these hanging gardens into the damp, hot closeness of the dim bottom region. The bright colors of many flowers glimmer like fireflies in the darkness of the forest. The outward splendor of the plants, however, is no more remarkable than their inner properties. Many species supply toxins for spears and blowgun darts as well as hallucinatory drugs. Many plants also have important pharmaceutical properties.

evenly throughout the year. Evergreen; three or more tiers; wide variety of tree species.

1.1 Lowlands
Hot.
Temperature: 72–82°F (22–28°C) throughout the year.
Annual precipitation: above 70 inches (1,800 mm).
Altitude above sea level: 0–2,600 feet (0–800 m).
Many-tiered; buttress roots.

1.2 Montane zone
Moderate.
Temperature: 57–72°F (14–22°C) throughout the year.
Annual precipitation: above 55 inches (1,400 mm).
Altitude above sea level: 2,600-6,900 feet (800-2,100 m).
Usually three-tiered; few buttress roots.

1.3 Mountains
(Cloud and fog forests)
Moderate—cool and damp.
Temperature: 50–57°F (10–14°C) throughout the year.
Annual precipitation: above 47 inches (1,200 mm).
Altitude above sea level: 6,900–10,500 feet (2,100-3,200 m).
Three-tiered, with many epiphytes; tree ferns.

2. Rain-green moist forests
Relatively large number of plant species that shed leaves periodically. Two to three-tiered; great diversity of tree species. Dry periods of up to four months.

2.1 Lowlands
Rainy periods. In appearance more or less similar to evergreen moist forests. Hot.
Temperature: 72–82°F (22–28°C) throughout the year.
Altitude above sea level: 0-2,600 feet (0–800 m).

2.2 Montane zone
Moderate temperatures ranging between 57°and 72°F (14–22°C) throughout the year.
Altitude above sea level: above 2,600 feet (800 m). Dry period. The upper canopy sheds leaves partially; few buttress roots; fewer epiphytes.

3. Rain-green dry forests
Periodically leafless for some time; one or two tiers; relatively small number of species, many of them xerophytes with thorns.
Since the length and severity of the dry period affect vegetation more than temperature, no altitudinal subdivision is required.
Dry period lasts from six to eight months.

Sometimes other forms of vegetation associated with a specific zone are described separately. Among these are the mangrove forests, which link the salt water of seas to the fresh water of rivers. These forests grow in the tidal range of sea coasts and establish themselves as pioneers on river deltas and banks as far inland as the water retains any saltiness. Most of the trees and shrubs growing here are specialized, and they attain remarkable stability by putting forth fast-growing stilt roots from the trunk and branches and sending them into the muddy bottom. These roots in turn encourage the accumulation of material suspended in the tidal water. Other species, such as the strange *Bruguiera*, even develop "breathing" roots that float on the water's surface. Comparable to the mangrove forests are forests growing in swamps and areas regularly flooded by fresh water. These forests are made up of trees that can survive long periods standing in water.

The aspect of tropical rainforests that probably impresses people of the temperate zones most deeply is the profusion of different life forms that present themselves in an almost unimaginable vitality. Giant trees reaching heights of 160 to 200 feet (50–60 m) and sometimes even 300 feet (90 m) rise above the rest of the jungle. So many levels of trees and bushes grow among them that they are almost hidden behind an impenetrable tangle of vegetation. The only hint of their existence is the huge trunks that often measure many feet in diameter and appear even larger because of the buttress roots that flare out at the bottoms. An immense number of different plants grow next to and on top of one another between the forest floor and the highest crowns. A striking feature of rainforests everywhere is the incredible variety of tree species, trees pushing up at all levels, all of them eager to reach the light, but often a tree has to linger in the shade, sometimes for decades, until better light allows it to grow to its full height. In the rainforests, tree species thrive that are much more tolerant of shade than even our maples and hemlocks, trees whose low requirement for light is already quite remarkable. In the tropics there are shade-tolerant trees that can survive in near-lightless conditions for decades without growing. They wait in the green darkness until an increase of light allows them to aspire to a life in the sun. In the meantime, they absorb the rain that filters down from the giants and give off large amounts of moisture, on which, in turn, other plants as well as animals depend for life.

Far above the forest floor, on trees, shrubs, lianas, and a stringy network of other plants, life forms exist that look as though they belong to another world. They need no roots to absorb nutrients and water from the soil; they find a footing on branches, tree trunks, or other plants of the canopy and absorb moisture and nutrients there. These plants are called epiphytes—plants that "grow on" other plants without feeding on them the way parasites do. All they require is a place to which to cling and a chance to spread and multiply. Their diversity and adaptability are astonishing. Who could overlook the variety, shapes, colors, and smells of orchids and bromeliads? Their showy flowers and pure colors stand out even in the darkness under a thick roof of leaves. They occur in a wide spectrum from white to dark blue, in almost all conceivable gradations and combinations of color. Sometimes they shine forth in full glory in clearings, on isolated trees after a forest fire, or along the edge of the jungle. At other times, finding them requires arduous searching. Some of them live in such secluded remoteness that only the initiated get to see them, but always they appear amid the lushness of nature with a beauty that never fails to move us. Our appreciation of nature, however, should be supplemented by an awareness of the following facts: Worldwide, orchids are found from the temperate climates to the evergreen wet tropics. There are over 750 genera and over 25,000 species of orchids. Every year, about 100 new species are identified. Their principal habitat is the tropical rainforests, but they are also found in Tierra del Fuego and in northern Scandinavia. Orchids may well be the most diverse plant family in number of species and variety of forms, and they may be one of the youngest to penetrate into extremely inhospitable habitats. Bromeliads, on the other hand, are restricted, with one exception, to tropical America. This family includes 46 genera with about 1,700 species.

In our temperate forests, ferns grow almost exclusively on the ground. In rainforests, however, they thrive not only in terrestrial form as tree ferns but also as epiphytes in all levels of the canopy. Between these two extremes are other kinds of plants, especially members of the *Araceae* family, whose flower clusters are enfolded in large, leaflike bracts. These plants obtain the water they need only from rain and moisture in the air. Nutrients are absorbed from the dust, humus, and other organic matter that accumulate in the trees. The plants have developed special organs that make this kind of life possible, and many have air roots with an absorbent outer layer that practically combs moisture out of the air. Similarly, the tomentum of some air roots, that is, a spongy mass of densely matted hair, traps water, dust, and organic matter, which are then assimilated. Thus, regular factories are at work up in the air. Other plants have leaves that are modified into pitcher-like shapes for collecting water and nutrients, or grooved to function as reservoirs. The world of air plants presents a most varied picture, which becomes even more complex if we include the semiepiphytes, that is, those plants—like our houseplant *Monstera*—that germinate in the ground, use their tendrils to climb trees, and, once the stem connecting them to the ground withers away, continue life as pure epiphytes.

The profusion of species characteristic of tropical rain-

An entire forest on stilts

Where tropical forests extend to the edge of the sea, the ground they grow on is subject to the ebb and flow of the tides. Trees respond structurally to this unusual ecological situation. Mangroves

(top left), for example, manage to hold their own by developing stilt roots that flare out toward the bottom and raise the tree's trunk and crown safely above flood levels. Such tidal forests not only line tropical sea coasts, but also grow in large estuaries, where the vegetation has to adjust to the constantly shifting salinity of the water. Trees other than mangroves (center and bottom left) also have developed finger-like prop roots and stabilizing crowns as an adaptation to their soils. Trees with prop roots can actually "move" by growing more roots on one side than on the other to take advantage of light. The nippa palms (above) growing along the banks of the Belait River in Borneo are not exposed to such ecological problems, and they grow with their stems in the water.

A symphony of shapes and shadows

Everywhere on the earth, rainforests give a similar impression of dense growth and marvelous shapes, of structural diversity, and of a wealth of species almost beyond belief. Being in

such a forest is never boring, because the scene that presents itself changes wherever the eye turns (left). The brush-like inflorescences of an albizzia from northeastern Australia, a relative of our locusts and acacias, are made up of numerous showy stamens (top). Individual, conspicuously yellow flowers (bottom) are borne directly on the trunk so that they will not be lost in a mass of dense vegetation.

Encounters of the third kind

The law of the jungle seems cruel and merciless only if regarded from a superficial point of view. Eating and being eaten are everyday events in this world. All living things have their nutrients recycled rapidly from one level to the next. In the wild, living things seldom die of old age.

Every spot is bursting with life

Rainforest trees are not so much individuals as habitats accommodating incredibly vast numbers of species. Epiphytes and climbing plants compete for every spot that offers support. They

overrun not only the host trees but also each other and create niches for all kinds of small animal life (right page). These life communities exist practically without contact with the ground. The unusual blue of the flowers borne by the fragrant jacaranda tree (top) makes a spectacularly colorful sight. Bright red, tubular flowers hang down from the canopy region on two slender, rope-like branches (bottom). These flowers are visited and pollinated by hovering hummingbirds.

forests is also demonstrated in the kinds of plant communities found there. A wealth of species thrive side by side instead of only a few dominating the forest. Individual stands are constituted of many different species, each of which is represented by only a few specimens. If we compare this to the forests of eastern North America or central Europe, we are struck by the fact that hardly any original forests here survive and that the regrown forests are made up of a small number of different kinds of trees.

An argument made by those who defend the cutting of the rainforest is that the forests of eastern North America and Europe were almost completely cut down at one time without terrible ecological effect. Now the peoples of developed countries are telling the Third World countries, where the majority of the rainforests are located, that they should not cut down their forests. This argument may have some political merit, but none ecologically.

Species diversity, greatest in the tropics, lessens considerably as one travels away from the tropical zone, whether north or south. As many as 200 different species of trees per acre are found in the rainforests, whereas in the northern temperate zones such as New England, for example, an acre of land might have only six to ten different species of trees on it. Not only that, in the tropics, the adjacent acres might be of an entirely different composition, with few of the species overlapping those of the original acre. The temperate forest acre, however, is surrounded by nearly identical acres of trees, other kinds of plants, insects, birds, and so forth. Thus, if a large part of the temperate zone is cut down, the remaining forest is similar enough in species composition to what was cut that it can act as a reservoir for reseeding and repopulating the destroyed areas. The same is not true of the tropical rainforest. The small areas that remain after extensive

cutting will not necessarily be typical of what was destroyed, nor will they have the species diversity of the larger area that would allow replenishment with the same species if there were an opportunity for regrowth. Another factor acting against the regrowth of the rainforests (and covered more fully elsewhere in this book) is the degradation of the already poor soils of the tropics when they are stripped of vegetation and exposed to the direct effects of the heavy precipitation of the tropics.

How much richer is the flora of the rainforests! At least half of all scientifically described plant species occur there. Thus far, about 25,000 species of plants—about one tenth of the total worldwide—have been identified in the Malay Archipelago (Borneo, Sumatra, Celebes, and the Moluccas). Among these, the orchids form the largest group, with between 3,000 and 4,000 species. Woody plants are also present in impressive numbers: The myrtle and the fig families account for about 500 species each, and there are over 700 different species of heathers. Trees with a minimum diameter of 16 inches (40 cm) at the base have been assigned to 2,500 different species, and scientists have identified about 400 species belonging just to the dipterocarps, a family that represents the tallest tropical trees.

Comparable counts made in the Philippines show about 3,000 species of trees. A similar picture of the wealth of species encountered in tropical forests emerges from a survey of Africa, in which the compositions of forests in different tree-growth regions were compared. About 2,800 to 3,200 different tree species grow in the lowland rainforests of the Ivory Coast, southern Nigeria, and the Congo, while in East Africa, in areas with relatively high precipitation like central Kenya, as many as 3,800 to 4,600 species have been documented. The numbers decline to between 1,000 and 2,000 in the African savannas and 500 to 1,000 in the semideserts of the Sahara, with

extremely arid desert areas yielding only between 50 to as few as 7 species.

The tropics are, on the whole, the domain of broad-leaved trees and shrubs, but a number of conifers also grow in tropical rainforests, generally at higher elevations or in localities offering special conditions. Some are restricted to the tropics, while others extend to subtropical regions. Worldwide, there are about 50 genera of conifers, about 20 of which, with roughly 200 species, thrive in tropical forests. The total area of rainforests that include conifers is estimated at about 86 million acres (35 million ha), and the heaviest concentration—over 49 million acres (20 million ha) with 7 genera of conifers—is found in Central America and in the Caribbean. The most prominent among the conifers here are pines, some species of which have been cultivated frequently. The greatest variety of tree-size conifers is concentrated on 20 million acres (8 million ha) of forest in Asia and Oceania, where 14 genera have been identified, some of which are made up of many different species. *Podocarpus* (yellowwood) is the only conifer genus to occur in all three major rainforest regions. It exists in over 100 species, some of which are merely shrubs.

The *Araucaria,* or monkey puzzle, genus of conifers has attracted special attention because these trees display such unusual shapes. The genus contains only 12 species and is limited to the southern hemisphere. The trees look like creatures from a distant past and seem to have nothing in common with the evergreens of the temperate zones. Many species grow to a height of nearly 300 feet (90 m) and have incredibly straight, massive trunks that, when they grow in dense stands, are free of branches. Because of the high commercial value of the wood they furnish, these trees are already on the brink of extinction. Among them is *Araucaria*

Many-storied treetops crowded together

In the tropical rainforest, there is no such thing as a clear and orderly arrangement of treetops. Tight crowding is the rule, so that individual trees are able to

push their way upward only if they are extremely slender. They cannot broaden into a crown until they have reached the canopy. Strangler figs start life in the canopy, thus getting a jump on their competition. They grow big and strong as soon as their roots find their way down to the forest floor.

The forest lives on water

Water is one of the dominant ecological factors that shape the structure and permit the self-perpetuation of the rainforest ecosystem. Water is generally received from above. On its way down from the foliage of the canopy, it forms rivulets and veils of droplets that water many other

sectors of this environment. Open, standing water (as in the Australian eucalyptus swamp, top left) is rather rare in a true rainforest. An abundant water supply lets small trees take root high on strong tree branches and grow until their weight proves too heavy for their hosts to bear (above).

The ancient genus of ferns

The diversity of species character-istic of rainforests also finds expression in what seems to be an infinite multitude of different ferns and fern structures. De-pending on where

ferns grow, their con-stituent parts fulfill the most varied func-tions. With very few exceptions, ferns need moisture and shade to thrive; that is why they thrive in the rainforest. Often they grow in the semidarkness of the forest floor; some-times they float in great numbers on lakes and rivers; they also colonize the trunks and limbs of giant rainforest trees. The ancestors of many of today's ferns once dominat-ed the continents for millions and millions of years. They grew to the size of trees and, in fact, formed the first primeval forests on earth. In the Middle Ages, strange magical powers were ascrib-

ed to these ancient plants. In 1612, a synod investigated the misuse of fern extracts in all kinds of witchcraft. Because popular superstition held that ferns blossom on Midsummer Eve and drop their seeds at the same time, it was believed that a brew made that night would make people invisible, bring them riches, and success in love. In the large photo (left) the small floating plants are water ferns. The larger floating plants are called water lettuce, which is not a fern but a flowering plant of the arum family.

Brightly colored fruits are more conspicuous

Primary colors are an aid not to be underestimated when it comes to the spreading of a species. Fruits with bold colors stand out against the various greens of their sur-

roundings and attract frugivorous birds and flying mammals. This considerably increases chances for rapid dispersal of indigestible seeds. The intensely bright pigments of the fruit from the so-called lipstick tree (*Bixa*) (top) are used by Indians in their ritual body painting. The bright yellow of balsam pears (*Momordica*) (bottom) has thus far not found a use by humans.

angustifolia, which grows in southern Brazil and whose wood is sold as Paraná pine. *Araucaria* from New Guinea include the Klinki pine (*A. hunsteinii*) and its relative, the Moreton Bay pine (*A. cunninghamii*), which is found not only in New Guinea but also on the east coast of Australia. These trees, among the most beautiful on Earth, grow to towering heights, form imposing limbs, and have crowns with shapes of simple architectural beauty. *A. excelsa*, native to Norfolk Island in the South Pacific, is grown around the world in pots and sold as a houseplant, known as the Norfolk Island pine.

There is no quiescent period in evergreen rainforests as there is in the forests of temperate climates; consequently the wood shows no clear annual rings, which help determine a tree's age. Continual decay is followed by continual renewal. This lack of dramatic change may suggest sameness, but closer inspection shows this impression to be inaccurate. The complex forest world is not constantly and uniformly green inside and out, but keeps flowering along the edges, in the forest interior, along the ground, in the middle stories, and in the canopy. The many different kinds of trees and shrubs, particularly the epiphytes—especially the orchids and bromeliads—as well as parasitic and climbing plants all have their different times of flowering. Here, too, we find tremendous variety: Some plants flower only at intervals of several years; others blossom several times a year; and some bloom all year. Seeds are produced throughout the year. In the rain-green moist and dry forests of the tropics there are, however, dry periods when leaves are shed; in some areas these periods are fairly regular. In the evergreen rainforest, nature works indefatigably all year and with a long view. The nutrient cycle of the temperate forest of North America and Europe take a different course. In the temperate zone, trees respond to

shortening light periods and the decline in warmth by withdrawing nutrients from the leaves and storing them inside so that they will be available again in the spring to help start new growth. The amount of water in the organs of winter-hardy plants is reduced and redistributed. Finally, the leaves fall to the ground, where animals and fungi break them down and they gradually become part of the soil. In much of the temperate zone, the cycle slows down or stops for a portion of the year.

In temperate forests, organic matter is incorporated in the soil in the form of humus and soluble minerals. A healthy forest floor constitutes a reservoir of major nutrients, trace elements, and water. This reservoir extends throughout the entire root area to a depth of 3 or many more feet below the surface, thus being available to shallow–as well as deep-rooted plants. As decaying plant matter is added to the soil, rocks and stones breaking up in the ground contribute minerals, thus completing the cycle of transformation from tree to soil via humus, rock, and mineralization and back to vegetation: a well-functioning system, as long as man does not interfere thoughtlessly.

The ecosystems of tropical rainforests function completely differently. Anyone seeing the black forest floor for the first time assumes that it is the same kind of friable, humus- and nutrient-rich soil, well interlaced with roots, that is found in the fertile forest tracts of eastern North America or central Europe. This impression is usually false because, as a rule, the soil of tropical forests is very poor and only a minimum of exchange occurs between soil and plants. Most of the nutrients circulate within the vegetation. Whatever organic matter develops is captured, transformed, and reassimilated somewhere between the treetops and the lower levels of vegetation. Whatever does drift to the ground is not given the time or the chance to turn slowly into humus. Millions of organ-

isms—insects, fungi, lower orders of plant and animal life, including many protozoans—go to work on the organic matter and absorb it. The dense mat of minutely ramified roots on the ground's surface is connected to a host of mycorrhizal fungi that also absorb, transform, and pass on substances to the vegetation. In the moist tropical forests, most of the nutrient cycle thus takes place between plants and not in the exchange between soil and plant, as it does in the temperate zone forests. Knowing this, we are not surprised to learn that most of the trees are very shallow-rooted, generally penetrating through only a surface layer of 4 to 12 inches (10–30 cm) of soil. That is why strong, spreading-buttress roots and multiple stilt roots, as well as lianas and other vines and creeping plants, are so important for support and anchorage in moist rainforests. But the peculiarities of this ecological system also show clearly why slash-and-burn methods will yield no long-term agricultural returns. The lush rainforest has nutrients stored in its vegetation and not in its soil. The nutrient elements stored in the vegetation either escape into the air, are hauled away as logs, or fertilize the ground in the form of ash or rotting plant material for a maximum of one or two years, after which time they are washed away because of the high level of precipitation and rapid decay. The soils have no reserves of absorptive structures, no regenerative powers, and thus no significant exchange or storage of nutrients can develop. These conditions also severely limit the effectiveness of later chemical fertilizing. Especially in the tropical regions, with their abundance of rain, cleared and burnt earth is dead earth. It takes a long time for species-rich forests to regenerate, and in some cases they may not regenerate at all. In many areas, only meager replacement communities will be able to grow up again.

Amazonia represents a unique situation, not only in South

Somewhere between darkness and dim light

Generally, little light penetrates into the bottom regions of the rainforest. Only around the edges of clearings and along rivers does daylight enter the lower sto-

ries of the forest from the side and allow plants to grow in the lower reaches. Large-leafed plants, almost black owing to the large accumulation of green pigments, try to make the best use of whatever rays reach the dark forest floor. In this permanent semi-darkness, it is easy to overlook arboreal snakes like the one shown above, which has wound itself in tight rings around a tree limb.

Surveying the forest

A solitary rainforest tree towering above the rest of the canopy has started its own particular blossoming season with an explosive burst of flowers—in complete disregard of the flowering rhythm of other trees. A philodendron has wound its way into the tree's still-bare branches. Philodendrons are lianas; some philodendron species are sold in great numbers as house plants throughout the United States and Europe. The tree's exposed crown also makes an excellent lookout for a pair of king vultures (right). For raptors and carrion eaters, the rainforest is almost a marginal biotope, for the food supply there is relatively sparse and somewhat inaccessible.

America, but also in the entire tropical world. It is the largest tropical rainforest region and also the largest forested area of any kind in the world. Amazonia has many unique features, and it has aroused curiosity and wonder in observers of all kinds. Alexander von Humboldt wrote in exalted language about the "forested zone of Amazonia" and coined the term *Hylää* for it, a word that is based on the Greek *hyle,* which means "wood" and sometimes also "matter" or "material." "Hylozoism" is the doctrine that all matter is animated. It is to Humboldt that we owe the first scientific accounts of the rainforest, but Charles Darwin, who came to Brazil on the *Beagle* in 1822, responded to this primordial forest with similar excitement. This widely traveled naturalist, too, was filled with admiration for the overpowering profusion of vegetation. How much diversity in nature is dependent on the availability of water becomes clear when we contemplate the Amazon River. Up to two thirds of all readily accessible fresh water on Earth is concentrated in the 2.7 million square miles (7 million km²) of the Amazon basin.

A famous event in the history of this region is the transplanting of rubber trees (*Hevea brasiliensis*) from the tropical rainforests to England. Seven thousand seeds from rubber trees were planted under glass in England's famous Kew Gardens, and many stories are told about this export, which dealt a severe blow to Brazil's economy. From the 7,000 seeds, 2,000 seedlings were obtained, which were eventually transported in small greenhouses to the English colonies in Southeast Asia. There the descendents of those seedlings, numbering about 3 billion, now account for over 90 percent of the world's natural rubber.

The entire "rubber rush" of the mid-1800s seems strange today. It brought to Amazonia droves of adventurers who hoped to get rich quickly like the hordes that flocked to California during the gold rush. In that period, about 1,800 plant species were discovered that yielded a rubber-like, milky juice. These included various small shrubs, lianas, and trees, among the latter the rubber-producing *Ficus elastica* and *Manihot glaziovii.* But only *Hevea brasiliensis* survived the boom, becoming an economically important natural resource, that is still in demand after 150 years and the invention of synthetic rubber. In the course of their raids into Cuba and Brazil, the Spaniards came across mahogany trees (*Swietenia mahogoni*), and in the second half of the sixteenth century, mahogany wood began to be exported to Europe. Because of its bright, reddish brown color and its easy workability, the wood was soon in such demand for furniture and the interior of houses that all tropical regions were combed for similar trees. Today, wood that is sold as mahogany comes from a variety of botanically different trees.

Included among the African rainforests is the east coast of Madagascar, an island in the Indian Ocean that is a world unto itself. Far enough away from Africa to prevent animal or plant immigration, the island has unusually varied fauna and flora, some of which are endemic to the island, that is, found nowhere else. About 60 percent of the 12,000 plant species occurring on Madagascar are endemic—an obvious sign of the island's early geologic isolation and also a striking demonstration of Darwin's theory of evolution. Comparable results of geographic isolation are found in the animal world. The rails of Madagascar, for example, are flightless, although they have short wings. They presumably were able to survive only because they have no aggressive enemies on the island. The tenrecs, a family of insectivores that resemble hedgehogs, have several distinct anatomical features. Instead of moles, rice tenrecs (*Oryzorictes*) burrow through the earth. In the tree-tops, lemurs, a form of primitive arboreal primate, survived

Bamboo groves in the rainforest

In the Southeast Asian rainforests, in clearings created by humans harvesting wood or left behind by ferocious storms or the collapse of a colossal ancient tree, small groves

of various kinds of bamboo often spring up. The trunks of these strange, tree-like grasses are still green after several years, even after entire decades (right). Bamboo grows at a breath-taking rate. In the permanently moist warmth of the tropics, the un-branched hollow shoots can grow as much as 1.5 feet (.5 m) in a day—a patient observer could actually watch this vertical growth take place.

All bamboo species are grasses and are directly related to our meadow grasses and cereals. The structure we observe in our common grasses—the stalk being subdivided by leaf-bearing joints into stiff segments—is also found in bamboo shoots. On the joints, there are

root buds that can send out roots if necessary. Bamboo stems are not continuous hollow pipes from top to bottom, but have solid layers that divide them into compact segments. This stabilization is needed to support the heavy foliage at the top and to withstand lateral pressures.

Rainforest "types"

For over a century, zoologists have been in agreement that *Homo sapiens* and other primates are closely related biologically. In spite of the philosophical and religious opposition and detraction the dis-

covery evoked, this view has been confirmed by comparative anatomical studies and molecular genetics. Of course, the primates that now exist cannot be regarded as the primitive forebears of modern man, but man and other primates do share a common ancestral line, from which the bipedal primates, or hominids, branched off about 10 million years ago.

because there was no pressure from competing species living on the African continent.

In Asia, the tropical forests of India, Malaysia (Sumatra, Java, and Borneo), the Philippines, and a number of other islands contain an abundance of tree species, including valuable commercial timber trees, that may be unparalleled elsewhere. The uppermost canopy is dominated by trees of the *Dipterocarpaceae* family. On Borneo alone, about 270 of the 400 species belonging to this family have been identified. This tree family is amazingly adaptable ecologically, occurring in Asia in almost all types of tropical forests. In rainforests, the family is represented by evergreen trees; in dry forests, by deciduous ones; and in rain-green moist forests, by all sorts of intermediary forms. Dipterocarpaceous trees grow on very different soil types, ranging from mineral earth to peat bogs, and from lowland plains to mountains. In many places, the trees of this family completely dominate the scene. They usually grow to a height of between 165 and 200 feet (50–60 m). Valuable timber is obtained from dipterocarpaceous trees especially from the genus *Shorea*. The family owes its scientific name to the two-winged fruits, which are quite heavy and therefore cannot disperse very far, found on its trees. It may be this immobility that has led to the amazing genetic diversity among the members of this family. Borneo, which is the third-largest island on Earth and is situated exactly on the equator, is a biological El Dorado. Not only are there many Meranti trees (members of the *Shorea* genus and thus of the *Dipterocarpaceae*) here—trees that are harvested or, more accurately, decimated for their much-sought-after timber—but Borneo is also home to 16 percent of the world's birds and to one of the world's largest apes, the orangutan. The mountain forests display a wealth of animal and plant life beyond all expectation.

The rainforests of Australia and nearby islands consist of a narrow strip along the coast of Queensland in eastern Australia and, more significantly, areas of New Guinea and islands in the equatorial zone of the South Sea. In Australia, acacias, a genus of woody plants belonging to the legume family, predominate. There are 700 to 800 different species of acacias, about half of them native to this continent. They include evergreen and deciduous plants, average to tall trees, and bushes, vines, and creeping plants, and they are found in tropical and subtropical zones, in rainforests and dry forests, even in savannas and semideserts. The flowers can be either unisexual or bisexual and are a showy yellow or an unobtrusive white. Some have leaves that are modified into thorns that protect the plants from being eaten. A related species growing in Central America has devised a different method of defense. A certain kind of fierce ant lives in tunnels inside the approximately 1 inch-long (2–3 cm) thorns located at the base of each leaf. The host tree supplies the ants not only with sugar from organs called extrafloral nectaries, but also with fats and proteins from specialized glands called Beltian bodies after Thomas Bel, who first described this form of symbiosis in 1874. Only after this relationship was understood did it become clear that the ants protect the trees against defoliation by plant eaters; they emerge in swarms to sting and bite intruders unmercifully. Their presence benefits the host trees in another way: The ants prune encroaching foliage and shading branches from nearby plants, thus reducing competition for light and consequently enhancing the vitality of their hosts.

In New Guinea, rainforests both in the lowlands and, especially, in the montane zone are still intact. In addition to deciduous trees, such as some eucalyptus and casuarina species that also occur in Borneo, various conifers of the southern hemisphere grow here.

One is struck by the realization, accompanied by a great sense of obligation, that the rainforest is a gene reservoir of unimagined and unimaginable dimensions, a pool whose breadth and depth hold tremendous promise. Scientists estimate that the evolution of the rainforests began 60 or 100 million years ago. Since that time individuals and species have crossed, types have been selected, strains have died out and new ones have emerged. Even now genetic information is stored, passed on, and, of course, transformed. Many plant and animal species have not been discovered yet. Nowhere else are there life systems of such ecological variety as in the moist forests. This, too, is a result of genetic diversity. Science is only beginning to explore this world, but we already know and are reminded daily that, as a consequence of our way of life, of the one-sided demands we place on the plant and animal world, of our exploitation and degradation of the environment, of our urge for progress, and of the hectic pace of change, we have and will have more and more need for the genes of wild organisms. These genes are in demand as an aid to our methods of producing animals and plants for our use, but the reserves of genes found in the tropics are also of inestimable value to medicine, not to mention developments unforeseen even in our time of advanced technology. All of humanity has a stake in the continued existence of tropical forests.

Among the more distant relatives of man are the New World monkeys, such as the black spider monkey (left page) and the Madagascar sifaka (large picture on left), both of which use their long, prehensile tails almost like a fifth hand when climbing. The orangutan

(above), with its extremely long forelimbs, is perfectly adapted for clambering in the canopy region of the rainforest. The orangutan, which lives in Southeast Asia, is a great ape and thus belongs to a group that includes some of man's closest relatives. African anthropoid apes, like the chimpanzee and the gorilla, are thought to be somewhat more closely related to man than the other living primates. Old World monkeys lack a long, prehensile tail, but they move across the treetops with remarkable agility.

Ernst Josef Fittkau

The Law of the Jungle: Living Lavishly on Next to Nothing

Until quite recently, it was believed that only extremely fertile soils could give rise to the lush vegetation of tropical rainforests. In addition, it seemed, the warm and humid climate must offer excellent conditions for agriculture and for raising cattle. This view turned out to be a tragic misapprehension of the facts.

In spite of all the biotic diversity, the population density of individual species is generally low. With the increase in body size, the number of individuals per unit of area diminishes further. Insects are the only exception; they are the hidden rulers of the rainforest.

Branchless trees terminating in flower heads

In the Ruwenzori Mountains of East Africa, with increasing altitudes montane rainforests give way to cloud forests and eventually to plant associations that are comparable to the plant life of the High Alps in Europe. Even at these altitudes, plentiful precipitation allows the growth of a rich assortment of plants that includes some unusual shapes. The pillar-like plants shown here are giant lobelias, related to the bellflower family. Species occur only within small, clearly defined ranges and are in some cases confined to a single mountain slope.

The poetry of creation

The dramatic composition of this almost unreal-looking photograph taken in the swamps of Venezuela might have been invented by a Chinese painter of the old school. In the fading light of the late afternoon, white herons and green parrots hang in the branches of a dying tree, looking like creatures from another world.

The magic of colors and shapes

Although orchids are a plant family that has a worldwide distribution—including Atlantic mountain slopes in Norway and extremely dry rock banks in the Himalayas—the tropics, especially the tropical rainforests, are the true center of diversity of these plants. Here the great majority of the approximate total of 20,000 species is found—not on the ground, as in most of the other areas of distribution, but in the airy heights of the rainforest canopy, in the form of epiphytes. The image of a richly planted flower garden crowded with the most exquisite orchids would fit well with the romantic view of the rainforests' exotic plant splendor.

As late as the first half of this century, the rainforests of the equatorial zone were among the least-known and economically least-exploited areas of the world. Not until man began to contemplate the conquest of space were attempts made to draw these regions into the realm of global economic development. Huge areas adding up to continental dimensions and practically uninhabited by humans seemed to offer space to accommodate the rapidly swelling world population, and a growing demand for raw materials presented a further argument for tapping the mineral resources that were suspected to lie buried there. Economic geographers had tried to draw attention to the many resources lying idle, especially in Amazonia, at a time when rainforests still attracted only naturalists and collectors of butterflies and orchids. The tropical jungle, an immense, wildly proliferating cover of vegetation, it was thought, could thrive only on very fertile soil. Furthermore, the steadily humid climate seemed to promise favorable conditions for agriculture and cattle raising.

Today, at least half the world's rainforest area has been opened to economic development; that is, the forest has been cut or burned to provide cleared land. But nowhere has anybody been able to prove that rainforest areas, once made accessible, can support long-term, large-scale agriculture, or that the forests can be logged on a sustainable basis. Ambitious settlement projects either have failed or have not remotely lived up to expectations. As a rule, efforts to turn rainforests into agriculturally productive land have resulted in useless, degraded soils. Modern development strategies have been, and still are, based on a fundamental misunderstanding of the possible ways in which tropical rainforests could be utilized.

To be sure, tropical rainforest regions have always supported humans in greater or smaller numbers, but these populations used the forest and its resources in such a way that it remained a viable environment for the users. This is still true for the last scattered tribes of forest Indians in South America or the Pygmies of Africa, as well as for the dense populations of rice farmers in Indonesia. In Southeast Asia, large-scale, intensive agriculture has been practiced for over one thousand years in areas that were originally rainforests. The volcanic rock found on Java and Bali produces soils that, if maintained properly, permit human settlement of a density not found elsewhere in rural areas.

The results of economic development in the hot, humid tropics show thus far that precisely those forest regions that had remained largely unaffected by humans until our century are generally not—as had been hoped—suitable for intensive agriculture or for the forest industry. The fact is that indigenous peoples developed technologies that had no long-term negative impact on the forest, and population densities fluctuated with the availability of land suitable for small-scale slash-and-burn clearing and with the quantities of foodstuffs that could be harvested in the forest year after year.

It is increasingly evident that the central question on which economic development in rainforest regions depends is the availability of nutrients in the soil. In order to grow, plants need not only air, sunlight, and water, but also certain nutrient salts. In the evergreen forests of the humid tropics, vegetation receives an abundant supply of energy from sunlight as well as plenty of rain all year round, but, apart from a few exceptional situations, there is a clear shortage of nutrients. Normally, plants absorb nutrients along with water from the soil. Nutrients are released through the weathering of rock material; some become part of the clay in the soil, and some are retained in humus substances during the breakdown of dead organic material. Only a certain amount of nutrients filters down in dissolved form into the groundwater. In the humid tropics, with their constant heat and humidity, soil formation processes occur 50 to 100 times faster than in the temperate zones. In old, flattened landscapes and in sediment-filled lowlands—types of landscapes found in especially large areas in Amazonia and on a smaller scale in Africa and Asia—soils can form that are very deep. The bedrock may weather and be transformed into clay minerals down to depths of 30, 40, or 100 feet (10, 20, or 30 m). Clay minerals, like other rock materials, are subject to further transformation and aging processes. Young clays, depending on the type of material from which they originated, can be rich in just those nutrients that plants need for growth. Potassium, calcium, magnesium, and phosphorus are held by the crystal structure of fine clay particles. In the uppermost soil horizon, plants gradually deplete the clay of the nutrients it once contained. At the same time, these mineral particles are also leached away in the course of further weathering processes, accelerated by the large amounts of rain and the continuous warm weather, and they end up in the ground water. Multilayered clay minerals thus gradually lose the nutrients they had and even lose the capacity to hold new nutrients.

In flat lands, where the soil lies directly on the bedrock, nutrient salts that are absorbed by the plants or that seep down into the ground water can continually be replaced through weathering and soil-building processes. On sites with even a minimal incline, slight but continual erosive removal of the soil surface helps get rid of worn-out, no longer very useful clay minerals. The flatter the terrain is, however, and the deeper and older the soils, the less chance there is for the stores of nutrients to be replenished through surface erosion or through ongoing weathering of the bedrock. With each season of

Scenes from the lives of lizards

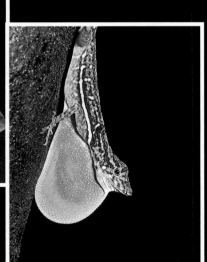

The *Agamidae* family, which includes over 300 different species, is a large reptile family. These lizards are diurnal animals with excellent vision, which makes life in the canopy much easier. The Eichhorn agama (large picture), which feeds primarily on insects, lives in the tropical forests of the Old World. Anoles, on the other hand, belong to the *Iguanidae* family, a group of lizards that occurs primarily in the rainforests of the New World. Male anoles puff up their brightly colored throat sacks either to make a threatening gesture in defense of their territory or to impress a female that is ready to mate (above right). The Graham anole is also an insectivore, but likes to sip flower nectar now and then (above left).

Without fungi there would be no rainforest

In the consistently warm, humid climate of tropical rainforests, fungi are omnipresent in an immense variety of forms. But appearance deceives here, too; normally, the visible parts of fungi are merely its fruiting bodies. The actual fungus consists of a pale, white, underground network of filaments in the poor rainforest soil. Fungi often surround the roots of trees and other plants, embracing them as tightly as a glove fits the fingers of a hand, and supply their plant partners with mineral nutrients.

A frog in a tight spot

This leaf frog clinging to the lower jaw of a juvenile caiman seems to be the victim of a serious misjudgment. It probably thought the caiman lying motionless in the water could be used for climbing, and it may even have danced around on the animal's nose. A single snap of the jaws could put an end to the frog's life, but there might still be a way out of the precarious situation: Frogs have glands in their skins that, when the animal is under stress, exude a stinging substance, making the morsel about to be swallowed distinctly less appetizing. Remembering this kind of experience, both parties are likely to avoid mutual encounters in the future.

Art works of the highest perfection

At first glance, the rainforest seems to be a symphony entirely in green. Only upon closer inspection does one find miraculously beautiful colors in all shapes. What is so striking again and

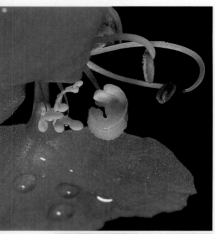

again is that nature's apparent whimsy always turns out to have a useful function.

planting, a certain portion of nutrients is removed from the soil in the form of agricultural products. Cultivation and harvesting can continue only until the store of nutrients in the soil is exhausted. In temperate latitudes, we take it for granted that soil that is cultivated has to be replenished with fertilizer to make up for the loss of nutrients. The same is not true of the inhabitants of the rainforest. In the traditional practice of nomadic agriculture, forest soil is fertilized with ashes from burning the original vegetation cover or with rotting vegetation. We know now that in tropical lowland rainforests, at least 90 percent of the available nutrients are bound up in living vegetation, the biomass. When forests are burned to clear the land, almost the entire supply of mineral nutrients is set free at once. This huge, one-time application of fertilizer as a rule supports only a few harvests; most of the nutrients are washed away by precipitation before the new vegetation has a chance to absorb them. The aged, kaolinic clays are by their nature only minimally capable or completely incapable of binding the massive amounts of released nutrients, and the humus substances that could ordinarily bind them are unable to do so because, with the drying out of the forest floor, they have been completely ruined. Thus the productivity of the rainforest soil is destroyed. Consequently, a new piece of rainforest has to be burned every two or three years—a self-perpetuating process without end. Native slash-and-burn agriculture involved small-enough plots so that the land could regenerate after the plots were abandoned. They could be replenished, in terms of both plant and animal species and nutrients from the adjacent land. Only where there are soils that are not too warm and that are still able to draw on mineral reserves in the remaining bedrock is it possible, after 10 or 20 years, to make renewed economic use of the secondary

forest that grows up after the burning of the original forest. This second harvest is bound to be more modest, and, even under these conditions, there is no true regeneration: The collapse of the system that recirculates nutrients makes deficient soils inevitable.

Probably the most nutrient-deficient, kaolinic clay soils anywhere are found in large stretches of the central Amazon region, in the so-called terra firma, sections of the Amazonia plain that do not flood. These soils were formed from sediments the rivers carried into the Amazon basin in the Tertiary period, that is, before the ice age. These sediments were carried into the Amazon basin from much-reduced mountains of ancient rock (the Guyana shield in the north and the Brazilian shield in the south). Most of the parent material of these soils must already have been quite weathered, sandy to claylike rock. The extreme paucity of nutrients of these regions is apparent in the chemistry of the water carried by streams in the rainforest. It is almost the same as distilled water; the concentration of salts in this water is about one thousandth of that found in forest streams of the eastern United States or in Europe. There is so little calcium in the water that no molluscs with calcareous shells live in the streams, nor are snails found on land because the uppermost layers of the soil are also devoid of calcium.

In keeping with the poverty of the soil, even the live biomass of the forest contains fewer nutrients than that of forests growing on more fertile soil. In the terra firma of central Amazonia, only one harvest is usually possible on land cleared by burning. Only relatively undemanding crops, such as pineapple, cassava, and sugar cane can be grown here. Pineapple and cassava take a full two years to reach harvestable size, and bananas, corn, peanuts, and beans cannot be cultivated. In better soils, cassava roots

grow to comparable size in as little as three months.

Local observation shows that people cannot live in these areas permanently without developing deficiency diseases. One especially noticeable sign is the unhealthy teeth seen even in young people. Even in pre-Columbian times, no Indian populations lived permanently in the plain of Tertiary sedimentation in central Amazonia, and, until this day, settlement has remained restricted to the fertile flood plains of rivers cutting through the Amazon lowlands, rivers originating in the Andes and in the Andes foothills. It is only outside the area of Tertiary sedimentation in the Amazon basin that human habitation extending far back in history is found in forests lying beyond the valleys of large rivers—namely, in the Amazonian peripheries located on the flattened shields and the Andes foothills, which consist of young, lightly weathered Andean sediments.

Central Amazonia is an example of a fully mature rainforest landscape. The forest has reached a stage that will ultimately be attained by all rainforests after a sufficiently long time. The young volcanic mountain landscapes in tropical Asia represent the other extreme. Natural erosion there accounts for the fact that enough surface material is carried away, even under a thick cover of vegetation so that the soils are continually rejuvenated by weathering bedrock, and periodic volcanic eruptions cover the earth with new ash. By making use of appropriate technology, such as terrace cultivation, harvests can be obtained year after year without need for fertilizers after the forest has been cut. Theoretically, crops could be grown here continuously until the mountains have worn down to nothing, the area has flattened out, the soils have grown deeper and deeper, and all the nutrient reserves in the upper soil levels have been used. The last stage in the aging process of a landscape is reached when even the clays disintegrate

Acrobats equipped to conquer heights

The pretty, red-eyed leaf frogs (left) are often found in the upper stories of Costa Rica's rainforest. The tips of their fingers and toes are modified into

suction cups and are thus able to cling to even smooth and treacherous surfaces. These frogs not only make their way upward on vertical stems and trunks by climbing and reaching, but sometimes also travel along leaf edges and stems, climbing upside down in a hanging position. The emerald tree frogs of the Seychelles also have sucker toes and are excellent acrobats (above top). Arboreal frogs feed on insects and their larvae, of which there is a great abundance in the canopy region.

Camouflaged hunters on silent paws

A large, carnivorous predator, the jaguar (left) is at the end of the food chain. Among its prey might well be a careless spider monkey (top) or the strange-looking bush dog (*Speothos venaticus*) (center). Brockets (*Mazama*) (bottom) are South American forest deer that are mostly nocturnal.

Rarities from the animal world

The ocelot (right) is an outstanding climber and swimmer. It hunts small mammals and, more often, birds and reptiles. Ocelots are an endangered species because illegal fur trade has

decimated their populations. The opossum (top) also has a valuable pelt. It is a marsupial and an omnivore. The aye-aye (bottom), a lemur, is one of the strangest primates. It lives in eastern Madagascar, is nocturnal in its habits, has incisor teeth that never stop growing, and feeds on fruit and nuts. The species is practically extinct because the Madagascans considered these animals evil omens and therefore hunted them mercilessly.

Famous for sluggishness

Although sloths are proverbially slow and sluggish, they are among the most successful larger mammals of the South American continent. There are five species, including the large three-toed sloth (top). A

sloth's pelt consists of an undercoat of short, fine hair and a layer of long, rough guard hairs among which algae grow. The green color of the algae serves as excellent camouflage. The fur of an immature puma is still delicately mottled (bottom). These spots also conceal and protect. They disappear completely as the animal reaches maturity.

Be embraced, all ye millions

The ever-humid, steaming rainforest is home to many curious creatures that fit properly into neither the plant nor the animal kingdom. They show traits that belong to neither of

these two classical divisions of life. The slime molds are one such class of strange organisms. Their common name, like their scientific name, *Myxomycetes*— derived from Greek terms meaning "slime fungi"—is misleading because slime molds have nothing in common with molds or fungi. They begin life as microscopically small spores that are carried aloft by the wind and transported over wide distances.

and disappear from the uppermost soil horizons. If the parent materials were predominantly granite and gneiss, as is the case in Amazonia, then sand is all that is left in the soil. These so-called podsol soils are found over large areas of Amazonia.

Most tropical rainforest soils lie somewhere between these two extremes—central Amazonia and the volcanic areas of Asia—and they differ widely in available nutrients. Fertility increases in proportion to the natural erosion due to the gradient of the terrain, but as a landscape flattens out and the soil ages, fertility decreases. In recent geological history, however, other factors— such as climate fluctuations during the ice age and the effects they had on the landscape—have repeatedly disrupted these simple processes of soil formation. It is still possible to explain the geochemical conditions as they exist on the different continents by referring to the processes briefly sketched above. To summarize the principles and processes at work on tropical soils, one could say that fertility—the nutrient reserves present in soil—depends strongly on the kind of parent material from which the soil is derived, as well as on age, average temperature, and rainfall. An understanding of these processes is also useful in determining how much they have affected the basic structure of ecosystems and how much human interference these ecosystems can tolerate.

Nutrients alone do not account for the quality of the rainforest soil, but we can skip over those combinations of factors that are responsible, for instance, for the soil's physical structure, its aeration, and its ability to hold water. No matter how different the soils of various locations may be in these respects, the tropical forests have adapted to them by developing an almost infinite variety of forms of vegetation and plant species. A thick cover of vegetation can grow on the most diverse kinds of soils as long as rainfall is heavy enough

throughout the year to keep the soil from drying out. Where soils have good water retention, as is the case with reddish clay soils, for instance, the forest can even withstand climate phases of sparse rainfall for a certain period. This is not possible, however, on very sandy, well-drained soils. On podsol soils, rainforest tree growth gives way to an entirely different vegetation within the same climatic region.

Rainforests depend on a humid climate. Real tropical rainforests can develop only where there is a minimum of 78 inches (2,000 mm) of precipitation distributed fairly evenly throughout the year. If, over several years, there are annual dry periods lasting more than two or three months with less than 2 to 4 inches (50–100 mm) of rainfall, the vegetation changes. The more well-defined such annual "dry periods" are, the greater the proportion of trees that shed their leaves during these times of low precipitation. This means that the normally dense canopy of the forest lets in more light. The sun's rays, 99 percent of which are otherwise absorbed year round by the trees' foliage, can now penetrate to the forest floor with full intensity and bring about considerable changes in the climate of the forest interior and, consequently, in the environmental conditions that prevail there. Temperature fluctuates more in the course of the day, as does relative humidity. In areas of evergreen rainforests, the monthly median temperature lies between about 75° and 79°F (24–26°C), with highs between 91° and 97°F (33–36°C) and lows between 64° and 68°F (18–20°C). Median daily fluctuations amount to no more than 12° to 14°F, (6 to 8°C). This is several times more than the annual temperature fluctuation, which is only 2° to 4°F, or 1 to 2°C, on the average. The average monthly relative humidity does not fall below 75 percent and in most cases remains considerably higher. The climatic data cited here apply only to lowland

rainforests up to an altitude of 1,000 to 1,300 feet (300–400 m). Evergreen rainforests extend, however, up to altitudes of 3,250 to 6,500 feet (1,000–2,000 m), where they give way to cloud and mountain forests. Upland or mountain forests differ considerably from lowland forests in their make-up; even at altitudes of 1,600 to 2,300 feet (500–700 m) the spectrum of tree species begins to shift dramatically.

The so-called inner tropical belt on both sides of the equator has a permanently humid climate. Adjacent to it to the north and the south are the outer tropical belts, which extend to the Tropic of Cancer and the Tropic of Capricorn, respectively. With increasing distance from the equator, precipitation becomes more and more concentrated in a shorter and shorter rain period. The average annual temperature decreases, while maximum temperatures rise and minimum temperatures drop. Relative humidity also fluctuates dramatically over the year. Eventually, precipitation diminishes and becomes highly variable. In response to these changes in climate, evergreen rainforests gradually give way to partially deciduous, seasonal rainforests, which in turn are replaced by humid savannas, dry savannas, steppes, and desert-like formations. With the change in climate from the inner equatorial belt to that of the outer tropical regions come fundamental changes in the processes of weathering and soil formation. In the equatorial zone with its continual rains, the soils of the lowlands are, as a rule, extremely low in nutrients, unless they are made up of young and only lightly weathered sediments. Farther from the equator, different geochemical developments can be observed, and the reserves of available nutrients in the soil increase. In semiarid to arid regions, finally, the accumulation in the soil of soluble chemicals produced by the weathering process can become high. Depending on the nature of the parent material and the evaporation rate, a crust of soluble salts can accumulate at or near the surface.

In the tropics, all intermediate stages between nutrient depletion and nutrient accumulation are found. The potential for agricultural utilization in these regions has been misassessed repeatedly, in complete disregard of the vegetation cover found. The fact is that basic ecological conditions in the tropics are extremely varied: In the inner belt, infertile soils receive abundant rainfall, while in the outer belts there are fertile soils that get only sparse precipitation. Between these two extremes there is a strip—much too narrow for extensive agricultural exploitation—with balanced geochemical and climatic conditions. Today's economic and political inequities between north and south derive, at least in part, from natural causes. In temperate latitudes, soil and climate conditions are much better suited to long-term, intensive agriculture.

Let us return to the evergreen rainforests that cover the most varied landscapes in the inner tropical belt. On all continents, tropical rainforests growing on comparable soils and terrain are structured quite similarly. The average height of mature trees in the Amazon region—115 to 150 feet (35–45 m)—may be somewhat less than that of trees in African and Asian forests, but the number of tree species, palms, lianas, and epiphytes is so huge that it is practically impossible to point out clear and striking differences. In the first place, it is very difficult to recognize by the trunk what kind of tree one is looking at: The thin, usually smooth bark differs little from species to species, as do the leaves in the crowns. Blossoms that could help identify a tree are visible only when they grow directly on the trunk, which is quite often the case, but many are far up in the canopy. Some plant families, such as bromeliads, the epiphytes so typical of the South American rainforests, are restricted to specific continents. In Africa and Asia, ferns

are a similarly characteristic class of plants. There are also many types of vegetation that occur throughout the tropics, though represented by different species in different parts of the world. The structure of the forest does not always follow the textbook model of three levels—canopy region, trunk region, and forest floor, or basement—very clearly. Individual trees that have grown exceptionally tall, the so-called emergents, protrude above the roof of the canopy. A well-developed tree forest has only sparse vegetation on the ground. There are few herbs and shrubs, and the undergrowth consists primarily of saplings. Flowers are rare in this basement area. One is most likely to become aware of flowering trees by the fragrance, and one is most likely to see them by following the rivers, where the banks are often covered with dense vegetation reaching—in contrast to the situation in the forest interior—all the way down to the water line.

Anyone visiting a rainforest for the first time will marvel at the surrounding lush greenness, especially in hilly or mountainous terrain. Visitors are likely to be disappointed, however because—apart from ants and some butterflies—hardly any animals are to be seen. Depending on the time of day, absolute silence may reign, interrupted periodically by the whirring of cicadas and only the croaking of frogs and toads or, more rarely, by bird calls.

It is hard to imagine that a life community on a single acre may contain as many as 200 different tree species. The fauna inhabiting the same area may include as many as 50,000 different animal species, the same number that is given for all the animal species that occur in the eastern part of North America or in central Europe. Fifty to 60 kinds of ants may live in a single tree. This almost equals the number of ant species in all of New York State. However, the huge army of different animal species is made up primarily of tiny arthropods. Tiny mites, minute spiders,

insects, termites, and ants populate the upper parts of the ground and the trees. In central Amazonia, beetles dominate in the treetops. Recent studies have shown that more than 905 species measure less than 2 millimeters. The same forests harbor the largest beetle of the world, the Hercules beetle (*Dynastes*), which is about 6 inches (15 cm) long. Bees, wasps, and butterflies are represented by innumerable species, and by far the greatest number of frogs and toads are found in the tropical rainforests. The same applies to lizards and snakes. Two thirds of all birds occur in rainforests. Mammals, on the other hand, are represented in rather modest numbers. The dominant groups are animals of small to moderate size: bats, rodents, and a number of biological forms that represent extreme adaptations to the rainforest biotope, that is, animals like sloths, armadillos, anteaters, pangolins, aardvarks and monkeys. Even in Africa, only a few large animals of the savanna penetrate the adjacent, partially deciduous forests. In the truly evergreen lowland rainforests, they are absent altogether. Antelopes exist there only in dwarf form, if we disregard the rare okapi.

Poor visibility is by no means the only reason why one sees so few animals, especially larger ones, in the rainforest. Even though the diversity of animal species is great, most species are represented only sparsely, and increasing body size markedly reduces the density of representation even further.

At the beginning of this essay, we discussed in some detail the extreme paucity of nutrients in the soils of low-lying tropical rainforests, especially in Amazonia. We also mentioned that at least 90 percent of the mineral nutrients of the entire ecosystem are locked up in the living, plant-based biomass. This raises the question of how rainforests can flourish in full maturity for millions of years on soils without discernible nutrient

When the spores settle on moist, decaying vegetation, such as fallen leaves or rotting wood, they germinate and produce flagellate protozoans, or swarm cells, that creep freely across the substrate in the manner of amoebas. They feed on bacteria and other micro-

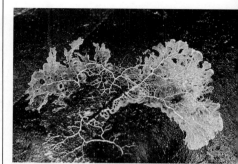

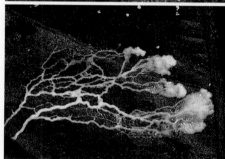

organisms. When two swarm cells collide, they may fuse. This is the starting point of a completely different life phase. Through repeated cell and nucleus division, a large, slimy mass of plasma is produced that may contain several hundred million cell-free nuclei; this is called the plasmodium.

Clowns among the rainforest birds

Toucans are lively rainforest birds of the New World whose most outstanding feature is their huge, brightly colored beaks. About 40 species of toucans are known. They feed mostly on fruit and nuts. They have developed great skill at harvesting fruit, tossing berries in the air with the tip of the bill and then catching them in the open bill and gulping them down.

A world of water

Voluminous, almost daily downpours send water hurtling earthward. The rain, split and branched into thousands of rivulets, passes through the canopy and runs down branches and tree trunks. In this pro-

cess the moisture is distributed over greater and greater surfaces, until it finally returns into the atmosphere by way of evaporation. A certain amount collects in rivers and forms mighty cascades over drops in the terrain. The Iguaca Falls in the border area between Argentina and Brazil are perhaps the most impressive example of a rainforest waterfall. The falls, 2.5 miles (4 km) wide, are split by rock outcroppings and islands into over 200 separate cataracts that tumble more than 260 feet (80 m) into a canyon (right page).

reserves. It has to be remembered, too, that with the seepage and the ground water, as well as with the streams and rivers that are totally devoid of minerals, nutrients are further washed out of the rainforests on a continual basis. Only one thing can make up for such a permanent outflow: rain. Indeed, scientific analysis of the precipitation has shown that rain water supplies the forest ecosystem with more nutrients—potassium, calcium, and phosphorus, for example—than are carried away in moving water. With these facts as a background, it still remains to be explained how the forest is able to keep the nutrient losses small enough to be replaced by nutrients captured by rain from the atmosphere. The shorter and more direct the nutrient cycle, the more reliable and steady must be the obvious balance between losses due to leaching and the meager supply of nutrients in the air. Available nutrients, whether in the form of fertilizing rain showers or of decomposing material in the ground, must be recycled immediately into the ecosystem in order to be retained.

A whole range of adaptive mechanisms that help keep the routes of the nutrient cycle short is apparent in nutrient-poor rainforest landscapes. Many of these mechanisms aim not only to retain released nutrients in the ecosystem, but also to use optimally the materials supplied by the rain.

By the time the precipitation that falls on the thick foliage of the canopy reaches the ground, its chemical composition is changed. In the course of running from leaf to leaf and dribbling down branches and trunks, the rain water passes over plant surfaces that are active in various ways and that give off substances as well as absorb dissolved chemicals. This exchange takes place especially where algae, lichens, and mosses grow in a dense mass on top of wood and foliage in the trunk and lower canopy regions. The surface layers of the forest floor

itself are permeated with a dense network of minute tree roots through which the water that soaks into the ground has to pass. In suitable spots, where rain water running down the trunk collects and runs off, roots even grow above the ground and are washed by the water. But the dense root system near the ground's surface has another, perhaps even more crucial, task: It guarantees—if only by being so extensive—that nutrients becoming available as the leaf mold decays are reabsorbed into the living biomass with as little loss as possible. The roots are able to do the job so well because of a symbiotic association between roots and fungi. Hyphae, that is, filaments of fungal growth, form on and invade the roots, forming the so-called mycorrhiza. This fungal network, which is either directly or indirectly part of the tree's root system, further permeates the ground and increases many times the surface area of living filter tissue that actively absorbs dissolved chemicals from the water that enters through the pores. In addition to absorbing water, the mycorrhizal fungi also participate actively in the breakdown of leaf litter. Ideal recyclers, they are essential in keeping the entire ecosystem functioning.

In the rainforests of central Amazonia, about 22 pounds (10 kg) of leaves, twigs, and branches fall annually on one square yard (1 m²) of forest floor. As a rule, the leaf litter forms only a thin layer on the ground because, after as little as two months, leaves are broken down completely by fungi and other soil organisms. In the permanently moist conditions found at ground level, tree roots are also able to rise out of the earth, moving into the immediate proximity of the litter. Where this happens, the fungi form a direct link between the leaf litter or the rotting dead wood and the tree's circulation system. In exchange for supplying plant nutrients, the fungi take from the trees substances that are otherwise not

readily available to them, especially carbohydrates and nitrogen compounds, which they need for the production of their own proteins. Without this symbiosis, this interdependent, closed nutrient cycle would not exist.

To keep the supply of nutrients evenly balanced also requires dealing frugally with available resources. This thriftiness takes many forms in the rainforests that grow in terra firma areas of central Amazonia. Reusable substances, for instance, and consequently nutrients, are withdrawn from the cells of older leaves before shedding time and are stored in the heart of the tree. As a consequence, the fallen leaves do not make good forage for the animals living on the forest floor, and fungi provide almost the only conceivable means of plowing back into the system whatever nutritive value is still present in the dead leaves.

Most trees develop seeds and fruits only sparingly. Seeds are generally packaged in such a way that they are difficult for animals to eat. There are few fruits that are edible for animals, and many leaf and flower buds contain substances that are repellent to animals. So-called flushing, that is, the rapid growth of leaves sprouting simultaneously on new twigs and the development of red color in these young leaves, is assumed to be a ploy to discourage hungry plant eaters. Mature leaves, as well as the tissues that surround bark, wood, and seeds, contain substances or structures that, by either mechanical or chemical means, prevent animals from feeding on them. The young leaves often lack these defenses, but because they all come out at once, animals cannot eat any large amount of them before maturation.

As soon as one moves from central Amazonia toward the peripheries—the old shields in the north and south and the Andean foothills in the west, including the alluvial valleys formed by the rivers descending

Bridging the elements

River valleys, especially those of the huge river systems in South America, almost always look like drowned landscapes. Here the most typical elements of the rainforest belt are combined: large

expanses of lowland and endless bodies of water that—despite their size—move only a fraction of the water mass that descends on the rainforest. In rainforest river landscapes like the one at the mouth of the Orinoco River shown here, the habitats of animals also overlap: A colony of herons will nest and breed only on land, but derives all its food from the waters of the river.

Where nature plays most liberally with colors

Just beyond the muddy mangrove coast of Venezuela, flocks of large silver herons and somewhat smaller silk herons gather. Mixed with them are bright

scarlet ibises, making a striking color contrast (large picture). Farther north, toward Central America, the scarlet ibis gives way to a similar ibis species that is pure white. Where the two species overlap, one finds mixed pairs.

Death and beauty side by side

The muddy, food-rich shallows make tropical mangrove shores highly attractive to water birds. Red ibises, herons, and brown pelicans scan for fish in the shallow, brackish lagoons. Predators

approaching a colony by either air or water are usually spotted instantly by at least one member of the colony, and consequently they present no major threat, for the entire flock will respond to a warning cry by attacking the invader. Sometimes, even smaller birds manage to drive away dreaded enemies, like the piranha (above), in this way.

Safety is greatest at the center of the colony. Nests close to the edge of a rookery are not so well protected and are therefore attacked by predators more often than those at the center. Although communal defense can provide effective protection against enemies, breeding in

colonies also has its disadvantages: Huge aggregations of birds actually attract predators.

from the Andes—conditions begin to change. With increasing amounts of nutrients available in the soil, the plant world becomes more generous toward animals. There are more and more seeds and fruits whose shape and consistency allow animals to eat them. The leaves are more nutritious for plant eaters; the budding tops of the palms growing here are no longer bitter and are even edible for humans.

Lecythidaceae, which include the trees that furnish what we call Brazil nuts, are a good example of adaptation correlated to the availability of nutrients. Species that grow on extremely poor soils develop few, small seeds and conceal them in woody pods hard as rock and several centimeters thick. Brazil nut trees (*Bertholletia excelsa*) are found only on the best soils in the northern and southern peripheral areas of the Amazonian rainforest. These triangular hard nuts are packed together in large numbers and encased, animal-proof, in solid, large round pods. Not even the world's largest rodent, the paca, can crack these pods. The Brazil nut tree's massive protection against animals that feed on fruit and nuts can also be seen as serving the ends of frugality in a different way. The heavy seed capsules, which take two years to form, remain where they drop, in the immediate vicinity of the tree's roots. Their chemical building blocks can thus be reabsorbed over the years into the tree's nutrient cycle. Related species in the same family, bearing sapucaia nuts, grow on the young and fertile alluvial soils of the Várzea River in the Amazon valley, which cuts through central Amazonia from west to east. These sapucaia trees form seed capsules that are larger than those of the Brazil nuts, the seeds themselves are comparable in size to Brazil nuts; but are covered with only a thin skin. The capsules hang upside down from the branches, looking like pots with large, round lids. As soon as the seeds are ripe, they drop to the flooded ground,

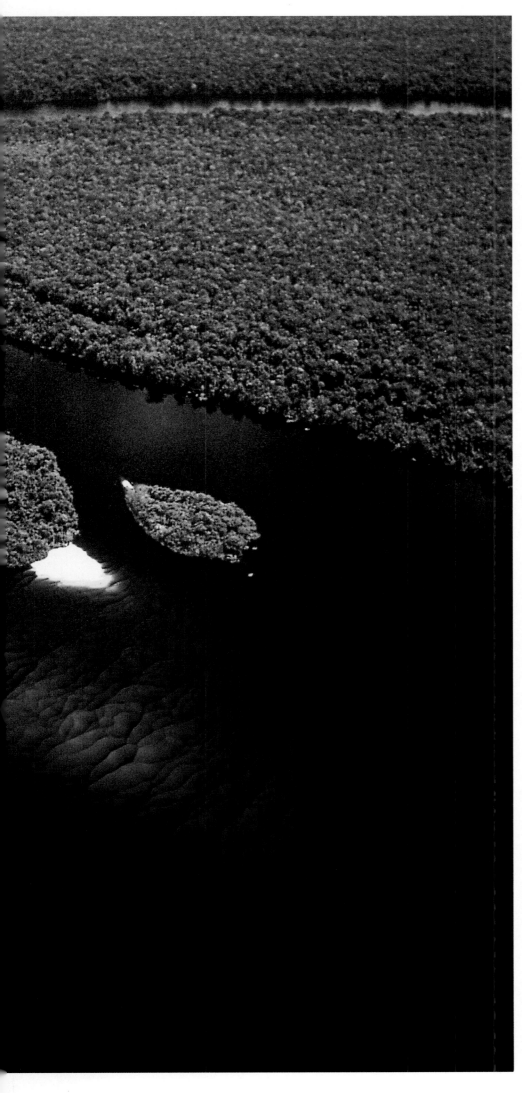

where they become food for fish. Where nutrients are plentiful, trees have evolved dispersal mechanisms that use strategies which also benefit the animals that are involved in dispersing their seeds.

The underlying bedrock, the relief of the terrain, and the age of the soils have combined to create a geochemical gradient in central Amazonia that extends from the periphery to the center, from the watersheds to the areas of Tertiary sedimentation. Both the vegetation and the animal world reflect this gradient, which is responsible for the differences in the various ecosystems ranging from the peripheries to the center. The scientific studies and observations conducted thus far indicate that with increasing impoverishment of otherwise well-structured soils in central Amazonia, the diversity of species displayed by trees, lianas, and palms becomes significantly greater. Not far from Manáus, more than 200 species of mature woody plants were identified on one acre. In peripheral regions, no comparable species diversity is found. As already mentioned, Brazil nut trees grow only in exceptionally fertile soils— usually where younger volcanic rock is layered over old granite and gneiss. Here the nut trees often grow in clusters, but the species diversity is much reduced. It is reasonable to assume that the greater the diversity of plants growing on a small area, the more self-contained the nutrient cycle in the jungle will remain. Different plants presumably need differing amounts of nutrients, depending on their age, their species, and the time of year. They absorb the nutrients directly or indirectly through their roots in staggered phases of activity. We may thus conclude that increased species diversity allows better utilization of nutrients released within the system or newly added by rain. From this perspective, the enormous variety of biological forms that characterizes the vegetation cover turns out to be a highly efficient strategy of

Rivers are not always life lines

Although huge masses of water continually circulate through the rainforest, the water is usually unable to collect and carry away many nutrients from the root horizon of the trees. The runoff

collecting in even the biggest river systems is therefore relatively poor in dissolved nutrients, and the water often is tinged yellow or brown from chemical-like tannins leached from the vegetation (above). The river systems of South America, even today not completely surveyed and mapped, dissect and segment the rainforest, but these waters are not arteries feeding the landscape because, instead of supplying the ecosystem with water, they merely conduct excess water away. On the other hand, rivers long provided the only way by which humans could penetrate to the heart of these continent-sized areas.

The miraculous world of leaves

Sometimes nature is profligate with color. Blossoms and leaves can be almost unbelievably many-colored. Nature furnishes many examples of purely aesthetic beauty that seem to owe their existence almost entirely to a playful impulse to experiment with colors and shapes. The tropical rainforest is full of miracles, and some of them can be admired in every single leaf.

A thriller from the animal world

Fer-de-lance snakes are passive hunters. They lie motionless, waiting patiently until their prey flies up to them. Attracted by the nectar of a heliconia inflorescence, a rufous-tailed hummingbird, somewhere between a bumblebee and a swallow in size, approaches. The tiny exotic bird just barely managed to escape this eyelash viper's fangs.

As though they were one

Disguise and deception are raised to the level of perfection in an ongoing game of hide-and-seek. A camouflaged creature remains invisible to the searching eyes of its predators because it blends into its surroundings. An animal that disguises itself to look like something else is seen but not recognized.

Flashy colors used as alarm signals

adaptation to a nutrient-poor landscape that—except for the lack of nutrient reserves—offers extremely favorable environmental conditions.

We have no conclusive scientific studies of the extent to which the geochemical gradient in Amazonia also determines the variety of animal life. We do know that at least the larger mammals occur in greater population densities as one moves from the center to the periphery of the Amazon watershed. To the best of our judgment, the distribution of many amphibians, reptiles, and birds is greater in the peripheral regions, especially toward the Andean foothills, where geochemical conditions are exceptionally favorable, and in the Guyana region. In the Amazon basin, the distribution of insect species—which scientists have not yet studied comprehensively but suspect to range in the millions—is still quite unclear, nor do we know how densely individual insect species are distributed. There is sufficient indication that the population density of many insect groups increases from the center toward the periphery and that many species are limited to the periphery. Thus, blood-sucking insects like horse-flies, biting midges, black flies, and mosquitoes are unknown in central Amazonia, except in the fertile valleys fed by rivers descending from the peripheries. Also lacking are the swarms of harmless sweat-licking flies and stingless bees that in the outer regions of Amazonia can be as much of a plague as stinging and blood-sucking insects. Apparently, there were never enough mammals in central Amazonia to maintain populations of insects that depend on blood from mammals for sustenance. The general absence of mosquitoes is ultimately linked to the geochemistry of the region, too. Mosquito larvae develop in small bodies of water, where they feed on algae. In central Amazonia the lack of nutrients is so great that in the pools left by flooding

forest streams not enough algae can grow to serve as an adequate food source for mosquito larvae. The few mosquitoes one does encounter have developed in the bromeliads in the treetops. The water collected in the leaf axils of these epiphytes is an ecosystem of its own, in which nutrients accumulate not only from rain but also from dead plant material and drowned insects.

Amazonia shows especially clearly how the complex interrelationships between soil fertility, vegetation, and the animal world work in rainforest ecosystems. If we apply what we have learned here to other continents, we will understand better why animals find better food supplies and therefore occur in greater numbers in Africa and Asia, where more favorable geochemical conditions prevail in most of the rainforest regions. In simplified terms, the interrelationships can be described as follows: If the soil is fertile and plants have adequate nutrient reserves, a large number of animals can be accommodated as consumers in the ecosystem. Food is offered to them in different ways: passively in the form of buds and leaves, and actively, as part of a dispersal strategy, in the form of seeds and fruits that are attractive and palatable to animals. This kind of life community is oriented toward harvesting by animals, and the success of its functioning in many ways depends on that harvesting.

As a landscape and its soils age, the nutrient reserves dwindle, and eventually the best strategies entail nutrient cycles that are as short as possible. To this end, animals are excluded from these strategies. Only those groups are welcome that serve a useful purpose, and this changes with conditions. A common strategy for survival includes pollinators, which are present in an incredible diversity of species as well as in huge numbers of individuals. These include bees, butterflies, flies, and many tiny beetles—all of them organisms

that consume only nectar and pollen, while helping the plant produce viable seeds.

Another important task is performed by termites that, together with many beetle larvae—some of which are huge—break down dead wood. On the other hand, a relatively small number of creatures feed directly on live plants, having succeeded in breaking through the chemical and mechanical barriers plants have devised to protect themselves against plant eaters. Many tiny insects, especially beetles, are found here, but we do not yet know enough about their way of life and their exact place in the ecosystem. Larger primates, which never occur in great numbers, also feed partially on plant matter. The more plentiful smaller primate species, on the other hand, live primarily on insects.

One group of animals that has overcome the various defense mechanisms of the vegetation most successfully is the leaf-cutting ants. In the course of evolution they have abandoned the traditional, not very specialized, robbing method of food gathering typical of ants and now live entirely on fungi that they cultivate themselves. Leaves that are nutritionally worthless to other animals are cut into small pieces, mostly at night, and stored in well protected, "climate-controlled" chambers in earth mounds, where they serve as a substrate for specific fungi that are found only in leaf-cutter ant mounds. These fungi draw all usable substances from the leaves and the ants regularly harvest the fungi to feed both themselves and their larvae.

Termites, too, subsist essentially on fungi. Fungi are absorbed directly with the dead wood that is riddled with them. More highly developed termites also establish productive fungi factories in their mounds, much as leaf-cutting ants do. It seems only fitting in the context of the nutrient cycles typically found in rainforests that the basic food of the small creatures inhabiting the ground should consist of fungi,

The hunting techniques of chameleons

Chameleons have adapted in many ways to life in the trees. Their extremities, for instance, have evolved into highly specialized climbing and grasping tools. Their eyes can move independently of each other, searching in several directions at once for insects, which the chameleon then captures and eats with the help of a long, sticky tongue.

Snakes are food specialists

Not all snakes are patient hunters that wait motionless in hiding until, with a venomous bite, they can launch a surprise attack on their prey. The cat-eyed snake living in the rainforest of Costa Rica

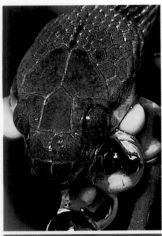

(top) specializes in eating the eggs of leaf frogs. How do snakes get into the treetops? There are acrobats among them, such as the arboreal boas and their relatives (bottom), which have developed prehensile tails that they use as climbing aids. They curl the end of their tail around a branch in a tight coil, raise their body, then wrap the front part of their body around the next-higher branch.

that is, microorganisms whose job it is to break down the litter that accumulates on the forest floor.

Cooperatives involving different organisms often prove efficient. We can safely assume that there are myriads of other, still unexplored, symbiotic relationships between plants and animals (involving insects, especially) that play crucial roles in the functioning of rainforest ecosystems.

The last link in the nutrient cycle is made up of the many organisms—arthropods as well as vertebrates—that control the plant and fungi eaters and that in turn serve as food for a higher level of consumers. One form of animal life that is always present in the rainforest is ants, which are found in an overwhelming number of species and shapes. They play a key role in keeping the food and nutrient cycle efficient. Together with termites, they in turn serve as food for many small and large vertebrates ranging upward in size to the giant armadillo and the ant bear of South America and the pangolins, or scaly anteaters, and aardvarks of Africa and Asia. Finally, central Amazonia is not lacking in giant snakes and large and small cats, such as the puma, the jaguar, and the ocelot. Because of their small number and nocturnal habits, however, these cats are rarely seen.

The clearly demonstrable connections between geochemistry, vegetation, and fauna in tropical South America are also at work in the forest ecosystems of the Old World's tropics. To be sure, geochemical conditions in both Africa and Southeast Asia are considerably more favorable. In the tropics of the Old World, there are no large areas of comparatively ancient and nutrient-poor sedimentation. The relatively narrow equatorial rainforest belt in Africa extends mostly over fairly degraded mountain formations and ends near the nutrient-rich arid zones to both the north and the south. In the east, it stops at the East African Rift. The Congo basin has

always had a considerable inflow of nutrients from surrounding regions. As in Amazonia, some of these nutrients are supplied in the form of rain. Except for a few geochemically impoverished areas on Borneo and Sumatra, the forests of the Asiatic mainland and the Indonesian islands have an abundant supply of nutrients. Young mountains, often covered with extrusions of volcanic rock, make possible the formation of very fertile soils. Here, rubber trees can be raised in plantations, while in Amazonia these trees grow only widely dispersed, even where there is exceptionally rich alluvial soil. Trees offer birds and mammals seeds and fruits in plentiful quantities. It is thus not surprising that in Africa and tropical Asia, fruit-eating bats and other mammals are much more common and grow larger than in South America. No doubt the existence of adequate food supplies was also a prerequisite for large animals like orangutans, chimpanzees, and gorillas to evolve in adaptation to their rainforest habitat.

The flora and fauna, as well as the presence of humans on the three continents, are affected by the geochemical downcurve that runs from Asia across Africa to South America. These geochemical conditions have always affected humans in their efforts to create a living environment for themselves. Humans have penetrated into the forest by choice or have been forced to retreat into it by necessity on all continents. They have made use of the opportunities the forests offered, submitted to the constraints of their environment, and adapted their way of life to the forest. Ultimately the availability of food—especially the limited sources of protein—determined human population density. The limits of the population that rainforest regions can adequately support are probably reflected in the average settlement density in these regions as it existed toward the end of the last century. A rough estimate is that there was about .4 person per square mile

in Amazonia, 4 persons in Africa, and at least 40 persons in Southeast Asia. These graduated numbers directly express the potential for utilization of the rainforests on the three continents. Today's overutilization of these regions ignores the basic conditions of rainforest ecosystems, the interconnections between the elements of these systems, and the inevitable consequences of overexploitation.

We have emphasized that in fertile volcanic landscapes, long-term agricultural use is possible without negative effects. In Africa, especially in the forests of the wide transitional zones leading to the evergreen forests, nomadic agriculture, facilitated by the open landscapes, has been practiced since ancient times. In Amazonia, human settlement based on nomadic agriculture existed only on the peripheries and in the valleys of the rivers that originate there.

Ecological and geochemical conditions have contributed greatly to the wholesale cutting and burning of forests in Southeast Asia and West Africa in the past few decades. As a consequence of this massive deforestation, truly vast closed forests now remain only in the Congo basin and in the Amazon region. The rainforests growing in the mountains of Southeast Asia are often made up of very tall trees belonging to relatively few species, which makes logging economically profitable. Lumbering conditions were similarly favorable in West Africa, where it was also possible to cut a large amount of good timber per unit of area. Thus far, central Amazonia, although easily accessible through its network of rivers, has not been attractive to the timber industry. Too many different kinds of trees stand next to each other, most of them consisting of wood that is not economically valuable to the wood products industry. The scarcity of nutrients results in slow growth, and, in addition, many substances that are incorporated into the tree's cells make the wood heavy and often brittle. Until recently the less species-rich and therefore economically more promising forests on the periphery of Amazonia were safe—like the forest regions in the Congo basin—because of their inaccessibility. This is no longer the case, however. Here, too, large-scale devastation of the remaining forest reserves has set in. Logging often starts with the selective cutting of especially valuable trees, sometimes only one or two per acre. Every tree that is cut takes several dozen others down with it, so that half the stand surrounding the cut tree is ruined or severely damaged—not to mention the com-pletely mangled forest floor. In the most favorable scenario, the forest is then left alone. Normally, however, land-hungry settlers follow the roads cut into the forest and complete the work of destruction. Forest areas that have been opened up are burnt over for short-term agricultural use.

We do not yet know how much damage is done to a rainforest ecosystem if single trees are cut and taken out with use of the least-disruptive harvesting methods. A complex network of interrelationships exists among a multitude of plants and animals, all of which depend on each other to a greater or lesser extent. The structures making up the ecosystems on poor soils seem to be especially varied and multileveled, and any interference in such forests is bound to have harmful effects. Irreparable damage is done where, as is the practice today, large tracts are cut down to make room for soybean and sugar cane plantations or for pasture land. The moment the protective cover of vegetation is removed, the degradation of the soil and consequently of the landscape begins. The sun dries out the upper layer of the soil. The humus substances that had accumulated as a result of fungal activity and activities of innumerable other soil organisms breaking down the litter are destroyed. Previously, kaolinic clay soils temporarily bound free nutrients

and prevented their leaching away, now the rain washes away the clay particles, which are no longer protected by a layer of leaf litter. Surface erosion increases at a rapid rate, and streams and rivers are muddied with soil material that is being carried away. The soils leach out and eventually become totally unusable for any kind of long-term agricultural production. The scarcer the forests become and the more the pace of deforestation accelerates, the more unlikely the possibility becomes that some day this land could again grow a protective forest cover. The plants and the animals that could do the job have been exterminated.

The rainforests are a component of our world that significantly determines the earth's climate. But above and beyond that, they are the most magnificent and complete manifesta-

tion of creation. We cannot shirk the responsibility of preserving the splendor of these forests, yet we must seek to protect the rainforests in ways that still allow utilization. Decimating the last remaining forests will not solve the social and economic problems that plague the rainforest regions. It will only magnify those problems to global proportions.

The law of the rainforest: diversity

The rainforests of Amazonia demonstrate especially clearly the correlation between soil fertility, vegetation, and fauna. As far as we can tell, the

range of many amphibians, reptiles, and birds is strikingly limited to the peripheral areas. There are also clear signs that the population density of many insect groups increases from the center toward the periphery and that many insects occur only on the periphery.

Josef Reichholf

Creation's Gene Archive: Where Life Overflows

The inventory of the species
living in tropical rainforests is breaking
all records. As many as 20,000 different
animal species may exist on several acres of
land within the rainforest. That is equal to
the number of *all* the animal species found in
the whole of the eastern United States.
Scientific estimates place the total number
of species in the tropical forest zone
as high as 20 to 30 million.

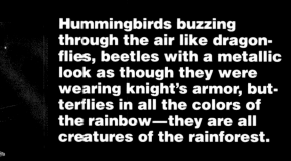

Hummingbirds buzzing
through the air like dragon-
flies, beetles with a metallic
look as though they were
wearing knight's armor, butterflies in all the colors of
the rainbow—they are all
creatures of the rainforest.

The most gorgeous roof on earth

No other biome contains the number of plant and animal species found in tropical rainforests. Research during the last few years has revealed that in the canopy region alone, there are many more insect species than anyone had suspected.

A seething biomass

The jungle is a colossal mass of vegetable matter. The biomass weighs as much as 400 tons or more per acre. By far the greatest amount of it is made up of trees and other woody plants, such as lianas.

Only flying could be better

The flying lizards—a form of agama—of the Southeast Asian rainforests cannot match the powerful, propelled flight of insects, birds, and bats, but they have the ability to sail elegantly from tree to tree or glide slowly to the ground.

The forest consists almost entirely of vegetation

The incredible denseness of rainforests where there are no extensive borders or large clearings has been created through mutual adaptation and competition over tens of thousands of tree generations. Such a forest is a closed ecosystem that seems static at first glance, but is highly dynamic, metabolizing and recyling substances at a breath-taking rate. Most of the biomass is made up of vegetation; animals constitute less than 1 percent of it.

The diversity of life-forms in the tropical rainforest regions is of unequaled magnitude. No other major ecological community or biome contains a variety of animal and plant species that is even remotely comparable.

Scientific investigations of the last few years have revealed staggering numbers of new insects, tiny beetles, especially. The canopy of the rainforest alone may have as many species as the entire earth was once believed to contain. Estimates that seemed valid even 10 years ago are now meaningless. As recently as 1980, scientists who systematically classify, describe, and identify new plants and animals assumed that there were somewhere between 2 and 3 million species worldwide; today all we can say with certainty is that this number is much too low. Presently, estimates range from 20 to over 30 million. If we assume that there may be 20 or 30 million different species, this implies that we now know less than one tenth of them. We have to look to the rainforests for the other 90 or more percent of this surprising profusion of species. The earth's other biomes have been more closely studied than rainforests, so most of the new species will be found in the rainforest.

Unfortunately, however, hundreds, if not thousands, of species are disappearing from the face of the earth every year, never to be seen again, as the rainforests are cut and burned by over 50,000 square miles annually. We have reason to think that since the Cretaceous period 65 million years ago—a time span hard for the mind to grasp—there has been no mass extinction of species comparable to what is happening in our time.

Every day, approximately 230 square miles (600 km²) of rainforest fall victim to the campaign of significant destruction that started about 30 years ago and has accelerated ever since. Day after day, uncounted numbers of animal and plant species dis-appear as a result of deforestation. They vanish, and no power on earth will bring them back, for extinction is final and irreversible.

With the exception of extinction, much of what we humans do to nature can be repaired. With the increased ecological awareness that has come in recent years, much damage has been reversed. Yet we witness the greedy exploitation of nature's greatest treasure, the most precious gift of life on earth, and remain largely passive, as though this massive extinction of life-forms were none of our business. Many industrial nations mobilize huge budgets and call on their best scientists to combat such environmental problems as the hole in the atmosphere's ozone layer or acid rain. But, in comparison with the sums devoted to study the damage sustained by the forests in the north temperate zone, only pennies are spent to explore the earth's storehouse of life in the tropical rainforest regions. It is not too surprising, consequently, that it has taken us until now, when the situation has deteriorated almost beyond hope, to awaken to the fact that these zones harbor many more species than anyone had ever suspected. Now we are too late even to name the plants and animals that have disappeared, let alone study them to discover qualities that could have benefited humanity.

All we can do is to try to save what is still there to be saved. At this time, at the beginning of the 1990s, barely half of the rainforest area that once existed remains. What is left amounts to about 2.7 million square miles (7 million km²), still a substantial chunk, it might be said. From the perspective of trying to preserve species diversity, however, it represents a portion shrunk to dangerously small dimensions. Many isolated stands and preserves remaining from the rainforests that spanned the continents along the equator in an almost unbroken belt a quarter of a century ago have become so small that it will be difficult, if not impossible, for them to last over time. They dot a sea of desolation like islands, and only a few exceptionally hardy species will manage to survive the coming years on these rainforest outposts. For the majority of rainforest species, the future looks bleak. They will languish for a while, then disappear, one after the other, or many all at once, as the size of their refuges shrinks below a certain critical point, for each species needs a minimum area of distribution if it is to survive. It is not enough for a few representatives of a species to be left somewhere in a refuge; under such conditions no stands can grow large enough to ensure continued existence. There has to be a minimum population, as scientists call the critical number of individuals that must be present in a given area for self-propagation. In the case of rainforest trees, for example, several hundred to a thousand trees of the same species are required; a handful will not do. But often there is not enough area for that many in the remaining stands of forest. That is why even preserves and national parks offer no guarantee of survival to the species contained in them. If the protected areas are too small and are no longer connected to larger tracts of forest, they may prove unable to halt extinction.

It may sound strange to hear that so many species are so severely threatened in the tropical forests. Are worried nature lovers exaggerating a little, perhaps, in an effort to save a bit more tropical rainforest than might otherwise remain? When land is cleared for agricultural use in tropical countries, is it not basically the same process that occurred long ago in other parts of the world? In the eastern United States, practically nothing remains of the original forests. The same is true in Europe and in many other parts of the world. With few exceptions—and even in these cases, the landscape has not been immune to human interference and change—land

A butterfly alights...

Butterflies have been appropriately dubbed flying jewels. Hardly any other insect group appeals to our senses with a comparable beauty of form and colors. A bright red *Dryas* butterfly has settled on the head of a spectacled caiman (large picture) and is drinking the salty lacrimal fluid. (Small pictures, counter-clockwise from the top) the iridescent *Thekla* butterfly belongs to the *Lycaenidae* family. The bright pigmentation of the *Delias* pair represents a warning color. The butterfly displaying an unusual blue and red color combination belongs to the family of *Papilionidae*. The metallic blue of the *Morpho* is produced entirely by the refraction of light, rather than by pigmentation. Glasswing butterflies are practically translucent because they have few scales on their wings.

...seldom all by itself

Butterflies settle by the dozens on the damp soil along a river to absorb water and dissolved minerals. The mouth parts of adult butterflies are so highly specialized that they are able only to suck up liquids. The sug-

ary nectar of flowers is often insufficient to maintain the proper metabolic balance, and they take advantage of any opportunity to increase their nutrient intake—even drinking the sweat off the skin of humans making their laborious way through the rainforest. The moth, *Chrysiridia madagascariensis* (above top) is day-flying and belongs to the large family of *Uraniidae.* Nevertheless, some members of this moth family are almost as beautiful as the brightly colored day-flying butterflies.

Each butterfly lives a solitary life

While in their pupal stage, butterflies register minute signals from their environment to determine the right time to hatch. When the moment has arrived,

hundreds of butterflies of a certain species appear all at once. They form no social ties, however, and only the presence of food or certain environmental factors cause them to congregate. Flying in swarms or group formations is therefore the exception rather than the rule. The exotically beautiful *Morpho* butterfly (above top) is usually seen singly. Even its splendid beauty is only transitory, for a butterfly's life is measured in weeks at best.

A silent strangler at work

Wildlife is rare in the tropical rainforest, and consequently the amazing diversity of species went unrecognized for a long time. No one suspected it because the animals were seldom seen.

A wealth of species beyond counting

Beetles must be by far the most successfully adapted order of animals—they make up more than one third of all known animal species and nearly two fifths of

all insects. They exist in the rainforest in a confusing array of shapes and colors, including conspicuous individuals such as the fire-engine-red fire beetle (bottom) from Sri Lanka and the leaf cockroach (top). All beetles can fly well. The hardened wing covers protect the wings when they are not flying; the wings themselves are transparent.

preserves generally represent "nature after human use," places like heaths, dry meadows, previously logged woods, lake shores, or artificial lakes. In the United States, the only places where the environment has remained in essentially its natural state are high mountain areas, deserts, large swamps, and a few small stands of virgin forest found in the Pacific Northwest and Alaska. Except for these places, which represent only a small fraction of the country, the land has been modified and shaped by over two hundred years of cultivation in many parts, but most of the original indigenous species are nevertheless still present. The animal species that have been exterminated in the United States in historical times can be counted on the fingers of one's hand. A considerably larger number of species were forced to retreat to neighboring regions to the south and north and are of great concern to those devoted to protecting nature, but most species still exist, only in small numbers.

It would seem, then, that the damage should not be that serious even if chunks of tropical forest almost as big as New York State are turned into arable land or wasteland. After all, there are still such vast expanses of rainforest left to which animals and plants can retreat. In North America, Europe, and other parts of the world, nature has managed on the whole to adapt quite well to man's opening up of the forests. No one today can imagine that a few thousand years ago, most of eastern North America was covered with closed forests. Hard as it may be to believe, these primordial forests were home to fewer species than the cultivated landscapes that have replaced them. Many plant and animal species—in fact, some fauna and flora, such as deer and robins, now found in the more open country of the United States—were once much rarer. Some other animals, such as possums and armadillos, migrated from their original

habitats in the southeast and west. Many of our plants, including most of our weeds, are emigrants from Europe. Cultivated landscapes are the work of man, and many species flourished in them until quite recently, when man began to introduce all kinds of poisons into the soil, apply excessive amounts of fertilizer, and create huge monocultures. Only then did the massive population decline of long-established species set in, leading to the situation we so much deplore.

It is this recent history we have to keep in mind if we want to understand why we cannot afford to remain calmly indifferent in face of the threat that looms over the tropical rainforests, the environment that holds the world's richest variety of species. We cannot hope that economic development and ecological coexistence in the rainforests will resemble what happened in the settlement of North America and Australia and, earlier, in Europe.

This brings us to the question of what is so special about the diversity of species found in tropical rainforests. What is it good for? How did it come about? How can we preserve it? We have to answer these three questions if we want to understand tropical rainforests and if we harbor even the slightest hope of saving at least a fraction of this immense variety for the future.

Let us begin by finding out what this diversity is good for. Only if we know what purpose it serves can we begin to understand its origins in the course of earth's history. Once we understand the evolution of species diversity in the tropics, we can seek ways to preserve this diversity. Even sustainable utilization of rainforest areas has to be approached with an understanding of the origin of species diversity; otherwise, even these practices will turn quickly into devastating exploitation.

Now we need to turn back to what goes on inside the rainforests. This forest ecosystem is

remarkable in many respects, and it differs markedly in its functioning from what we are used to in north temperate forests. Earlier chapters of this book discussed some of these topics in detail. What is of special importance in this context has to do with how nutrient cycles function in the rainforest.

A rainforest is made up of an enormous mass of plant material. The weight of this material amounts to 400 tons per acre (1,000 t per ha) or more. By far the greatest part of this plant biomass is made up of trees and other woody plants, such as lianas. The average biomass of rainforests is two to three times as great as that found in nontropical forests.

This huge amount of vegetation turns out, upon closer examination, to support few animals. The average visitor to the rainforest is inevitably surprised that almost no large animals are to be seen in this vast forest, and even biologists have to search a long time before they find what they are looking for. In abstract numbers: The 400 tons of vegetation per acre are matched by only 40 pounds (50 kg) of animals. Even if we add the small organisms that live in the soil, we still end up with no more than 166 pounds (200 kg), not even the equivalent of one cow.

Because larger animals are rare in the tropical rainforest, we remained unaware for a long time of the immense diversity of animal species there. No one suspected it, because most of the animals there were seldom seen.

The numbers quoted do not, of course, apply to all the rainforests in the tropics. There are major variations from continent to continent and among different regions within the rainforest zone. The forests of Southeast Asia, for instance, contain considerably more wildlife, especially large animals, than those of Africa. Amazonia scores the lowest by far. The numbers cited above, which reveal so blatantly the striking disparity between vegetation life and animal life, are based on Amazonia, the center of the largest rainforest expanse on earth.

What does this disparity indicate? Why are animals so rare in Amazonia, and why are their numbers so much lower in other rainforest regions than in tropical steppes and savannas?

Science has the answer. Animals are so rare because of a lack of food. Rainforests do not produce a surplus that can serve as an abundant food supply for animals. What the forest gives, it yields only in scant quantities. Much, indeed most, of the plant matter is poisonous for animals. The trees, by far the largest part of the biomass, produce innumerable poison combinations to protect themselves against the threat that plant-eating animals present to their vitality. Only a very few animal species or groups of animals succeed in finding a way around these defenses. Examples are ants of various kinds and termites, which can be seen wherever one goes—if one pays attention to such small creatures. Ants often amount to more than half of the animal biomass in tropical rainforests.

One group of ants, the leaf-cutting ants, has been especially successful: The leaf-cutters' trick consists in feeding leaves, cut down to proper size by their sharp mandibles and chewed to a pulp, to fungi they raise in underground "gardens." The fungi are unaffected by the poisonous substances in the leaves and absorb only what they need for their growth and for forming spores. The rest is discarded. The ants live on the fruiting bodies of the fungi. The large termites of the genus *Macrotermes* have evolved similar methods. They, too, cultivate fungi for food in special nurseries.

The role fungi play in rainforests appears even greater if we turn our attention away from the animals and focus on the trees. Almost all tree species in the tropical rainforest have evolved a symbiotic relationship between their roots and fungi. This association is called mycorrhiza. Fungi also help orchid seeds, which are no larger than grains of dust, germinate and develop into healthy young plants. Fungi can break down dead plant material rapidly, thus making recyclable nutrients available again quickly for the trees' growth. Fungi also help decompose animal cadavers. They are present everywhere in tropical forests because the humidity and warmth there offer optimum conditions to these strange, often undervalued life forms halfway between plant and animal. Without fungi, tropical rainforests could not function as the highly self-contained ecosystems they are, in which practically no mineral nutrients are lost.

From this perspective, plants, fungi, and animals fit together in one unified system, forming an all-inclusive symbiosis whose purpose it is to keep circulating the meager supplies of nutrients, especially inorganic salts—such as magnesium, potassium, sodium, and calcium—and phosphorus and nitrogen compounds, which are needed for the production of protein. Ninety percent of these nutrients, which are essential for life to flourish, are being passed back and forth continuously among the different life-forms of the rainforest. It is crucial to let as little as possible escape into the ground water, for whatever ends up in the groundwater is lost to the forest. Of course, leaching cannot be prevented altogether, no matter how self-contained the nutrient cycle may be. But whatever losses occur are offset by precipitation, because minute amounts of nitrogen, phosphorus, and inorganic salts are contained in dissolved form in the rain water. The tropical rainforests, then, function like gigantic nutrient filters, through which almost nothing escapes that can be of use to the organisms.

Most species have adapted to this way of life. They are as thrifty in their use of precious nutrients as can possibly be imagined. Now the diversity of species suddenly begins to make sense: Diversity magnifies the efficiency of the "nutrient trap"—which is what a rainforest really is—because the many, many different species fill all conceivable niches.

Forty, 80, or as many as 200 different kinds of trees growing on 1 acre do not represent a whim of nature, but are a necessity that makes survival possible under conditions of extreme nutrient shortage. The rainforest soils are depleted; they contribute practically no plant nutrients. Thus, everything the forest needs to sustain itself it has to conserve within itself and supplement from the air. Such a system can work only as long as the forest retains its density and only if all avenues of nutrient loss are eliminated. The rainforest cannot afford any leaks. Species diversity is one thing that prevents leaks. Each tree species has developed its own specialty for utilizing to the fullest the available nutrients. That is why few trees of the same species are found growing next to each other; only after a number of other kinds of trees have "cycled through" that location can an earlier species return.

Animals help in this process. They carry seeds and fruits away from the parent tree and sow them, so to speak, in new places. They also take care of pollination, and they defend many vulnerable trees against plant-eating animals. In return, the trees produce special secretions on which their protectors feed.

The larger kinds of animals that exist in the tropical rainforests are rather small and few in number in comparison to their relatives living in the steppes and savannas, and they are sparsely distributed. A group of medium-sized monkeys living in central Amazonia needs a forest area of at least 1 square mile. In the case of capuchin and howler monkeys, 1 square mile (1 km²) generally supports barely 20 individuals. An average group consisting of 10 to 15 monkeys

Intricate beauty of detail

At first glance, the difference between cockroaches and true beetles is not always apparent. The ball cockroach (top) has boldly marked wing covers, while the pollinating leaf cockroach (bottom) shows metallic light reflections. The life cycle of cockroaches includes no larval and pupal stages; the young nymphs simply resemble the adult insect more and more each time they shed their skins. Beetles, on the other hand, may spend months or even years as larvae caterpillars (grubs) before they emerge in their adult form.

A superabundance of nesting sites and food

The spatial complexity of the rainforest with its contact associations—a tangled intermingling of tree trunks, branches, and foliage—gives

rise to an abundance of microhabitats. Birds, especially, being able to cover distances effortlessly in direct flight, have made this highly structured environment their own and over millions of years have diversified into a huge number of species. Rainforest birds represent an incredibly wide range of species, with truly exotic plumage and all conceivable kinds of dietary habits. The black-headed oriole (above) fits perfectly into this environment.

Motionless in the tangle of branches

Arboreal snakes generally merge into the background of their habitat, their coloring either conforming to the predominant shades of green or adopting the irregularly mottled aspect of a

branch covered with epiphytes. When lying motionless in the tree branches, these snakes often appear to be a permanent part of the vegetation, especially if their shapes melt into the surrounding pattern of light and shadow. It is often hard to spot a vine snake (top) or a tree viper (bottom)—and the discovery may come too late. Being cold-blooded, snakes have a considerably more sluggish metabolism than birds and mammals; they live at a slower pace and their life span is quite a bit longer than that of warm-blooded creatures of comparable size.

therefore needs an area of between .5 to nearly 1 square mile (2 km²). According to our understanding, however, a minimum population of at least 500 individuals is required to ensure the survival of these species. Therefore, sheer arithmetic tells us that an area of 25 square miles (60 km²) would have to be set aside for these monkeys. This is more than the average area of many of our wildlife preserves. A pair of jaguars requires as much as 115 square miles (300 km²)!

Many kinds of birds, too, occur in very low densities. One square mile (1 km²) of tropical rainforest in Amazonia may contain several hundred different kinds of birds, but not one species has a population density that would ensure its survival if this square mile of forest were to become isolated. The scarcity of most rainforest birds is due to the high number of predator species and to surprisingly low food supplies. Birds could theoretically breed all year in the rainforest, but because of the scarcity of food most small birds attempt to breed no more than twice per year. Even then, the average clutch is considerably smaller than that of comparable birds living in the temperate climate zone. In temperate regions, the days are several hours longer during the summer—that is, during the breeding season—than in the tropics. Thus the parent birds have more time to find food for themselves and the nestlings. In addition, forests outside the tropics offer a much greater supply of qualitatively better insects during the summer.

In north temperate latitudes, most insects that occur in great quantities contain no poisons, whereas the overwhelming majority of tropical insects retain in their bodies poisonous substances from the plants they eat, as protection against animals that may want to eat them. Many tropical insects also have warning coloration to signal their poisonous nature. Other species try to benefit from this principle and mimic the warning coloration and markings of these

unrelated species in order to be thought inedible. The deception is often so perfect that even the sharp eye of a bird fails to detect the minute differences that could give the imitators away.

Mimicry, optical deception, and camouflage are preeminent features of animal life in tropical rainforests. Why do they play such a large role? Apparently, most species cannot afford the rate of population loss due to predators that is the norm in nontropical regions. Survival of the individual is more crucial in tropical forests than in forests of the temperate or cold regions. Many butterflies, for instance—insects that generally survive only a few days in northern latitudes—can live for months in tropical forests. Mass gatherings of insects are rare; when they do occur, it is usually in locations where rivers have deposited soil that is rich in minerals or where there are cadavers and excrement. In such spots, one may come upon colorful masses of butterflies that suck the juices from the dead bodies and the excrement as though intoxicated. This behavior, too, reveals the paucity of nutrients.

Let us summarize: Species diversification is the response of tropical nature to conditions of extreme scarcity. It is not a luxury made possible by the constant warmth of the tropical climate. Species diversification is at the heart of the forest's functioning. The forest is as dependent on a great diversity of trees as the trees are on a great diversity of insects. The food chains and the food networks that develop in tropical forests are closely interconnected. Abundance is rare and of brief duration. The fertility that makes possible the luxuriant growth of the forests is not contained in the soil or in the soil's upper-most layer, the humus, because this humus layer is almost non-existent. The fertility is in the forest itself. It is the forest that contains and subsists on the nutrients, transforming them, passing them on, recovering them, and reusing them. The

result is an awe-inspiring system that is capable of perpetuating itself. New life is born continuously and, in a cycle that has repeated itself for millions of years, a diversity of species has developed that is richer in information about life than all the libraries of humankind put together.

The multitude of species in the tropics contains potential solutions to environmental problems, solutions that we cannot imagine because we have not yet recognized the problems. Innumerable species must have had to contend with newly arisen, unfavorable conditions in the course of their evolution, long before man appeared on the scene. Their modes of solving problems are not necessarily the ones we adopt, even if we use the same substance that a tree, for instance, has developed to counter stresses of a different sort. Take quinine, for example. This substance, derived from the bark of cinchona tree, may have been produced originally to protect the trees against beetle larvae or other insects. Quinine was for several centuries the only effective cure we had for malaria, a disease to which trees are not subject. This example shows how, beyond its immediate function, a given substance may have entirely different potential uses, many of which will not become apparent until a need arises—assuming, of course, that the species producing the substance is still in existence.

These thoughts bring us to the question of how adaptations evolve in the first place. How did this immense number of different species originate? Was it the benevolence of tropical nature with its even, warm temperatures and high humidity that allowed life forms to experiment with all conceivable combinations to test their viability?

One thing we know beyond any doubt: Adaptation does not happen overnight. It takes time. The process of adaptation involves testing over many generations. Most of the species

Adaptation to all kinds of environments

The tree boa (top), which measures several yards in length, has a relatively moderate need for food. The doll's eye tree snake (bottom) is nocturnal;

it is seen in broad daylight only if it has been disturbed in its day-time hiding place. The small white-headed snake (center) does not climb trees, but lives in the leaf litter on the forest floor.

An orgy of color in the jungle

It is hard to imagine animals more gaudily attired than some of the leaf frogs of Central and South America. Some species show a sharp contrast of yellow and black; others combine deep or-

ange, iridescent blue, metallic green, or bright red with blue-black legs, striped sides, spotted backs, or net-like markings on the nape. They present an almost incredible display of color. The females or—more commonly—the males guard the eggs, wetting them as needed, until they hatch. Now comes the most re-markable thing of all: The tadpoles are carried piggyback by

their parents to the treetops, where they are deposited in small bodies of water such as water-filled knot holes or miniature swimming pools in the rosettes of bromeliads. The leaf funnels of these members of the pineapple family hold water vitally important to leaf frogs.

The scientific name of poison dart frogs is *Dendrobatidae,* or leaf climbers, and it describes them aptly. Many of them feed their offspring repeatedly with infertile eggs or move the tadpoles to other minipools with a more plentiful supply of mosquito larvae or other live food.

Leaf-cutting ants

The ants climb onto leaves and cut circular arcs around themselves, with a radius about the length of their bodies. Then they grasp the pieces of leaf between their mandibles and antennae and raise them like sails to be carried in long columns back to the nest. There, smaller worker ants pick up the leaves and masticate them into fine pulp, which they carry into special fungus-growing chambers. These fungus cultures provide the protein-rich food on which leaf-cutting ants live

A ring of poison brewers

With a few exceptions, all the approximately 500 species of passionflowers are found in tropical America in the form of shrubs, trees, and lianas. All of them belong to the same genus, *Passiflora*.

Just as unusual as the diversity contained in the genus is the architecture of the blossoms, in which some of the generally hard-and-fast rules of flower structure are playfully broken. Passionflowers have three protrusions on the underside, which look as though they were part of the calyx, but are made up of modified leaves. The bowl-shaped flower receptacle, from the edge of which the perianth arises, is located above them. The perianth consists of five sepals—which look much like petals but are recognizable as sepals by their greenish tips—five petals of the same

color, and a large number of conspicuously colored filaments that from a distance look like a mass of pollen-bearing stamens, but are completely sterile. The function of the latter structures is purely visual—they advertise an abundance of pollen, which is, in fact, nonexistent.

Some passionflowers develop into delicious-tasting fruits. Passionflowers are also highly attractive to the splendidly colored butterflies of the *Heliconiidae* family. These butterflies are a rare exception because they feed on pollen and thus act as important pollinators. The butterflies also lay their eggs on the passionflowers. Being overrun with consumers from the animal world endangers plants, however, so several passionflower species have developed a special substance (cyanogen, a glycoside that gives off cyanic acid) to discourage unwelcome guests.

Danger lurks even in paradise

The green palm viper is one of the dangerous poisonous snakes in the cloud forests of Costa Rica. Among its dreaded relatives are the bushmaster, the puff adder, the fer-de-lance, and all the

rattlesnakes. The mere sight of a snake generally triggers panic and flight in monkeys. These responses may go far back in evolution and are still present as reflex reactions in humans as well. Gibbons (above) are anthropoid primates living in the rainforests of Southeast Asia; they climb and swing acrobatically through the canopy. They are not quite so close to our own evolutionary line as are the African anthropoid primates.

that exist today are at least several hundred thousand years old; many of them probably have a history of more than one million years. Uncountable generations had to succeed each other before the mutations that had proven their usefulness could prevail.

In this respect, the tropics did offer very favorable conditions. Even during the height of the ice ages—which we think of as the distant past, even though we may now be in the midst of an interglacial stage that started some 100,000 years ago—large expanses of rainforests survived in the center of the tropical belt. This biome has lasted for many millions of years. Moist tropical forests may have existed continuously since the Mesozoic era (about 65 million years ago), or even longer. Precise details are of no great consequence in this context. What is important, though, is that the diversity of species did not arise during a few millenniums, but took several million years to evolve. The fact that quite a few of the larger animals and plants found today in the tropics have to be considered particularly ancient attests to the continuity of tropical living conditions. Climatic changes, especially during the last 1.5 million years or so, have been much more dramatic in the nontropical parts of the world than in the tropics.

Evolution thus had plenty of time to proceed and experiment with innovations. By itself, this is not enough to explain conclusively the extraordinary diversity of species found in the tropics. Constant living conditions also have prevailed for many millions of years in the depths of the oceans and in tropical coral reefs, yet these habitats—although undeniably characterized by a great variety of species—in no way match tropical rainforests. Continuity has to be periodically disrupted to a certain degree for a great diversity of life-forms to arise. Disruptions of habitat are practically unknown in the depths of the oceans. The deep-sea world is by far the most

stable environment on earth. In tropical coral reefs, global currents mingle the waters, thus keeping conditions constant. There are few coral reefs in the Atlantic Ocean, which is separated by the land mass of the Americas from the tropical Indo-Pacific Ocean and therefore accessible only by way of non-tropical waters, around the tip of Africa. What coral reefs exist in the Atlantic Ocean are located in the Caribbean, a section of ocean that was cut off from the Pacific only about 3 million years ago, when the Isthmus of Panama finally formed a continuous land bridge connecting North and South America. In terms of evolutionary time spans, this is a very short time: Life in the ocean can easily spread from one ocean to another, which also tends to reduce species diversity and keep the various oceans somewhat uniform.

The situation is quite different in the tropical rainforests. These forests occur on different continents and on oceanic islands in locations that are geographically isolated from each other. The large rainforest regions of Amazonia, Africa, and Southeast Asia are widely separated from each other, with thousands of miles between them. This separation itself, having lasted many millions of years, is enough to result in differences of development. Differences of this kind can be seen, for instance, between the primates of the Old World and the New. A number of species of New World primates have developed a prehensile tail that serves as a kind of "fifth hand." Old World primates have evolved along other paths: They produced the stock from which we, the human race, have sprung.

Apart from these major geographical divisions, which resulted in independent evolutionary directions, other, smaller, changes have occurred in more recent geological times, in the Tertiary period and the Pleistocene epoch. During these times, the rainforests underwent numerous declines and expan-

Tricky carnivores

A great many epiphytes belong to the huge orchid family, the great majority of whose species world-wide grow on trees. Another group of extremely fascinating epiphytes is made up of pitcher plants, belonging to the genus *Nepenthes*. The pitchers range in size from egg cup to beer glass. Presumably, the pitchers originally evolved as water storage, but later they also began to serve as traps for small animal life, which provides nutrients that are rare in the rainforest.

A glimpse of paradise

From the inhospitable world of the polar ice caps to the humid, warm jungle regions near the equator, billions of birds live in many kinds of environments. However, this profusion of birds is not evenly distributed over the globe. Although some deserts have scarcely any breeding birds, many bird species

lead an idyllic life on remote islands, along the shores of warm seas, on the marshy banks of wide rivers, and in the lush natural forests of the southern hemisphere.

sions resulting from fluctuations in the global climate. Thus, at the height of glaciation, rainforests were much smaller than today. What rainforests survived during the ice ages were probably restricted to the zones that now receive the greatest amounts of rain. Between them, deciduous forests and savannas sprang up, creating many separate islands of life where evolution proceeded in many distinct directions. These changes had the effect of isolating many species in locations where they continued on their individual evolutionary paths and where they became endemic, that is, peculiar to a particular locality. Amazonia is full of such islands of endemism, a discovery that we owe to German ornithologist and geologist Jürgen Haffer.

Fluctuations in the size and distribution of rainforests must have occurred even earlier, in the Tertiary period. Every phase of shrinking created the conditions for variations in species to arise. Then, when the forests expanded again and the descendents of what once had been a single population converged again, they often were no longer the same species and could not breed with each other. Different species, formed from what once had been the same species. The great

number of small ranges of individual species in tropical rainforests are another source of species diversity—and a special problem to efforts to preserve this diversity. If many related species exist geographically separate from each other, it becomes much more difficult to save a large segment of this species spectrum in a few nature preserves. The entire area must be preserved It is not enough to protect sufficiently large pieces of tropical rainforest to ensure diversity of species; the pieces also have to be geographically distributed in the right way. Only then will they be able to include a significant portion of the world's genetic pool and preserve it for the future.

This brings us to our third and most important question: How can we assure that the rainforest's vast diversity of species will continue to exist? The outlook is not altogether bleak, but we have to act quickly. The most important thing is to establish large preserves quickly. But what should be the principle of selection? From all we can tell, the key criterion should be the availability of mineral nutrients in the soil. Where mineral nutrients are plentiful and where sustained agricultural use seems possible, even relatively small preserves

will have a beneficial effect for the preservation of species, because greater productivity of soil goes hand in hand with less species diversity and with higher population densities. Consequently, reserves such as the ones established in Costa Rica, on Bali, and in southern India are likely to serve their function, assuming they are well run and supervised. The picture is very different in areas of nutrient-poor soils, as in Amazonia, the Congo basin, and large parts of Borneo and Sumatra. There, forest reserves have to be made on a much larger scale. The forest can not simply be pushed back into remote and inaccessible corners. Instead, the location of the reserves has to take into account a region's degree of species diversity. Diversity is greatest where the soils are poorest. Implicit in this statement is the notion that areas with high species diversity do not lend themselves to ongoing crop production. These areas should therefore be left alone and regarded as nature's pharmacy. In this way, forests that are spared now may, even in the near future, yield a richer return in the form of priceless substances—pharmaceuticals, ornamental plants, food, and many other forest products.

Bruno P. Kremer

Hanging Gardens in the Cloud Forest: Where the Flowers Grow on Trees

Trees and other plants thrust toward the light in an extravagant abundance. More plant life thrives here on the tiniest plot of ground than anywhere else on earth. The natives call the most magnificent and miraculous flowers "daughters of the air"—bright orchids that glow like colorful Chinese lanterns in the roof of the jungle.

The diversity of plants in the tropical rainforest, ranging from cannonball trees to plants that furnish life-saving medicines, is fascinating and breathtakingly beautiful.

Symphony in green with red accents

The rainforest is never monotonous. Harmonies composed of the most varied nuances of green are displayed in the leaves, shoots, stems, and bracts of the vegetation. Flowering woody plants attract little attention in this emerald sea, but individual trees that interrupt their green phases and sprout new leaves—whether in conformance to individual inner timing or to rhythms inherent in the species—do stand out. The new foliage lacks green pigmentation at first, but often sports a vivid, youthful red, under whose reflective cover the permanent green pigmentation begins to build up.

To be conspicuous at any price

The dispersal of fruit and seeds is of utmost importance in the dense rain forest. Developing organs that help seeds travel through the air does not always achieve the desired end. Much more effective is dispersal by animals, which eat the fruit and thus spread the seeds. Of course, the food has to be attractively and conspicuously packaged, as these soapberry fruits demonstrate so vividly. The contrast between the scarlet outer rind and the white, edible inner layer could hardly be more striking; it is bound to attract birds.

Green stage, brilliant actors

Viewed from close up, the overall green of the rainforest vegetation (right page) reveals details of amazingly varied design. The strange-looking inflorescence of a ginger plant (center) or the

flowers of a related species that have bright-red petals (bottom) are examples of exquisite design, as are the many kinds of fungi that break down dead wood (top). Among these fungi are the penny-sized Teuerling, whose fruiting bodies look like miniature birds' nests.

Anyone who wants a true, three-dimensional impression of the tropical rainforests ought to fly over such a forest at low altitude. This is the only way to see how the innumerable treetops intermingle and interlock, each tree trying to outgrow the others around it, each trying to exert greater competitive pressure, and all of them combining to form an irregularly undulating surface that extends from horizon to horizon. From the air, a virgin rainforest looks more like a deep, shoreless sea, its waters heavily rippled, than a forest made up of thousands of individual trees. Uniform stands of trees such as the ones we are used to seeing in the evergreen and deciduous forests of our climate regions are almost never encountered in a primary rainforest. The first impression rainforest vegetation makes on the newcomer is one of nearly absolute, unsurpassable chaos. A tropical forest has nothing in common with the neatly arranged, practically ruler-drawn rows of trees that make up our pine and poplar plantations in the southern United States. In tropical rainforests, an extravagant abundance of trees and other plants is massed together and strives upward. In a tiny area, more vegetation thrives than anywhere else on earth. The lush growth of tropical forests has been called a green hell—a response understandable from the point of view of people from more northern climes used to forests of an entirely different nature. "Green hell" implies entrapment, having to relinquish control, being at the mercy of the unknown, danger—in short, loss of autonomy.

To be sure, a rainforest is no place for a civilized Sunday walk. Real, concrete dangers lurk here, in the shape, for instance, of animals with deadly poisons at their disposal, poisons they may use to overpower prey or simply to defend themselves. Nor do the eerie dimness and the tangle of obstructing roots, tree trunks, vines, and foliage—all dripping wet—add up to a pleasant atmosphere. For people pampered by the conveniences of civilization, this environment feels more like hell than heaven. But let us keep in mind that tropical rainforests did not evolve for the sake of providing an environment tailored to man's needs and desires. Man, especially man as colonist, is almost always an intruder, a disruptive force in a world that is still in its primordial state, a world in which the creative, apparently chaotic diversity of nature is evident everywhere to all our senses. But as a biome—that is, as a major ecological community—containing more species than any biologist could ever hope to count, the rainforest is indeed a kind of paradise. It is an incredibly complex, perfectly interconnected and well-functioning ensemble of many individual species and life communities.

Equipped with all the destructive technology at his command, man set out several decades ago to attack, restructure, and exploit the ecosystem of the rainforest. One could speak of a new expulsion from paradise, but the metaphor is no longer appropriate because there is no place left for the exiled to go, with the world population that is expanding beyond control. Pressure from this population of over 5 billion people has forced humans to exploit even inappropriate environments. What is happening in the tropical forests—the destructive potential unleashed there, deforestation, the irreversible degradation into wasteland—is about as far removed from a paradisiacal state as can be imagined. Man may be turning the rainforests into hell after all.

There is no doubt that today's rainforests are the most species-rich and the most highly developed and complex life communities to be found on land. They represent plant associations that have to be described in superlatives. With an awareness of the time span of many million years during which life evolved on land, we can assert with a fair degree of certainty that the rainforests are quite old ecosystems. Their organismic history, in fact, goes back to the first plant associations that ventured from the seas onto the continents during the Devonian period 360 to 400 million years ago and spread relatively soon afterward over the entire surface of these continents. Of course, these plant pioneers of the Devonian period exhibit no similarities to today's rainforest vegetation, but it is noteworthy that the very plant forms that first colonized solid land are related to some species and genera still flourishing in tropical rainforests today. These archaic plant types look like living fossils next to modern rainforest vegetation and are in fact called living fossils. There are modern equivalents, for instance, of extinct primordial, leafless ferns of the Devonian period, namely, the whisk ferns belonging to the genera *Psilotum* (in American rainforests) and *Tmesipteris* (in New Zealand/Australia). Of the frond-type ferns, the especially ancient giant ferns (*Marantiaceae* family) are also restricted to the rainforests. Members of the *Angiopteris* genus that have frond leaves up to 16 feet (5 m) long are found only in Southeast Asia; the *Danaea* species, only in the tropics of the New World. All these ferns have changed their appearance very little since the Carboniferous period. They are representative of life forms dating back to a distant past, as are some other types of ferns, like the genus *Schizaea*, ferns that are called curly grass because they look like grass with forked blades, and the genus *Lygodium*, or climbing ferns. Among the gymnosperms, too, primitive forms that go back especially far in geological history are restricted to rainforest regions. Among them is the genus *Agathis* of the monkey puzzle family of conifers (*Araucariaceae*). The evergreen tropical rainforests turn out to be ecosystems that allow us to reconstruct major episodes from

Fireworks of form and color

Form and color have definite functions in nature. Flowers that are visited by birds and depend on them for pollination shine forth in bright-red hues. The appearance of a flower does not always give exact clues about the nature of the expected visitor, but even the flowers of begonias (top), spider orchids (center right), *Maxillaria* orchids (bottom left), and crimun (bottom right) are designed to appeal to specific guests. Pollination has been aided by the wind in the case of the *Chamaedoria* palm inflorescence (center left). Wind-pollinated plants tend to have smaller and less showy flowers.

Deception as a strategy of survival

In the rainforest, all kinds of things seem to be part of the vegetation, but upon closer inspection turn out to be of quite a different nature. Animals adapt themselves in shape, color, or

posture to imitate plants so well that they routinely fool the eye. Thorn bugs (bottom) look like exceptionally well-developed thorns, which many rainforest plants use to climb on other vegetation. The bugs match their model perfectly, not only in size and shape, but also in the angle of the thorn's tip. Warning coloration (top) does not always do the job by itself. These tree cicadas also arrange themselves on a branch in a pattern that imitates that of flower buds emerging from the bark.

the complex evolutionary history of life on land. They present a profile of what happened during almost half a billion years in the evolution of plants on various solid terrains. The rainforests are a living archive, both of traces of the past and of evolutionary history up to the present.

When people speak of evergreen, permanently moist rainforests, it is clear that the reference is to the huge, natural complexes of vegetation that occur in the tropics. What is less clear is that the term refers to forests of very different compositions, growing on different continents. "Rainforest" is at best a collective term. We have to remember that the area of distribution of these forests forms a irregular belt near the equator running east to west for more than 13,700 miles (22,000 km). The rainforests of different regions are widely divergent in structure and in composition of species. They are much more varied than the forests of temperate latitudes. The extravagant profusion of rainforest vegetation, the huge diversity of species, and—perhaps more than anything else—the inaccessibility of rainforest interiors have in the past stood in the way of detailed descriptions of individual forest types. Even with the aid of computers, we still do not get much more than a vague picture of staggering complexity and amazing species diversity. Our knowledge of the huge rainforest ecosystem necessarily remains incomplete and preliminary. Whether we will ever have a complete and systematic description is doubtful in view of the rapid disappearance of the remaining rainforest reserves.

A walk in a forest of eastern North America that is kept in a natural state can be refreshing to body and soul, but it does not expose one to a bewildering multitude of species. Walking in woods composed of maple, oak and hickory, or fir and pine, one can take in, almost at a glance, the tree species that make up the bulk of the woods and determine the plant community.

Usually there are no more than two or three different characteristic, dominant tree types, and even if one counts and includes all the shrubs of the lower story, one still ends up with slightly over a dozen different species of trees and woody plants. The picture is very different in the tropical rainforests: The number of tree species in a stand is almost paralyzingly large. In contrast to our deciduous forests or our coniferous woods, where the same few species grow next to each other in clusters and big stands like herds of sheep, in a tropical forest almost every tree belongs to a different species. To represent the composition and species density of such a forest community on a bar graph would, in almost every case, produce a mile-long row of short lines. An area no larger than a football field is likely to contain 50, and often over 100, different tree species that usually belong to totally unrelated botanical families. Even more surprising, on an adjacent plot there may be 100 completely different species.

Around 1970, the first attempts were made to determine relatively accurate numbers of the tree species making up the rainforests of northeastern Australia. Seventy stands, yielding 513 different species, were counted. In a primordial Malayan lowland forest, 375 tree species were found. It is probably safe to say that, on average, a stand of rainforest has about 100 times as many different trees and woody plants as a stand of equal size in the woods of eastern North America. A botanical inventory of trees in an area occupying 1 acre, not to mention 1 square mile, is an enormously time-consuming undertaking, even apart from the difficulties of trying to identify accurately the species found. Only rarely does one come across some types of rainforest where the species composition is a little less complex. In some rainforests in Malaysia, trees of the *Dipterocarpaceae* family dominate, but even these forests appear incredibly rich in species when

compared with North American forest types. As a general rule, the number of tree species declines with decreasing annual precipitation. In Venezuela, an average of 38 species per acre of evergreen rainforest has been counted; in rain-green moist forests, the number is 25, in rain-green dry forests, less than 17; and in dry thorn forests only 5 species were found on a plot of the same size. The number of species per acre also diminishes toward the cloud forests of higher altitudes: At 6,500 feet (2,000 m), there are still more than 21 different tree species, but 3,000 feet (1,000 m) higher, in the montane zone, only about 6 species were found per acre. The most luxuriant rainforests are thus located at low altitudes, where there is a great deal of precipitation, and it is here that the forests are densest, with between 83 and 416 trees per acre.

Where there is such a large and confusing diversity of species, it is naturally difficult to determine consistent patterns of spatial distribution. In a forest with a closed canopy, natural rejuvenation can occur only in small areas, for example, when gaps are created by a gigantic tree toppling over because of great age or because it is struck by lightning. Only there do seedlings get a chance to grow in the newly created opening. These breaks in the canopy close again relatively rapidly, and it is extremely interesting to observe which of the potential competitors succeed in making their way to the top. Often it is the microrelief of the soil surface, with the complex environmental conditions it creates, that determines which species germinate and grow. Differences can be due in part to termite nests, of which there are often a great many in the ground—although in a closed stand one is generally quite unaware of them. It has repeatedly been shown in limited areas of observation that seedlings grow noticeably less well in the root sphere of their own species than do competing seedlings belonging to different species. We assume that an exceptionally fine-tuned mechanism is at work here, which almost automatically ensures a constant turnover in species from generation to generation. This process is responsible for the varied, mosaic-like character of stands of trees that is so striking. It thus seems clear that rainforests are based on the principle of rotation. A certain species of tree can return to the spot where it once grew only after many generations have passed. This explains why no individual species dominate in the rainforest and why one almost always encounters species-rich tree stands of a surprisingly stable composition. This stability, however, is achieved at the cost of a fierce competitive struggle among the species. In their first stages, the seedlings have to fight for life in the darkness of the forest floor and, in addition to suffering from a growth-inhibiting lack of light, they have to contend with the competing roots of larger plants. Another startling fact is that tree seeds often lose their viability after only a few weeks. The principle at work here is: now or never. Because seeds are produced in great quantities, reserves of seeds can be dispensed with.

In the rainforest there is no real danger of not seeing the forest for the trees, but there is a danger of not noticing the inner structure of levels in the abundant vegetation of a dense stand of trees. One is generally unable to see very far, because tree trunks and foliage obstruct one's view in all horizontal directions as well as upward. But if one has a chance to look at the forest's edge along the banks of a body of water, if one sees a clearing torn into the forest by a storm, or if one can look out on a hillside covered with montane rainforest, the different levels of forest vegetation are much more apparent. Again one is immediately struck with how different these forests look from trees in the north temperate zone. Most rainforests do not display a clear

division into different stories conforming to the classical pattern of tree, shrub, herb, and moss level. Instead, the vegetation presents a much more variegated, irregular, confused, and disorderly picture—something close to a pleasant chaos. There is no obvious principle of organization discernible at first glance in this green tangle, especially because the enormous diversity of species creates a visual impression of randomly assembled color dots rather than recognizable shapes with clear outlines. Evergreen, permanently moist rainforests are not made up of trees of one height; instead, several stories are formed by staggered, variously shaped treetops. The canopy can be divided into at least three different tiers, although these tiers merge with almost no visible transition points. To be precise, the various stories of the canopy are interconnected by any number of "split-levels." Heights of nearly 200 feet (60 m) are reached by the proverbial forest giants—almost always isolated trees, apparently of great age, clearly towering above the other treetops. These trees give the canopy its irregular, restless appearance, making up a top layer with many apertures. The next-lower story does not form a completely closed roof either, but it is much less transparent than the first. In this tier, we find trees 65 to 100 feet (20–30 m) in height, trees that are closer to the dimensions we are accustomed to in our own forests. Below the 65-foot (20 m) line begins a claustrophobic crowding of many slender tree trunks and almost completely unbroken layers of foliage, with the greatest concentration of vegetation occurring between 30 and 50 feet (10–15 m) from the ground. A clear shrub level, as we know it from our forests, reaching up to about 15 feet (5 m) and making up the ground story, is largely absent in rainforests. Only here and there, in places where the undergrowth is not high, do young saplings try to push up. The sunlight, on its long way down through the

many layers of foliage, loses more and more of its power. By the time the rays reach the forest floor, only 1 percent or even .1 percent is left of the light that strikes the uppermost canopy. Thus, the bottom regions of the rainforest are at least as dark as the thickest conifer forests of the Pacific Northwest. Under such dim light conditions, leafy plants cannot thrive, and the rainforest floor is bare of lush herbs and velvety moss covers. Consequently, all one sees growing is a profusion of tree trunks ranging in girth from slender to mighty.

The forest is always dense, but it is not nearly so impenetrable as sometimes depicted in adventure novels, where these forests are routinely confused with jungles. Unlike rainforests, jungles are usually made up of relatively low-growing vegetation, so that lots of sunlight floods the ground, giving rise to scrub growth that is impassable. Such tangled thickets, if present at all, are found on the edges of rainforests, along riverbanks or in places with extensive storm damage, where hundreds of species suddenly compete simultaneously to gain a foothold. We have said that the basement floor of the rainforest, though hot, humid, and oppressively dark, is relatively easy to make one's way through. Still, a walk through the rainforest is by no means what could be called a pleasant stroll. Dead tree limbs and trunks block the way everywhere and prevent rapid progress at least as effectively as tangles of thick, green vegetation. Climbing over masses of dead wood is not a particularly pleasant experience. Insect larvae, fungi, and other agents of decomposition immediately set to work on the debris, transforming it. In the perpetual moisture beneath the leaf litter, punky wood instantly turns into sticky mush when stepped on, and all kinds of unusual root formations of rainforest trees put up barricades on the forest floor. Among these are the strange buttress roots, some as high as 30 feet (10 m). They look like huge

Camouflage is of the essence

As long as the short-antennaed cicada sits motionless on its branch (top), it is practically invisible. With its strange pattern of spots and the thorn-like protrusions on all parts

of the body that blur its outline, this creature is easily mistaken for part of the moss cushion on which it rests. The disguise lets it blend into its surroundings; thus it remains undetected, whether it is stalking prey or trying to hide from a predator. The butterfly that is resting on some dead leaves (bottom) is just as hard to spot. The posture and colors of the wings perfectly match the shapes and shades of the surrounding brown.

Every branch is like a hanging garden

Species diversity is a term that applies to all parts of the tropical rainforest ecosystem. This heavily laden branch contains many more hidden species than even the obvious, immediately apparent wealth of plant life would suggest. Among the hidden beauties are the delicate filigree of a console fungus (above), the mysterious purple of an epiphytic orchid (below), and the fascinating combination of shapes of a gorgeously colored *Cochliostema* blossom (bottom).

planks that have been leaned upright against the tree trunk, with the bottom ends flaring out wide to all sides. These root walls are reminiscent of the straddling support legs that prevent tall building cranes from toppling over. The similarity is not coincidental. The weight distribution in tall rainforest trees is indeed somewhat precarious. Not only are the trunks rather slender in relation to their height, but they also have to support a wide, umbrella-shaped crown high in the air. Solid anchoring at the bottom is absolutely essential to counteract shear force and leverage. Yet the roots are unable to penetrate deep into the ground because they cannot withstand the constant wetness of the lower soil levels. One other reason for the shallowness of the roots: No nutrients can be gained from going deeper; if any fertility exists, it is at the surface. Almost the only remaining solution to the problem is to develop mass above the surface of the ground, in combination with a thorough penetration of the uppermost inch or so of soil with a fine network of roots. Stilt roots, often many feet tall, serve a similar function. These roots are not put out only by mangrove trees in the tropical tidal forests, but are also widespread in lowland rainforests. In mechanical terms, they are comparable to the tripods that photographers use and to other kinds of stands that lend greater stability by using more floor area. Stilt roots also do not reach far down into the ground. Shortly after disappearing under the surface, they form long, horizontal root branches. Thus the soil volume actually available to the trees is always relatively small. In the rainforest, there are no plants with taproots that reach down to the bedrock. Rainforest soil always receives plenty of water and warmth and is therefore far from dead. For abundant, pulsating life to develop, however, there has to be an adequate amount of light. It is not surprising, therefore, that most of the life in rainforests is

found in the higher regions, in the complex world of the canopy. A closer look into these parts promises some unusual phenomena among the plants found there and their relationships.

The crown region of rainforest trees offers much better living conditions than the ground, but any plant wanting to enjoy the advantages of the canopy must first grow out of the dim basement region and push upward as fast as possible. Creeping and climbing plants expend most of their energy on vertical growth in order to reach a place in the sun. They do not develop trunks strong enough to support their own weight, but instead use the trunks and branches of trees and other woody plants for support. These kinds of plants are called lianas. Almost one tenth of all the plant species in the rainforest are lianas, and more than 90 percent of all known liana species occur in tropical forests. They belong to quite different plant families, but they all use the same tricks to work their way up the things to which they cling. There are, for instance, the climbing plants, one group of which is made up of many species and that uses long, relatively stiff lateral branches that stick out at right angles from the main stem to grow into the gaps among branches of other plants, thus assuring themselves of what might be called a window seat. They assure a good hold for their shoots by developing prickles or hooklike thorns that attach themselves to any available surface. These thorns, often sharp-edged and hard as steel, act as climbing irons and permit the vine to reach up quite far for the next foothold. The staghorn fern (*Gleichenia linearis*), which occurs in tropical regions all over the world, functions in this manner and, thanks to its extremely vigorous growth, fills in any gaps in the vegetation and even spreads in an unbroken cover across small streams. The notorious Rotan palm is an even more impressive climber. The midribs of the leaves, which

themselves are very long, extend beyond the leaf blade in slender, whiplike strands armed with ferocious barbs. The slightest breeze sends these strands swinging through the air to search for gaps and anchoring sites, thus helping the main shoot's ascent to higher levels. The vertical growth of these palms continues undiminished for many decades. Thus, climbing palms, of which there are many species, can reach impressive lengths of 650 to 1,000 feet (200–300 m) even though their main trunk stems grow no thicker than a few inches. When the older leaves die and fall off, the basal sections of the climbing palm lose their hold and slip off the surface to which they previously clung, and thus the garlands and ropelike webs hanging between the trees come into being. All kinds of small and large animals use these natural suspension bridges as aerial pathways through the treetops. In addition to these vines that use modified shoots for climbing, there are others that have successfully adapted their roots for climbing. They cling as close as possible to the trees supporting them and develop masses of fine roots at the points of contact. Like millipedes, these plants creep up the plant that supports them. We see the same phenomenon in vines such as ivy or Virginia creeper that climb and cover trees and walls in our latitudes. Some of the tropical tree climbers develop special leaves just above their fine clinging roots. These leaves create pockets of shade and moisture, where the root organs not only search for unevennesses of surface and other features that facilitate attachment, but also take advantage of the streams of water cascading down the tree trunk to satisfy their need for moisture. Many plants of the arum family belong in this group of vines, quite a few of which are cultivated here as popular houseplants, such as the genera *Monstera, Philodendron,* and *Scindapsus.* The plant that supplies vanilla beans is also part

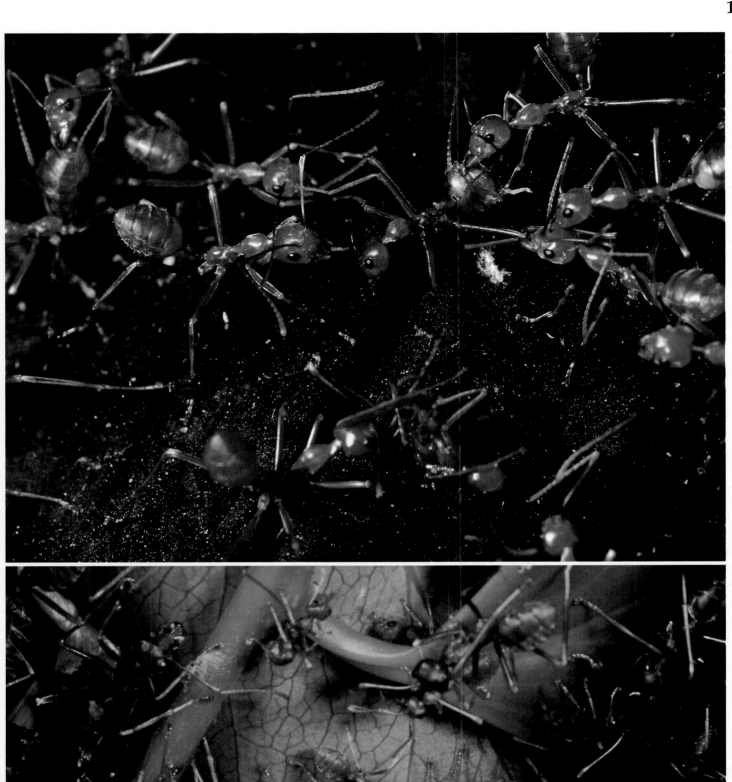

Ants stitching a living seam

Weaver ants of the genus *Oecophylla* have gathered here to staple the edges of adjacent leaves together with their mandibles. Each leaf is like a piece of material, neatly attached to the edge of the next one. In this way, large, dome-shaped structures are gradually formed, in which the ants can set up their brooding, living, and storage chambers. Often, hundreds of ants climb on top of a leaf, using their body weight to give it the desired shape. The future seams are held together by muscle power, each ant acting as a pin long enough for the sticky filaments of the larvae to harden in place. Over a period of weeks and months, a solid protective nest is built. This building job requires a remarkable degree of coordination. In earlier times, Indians used the clamping reflex of these ants to temporarily stitch gaping wounds.

Filled to bursting

No open space goes unused in the rain-forest ecosystem. Branches lying on the ground, toppled trees, and light gaps resulting from the collapse of a limb or an entire tree crown are taken over by vegetation so thick

that the forest floor is soon submerged again in dimness (large picture). What is true for the forest as a whole also holds true on the micro-scopic level. The air and search roots hanging from the canopy serve as a substrate for algae, lichens, and mosses (top). In the bottom picture are seen strange, club-shaped parasites that live on the roots of trees and produce nothing but flowering bodies for their own reproduc-tion. Ants carry off the seeds, which are high in energy.

of this group. It is a climbing orchid that develops longish clamping roots that reach around their support like hoops around a barrel and thus provide a strong hold.

There is a third method that helps plants gain access to the upper tiers of the canopy. Many lianas have tendrils or curling shoot tips that constitute grasping organs of high tactile sensitivity. These organs move through the air seeking suitable holds. Once a plant that serves the purpose is found, they wind around their partner in several loops and solidify the connection by quickly turning woody. The most imposing tropical lianas proceed in this manner, which is basically the same method used by our vetches and garden peas. Many winding lianas do in fact belong to the pea family. One of them, the genus *Entada,* beats all records of longitudinal growth: These plants can grow to between 1,000 and 1,300 feet (300–400 m). They climb all the way up the trees that serve them as support, then continue to grow horizontally, spreading across the canopy.

Lianas make up a considerable portion of the foliage, at least in the middle tiers of the canopy, and thus represent serious com-petition for light and nourish-ment to smaller trees. On the other hand, lianas have a hard time pushing through the largely closed canopy region because, as plants that germinate in the ground, they first have to pass through an area of deep shade in the lower regions of the forest. Many liana species have extremely dark green leaves—that is, the leaf tissue contains enormous amounts of chloro-phyll, so that at least some food can be manufactured through photosynthesis, making use of whatever dim light makes its way through the thick foliage cover. At this early stage of growth, specialists that have adapted to poor light conditions are at a distinct advantage. Lianas de-pending on plentiful light can prosper only where storms have created some openings among

Contrasts and contours

It is not always only the flowers that attract attention with their eye-catching colors and shapes, trying to lure wide-ranging pollinators; adjacent plant parts, too, are often involved in the enticing display. Thus

the bright carmine bracts of a ginger inflorescence (top) present a tempting sight to birds that visit flowers. Vines wrap themselves around tree trunks offering support. Their leaves hug the bark as tightly as they can, and under this protective cover, special roots often form to help absorb water.

Heavy burdens adorn the crowns

Epiphytes growing in the rainforest canopy weigh heavily on the branches of the treetops. They also provide innumerable minihabitats in which all kinds of animals live or hide. An entire ecological community is suspended from the lofty height of a tree branch

(top), looking like a lavishly planted hanging basket of flowers. The life of such an individual community may be temporary, but it forms part of an incredibly dynamic and ongoing interplay of forces. Unfortunately, much of the flowering beauty of the rainforest is not within eyeshot of the rainforest visitor.

the trees. Riverbanks also offer an opportunity to occupy a place in the sun.

Things are somewhat more propitious for plants that start life higher, in the tree branches, for example, and are exposed to light from the outset. Fruits and seeds that depend on animals for dispersal are usually equipped with features that make them stick or cling readily to available surfaces. These plants are thus well adapted for establishing themselves in the canopy region. They start out by germinating like any other plant. Initially, they grow a modest system of shoots and leaves and send off long aerial roots and search roots that travel down a host's trunk. As soon as the roots reach the ground and have access to more nutrients, a fierce and ruthless competitive struggle ensues. The tops of the initially harmless, epiphytic vines quickly branch out, shading the vegetation around them. The roots swell into sturdy pillars that clamp themselves around the host tree's limbs and trunk, preventing any further increase in girth, and eventually establish a deadly strangle hold. These plants are, in fact, called stranglers. Any tree with such a strangler in its crown is doomed. By the time it dies, however, the strangler's choking roots have become strong enough to form a fake trunk capable of supporting the plant growth at the top. The strangler has taken the place of its victim. The strangler figs (genus *Ficus*), relatives of the rubber tree, are especially notorious. The largest strangler fig discovered thus far covers an area the size of four football fields with its aerial supporting roots. Stranglers are not restricted to the *Ficus* genus (part of the mulberry family); some are also found in the dogwood and myrtle families. And life being what it is, one strangler will sometimes grow on top of another.

One is constantly tempted to resort to superlatives when describing the rainforest. The most gigantic trees are found here, the most shade-tolerant

plants, the largest inflorescences, the biggest individual blossoms, the most successful climbers, the most sophisticated stranglers, in an incredible variety. By far the most interesting plants, though, are the many epiphytes found in rainforests. These are plants that have lost touch with the ground, so to speak, and live in more elevated regions, preferring to start life in special sites up in the trees. Epiphytes grow high up on tree branches, but unlike parasitic plants, they do not sap the strength of their hosts by diverting valuable nutrients to their own use. They are, nevertheless, a burden on their hosts because of their weight, and it is by no means uncommon for such hanging gardens to tumble to the ground because the lush epiphytic growth finally proves too heavy for the supporting tree limb. If vines, wrapping themselves around and climbing anything they can find, add variety to the rainforest canopy, even greater variety is furnished by the many and often very colorful epiphytes, and the animal life that accompanies them.

One of the most crucial factors in the life of epiphytes is regular, reliable access to water. Epiphytes are unable to tap moisture and dissolved nutrients in the ground with their root organs as other plants do. Instead, they are totally dependent on rain water. The precious liquid, which usually arrives in the form of heavy cloudbursts, runs off much too quickly to be captured by roots or other absorptive organs, so most arboreal epiphytes have developed special adaptive mechanisms to catch and store water. In one widespread adaptation, leaf bases fuse to form funnel-shaped cisterns. In some epiphytes, basal leaves are modified into watertight tubes or pitchers. These collection tanks not only contain impressive amounts of water, but also accumulate dead organic matter, which is gradually transformed into humus. Roots grow into these tubular leaves to take advantage of this nutrient

resource. Thus the basal leaves of *Dischidia* plants (members of the milk-weed family) act as pots for the plants. Other plants, especially arboreal ferns, form sizable pockets with their basal leaves, behind which humus can accumulate, making up a mass of matter that always yields a certain amount of water to the roots through capillary action. In addition, many epiphytes have tuberous swellings or fleshy, tough leaves—always a sign that the plant is maintaining water reserves and that it is economical in its use of this resource. Unfavorable as growing sites high in the trees may seem in many ways, they by no means represent a marginal environment. Otherwise, we would not find there such an amazingly large array of species belonging to all kinds of plant families. It should also be noted that mountain rainforests are noticeably richer in epiphytes than are lowland rainforests, because in mountainous regions precipitation comes more often as fine, misty rain than as a violent deluge. Prolonged, gentle rain restores the water balance of epiphytes noticeably better than do brief, heavy showers.

A large number of epiphytes belong to the huge orchid family. In fact, many more orchid species grow on trees than on the ground. It is hard to say how many orchid species there are in the rainforests. They may number around 10,000, or there may be 15,000. What is especially fascinating in the ecology of these plants is the incredible variety of ingenious adaptations their beautiful flowers have undergone to attract specific pollinators. In one instance, male euglossine bees visit the blossoms of bucket orchids (genus *Coryanthes*) solely to perfume themselves with the flower's fragrance in order to impress the queen. Some orchid butterflies and in fact attract the attention—as well as the furious attacks—of male swallowtail butterflies (*Papilio*), which mistake the flowers for rivals. In this way, pollen packets are

reliably passed on to other blossoms of the right species. Other orchid species briefly hold visiting insects captive inside their flowers to make sure they pick up a load of pollen. Some orchids have adapted their shape and color to appeal to nectar-seeking hummingbirds, while others attract bats as pollinators. Variations in the biology of flowers range from nectar-dripping juice stands to the equivalent of girlie shows, for there are orchid flowers that masquerade as attractive sexual partners for their (preferably male) visitors.

Among the most intriguing epiphytes are the strange pitcher plants of the genus *Nepenthes* that are found in Indo-Australian rainforests. Their pitchers, ranging in size from egg cup to beer glass, are modified leaves. The normal leaf functions are left to the leaf stems, which are flattened. It thus looks as though the pitchers were hanging from the elongated points of ordinary leaves. The original function of the pitchers was probably to store water, but later their role expanded to include entrapment of small animal life, for ants, beetles, and spiders easily lose their footing on the smooth surface of the pitcher's lip, then slip and drown in the liquid inside the flower. Special diges-

tive enzymes given off by the plants gradually dissolve the prey captured in the pitchers, transforming it into nutrients for the plants. Characteristically, though, a number of insects and insect larvae have developed a resistance to the digestive enzymes in the pitchers and even choose to live there, competing with the host plant for food because they eat the drowning victims.

Bromeliads, a plant family composed of a great many species, some of them extremely beautiful, are restricted to the tropics of the New World. The pineapple plant, a member of this family, is one of the few species that do not grow on trees. In the leaf axils of many bromeliads are miniature aquariums, almost always inhabited by certain fauna. One finds there a varied inventory of life, ranging from single-celled protozoans to mosquito larvae. Some of the brightly colored tropical tree frogs of the genus *Dendrobates* spend their entire early developmental phase in these minipools. Biologists have observed these frogs carrying their newly hatched tadpoles into bromeliad plants and distributing them among the tiny water tanks of different plants, thus making sure that there will be enough food for as

many offspring as possible.

Ants play a special role in the life of many epiphytes because, on their collective excursions and migrations, they disperse the plants' seeds over the branches of neighboring trees. They are thus responsible for establishing regular epiphyte plantations. Many species have seeds with small, fatty, and apparently tasty appendages that ants enjoy. It is consequently not surprising to find the same kinds of epiphytes sprouting frequently from ants' nests. These epiphytes belong mostly to the bromeliad, pepper, and arum families, and—because they have extremely light, airborne seeds—to various species of the orchid family. In antiquity, the Hanging Gardens of Babylon were celebrated as one of the world's seven wonders. They still exist today in a different form, as colorful flower baskets suspended from the branches of trees in the rainforest and tended by ants.

Riding piggyback on top of one another is not unknown among epiphytes. Not only ferns, but flowering plants as well, take root in forked limbs, cracks in bark, cavities produced by rot, and other suitable growing sites, as long as these sites are sufficiently high in the forest. Even the tiniest plant organisms, such as mosses and algae, establish themselves on the trees. Lichens, too, should be mentioned here, strange organisms that evolved from a permanent association between fungi and microscopic algae. Lichens are no longer regarded as true plants, but as a form of fungus with a physiologically highly specialized mechanism for food absorption. The distribution of these different life forms often breaks any rules one might have formulated on the basis of the habitats different kinds of plants usually select. In tropical forests, mosses may grow on top of lichens, and thick moss cushions often provide the germinating environment for flowering plants. Conversely, algae, lichens, and mosses also colonize conveniently located organs of larger

A labyrinth of cushions and garlands

The green burden of vegetation resting on tree limbs and branches can stay alive only because sufficient moisture is available from the air. Additional water resources are tapped by special mechanisms, including specialized moisture-collecting leaves that

hug the tree trunk closely and have root hairs for absorbing extra water from the moist spaces created by the leaves (top). By resorting to such devices, plants that grow far from the soil are able to produce flowers of exquisite beauty (bottom).

A wealth of medicines from the rainforest

Among the tens of thousands of plant species growing in the rainforests are a large number that possess healing and other medicinal properties. Some of them have been traditionally used by rainforest dwellers. One plant remedy used by them is pokeweed berries (large picture), which are effective against parasites of the scalp. The substances of many other kinds of plants are still relatively little studied and tested.

Exquisite exotic beauty at all levels

Epiphytic orchids, which produce flowers of unusual loveliness, may contribute more to the floral decor of arboreal plant com-

munities than any other kind of plant. Thus far, more than 10,000 different orchid species— some of them almost impossible to distinguish from each other—have been identified in the canopy region of rainforests. The showy *Thunbergia* (top) belongs to a family whose leaves provided the model for the decorative motifs that appear on the columns of ancient temples. A *Dillenia* (bottom) presents its attractively colored seeds in an opened capsule.

epiphytes, and in this way mini-gardens of great complexity come into being, forming communities that almost defy efforts to tell which plants grow on which substrate and which depend on which others for sustenance. In evergreen rainforests, one often sees another phenomenon that is practically inconceivable in our leaf-shedding forests and in the few evergreen woods in the central United States: Algae, lichens, and sometimes mosses as well grow on the leaf surface of ferns and flowering plants.

The vegetation of the rainforest is complex and many-tiered to an extreme degree. High above the forest floor, independent ecosystems have evolved that no longer have much connection with what happens in the lower regions. They are a world that has moved quite far heavenward.

In our temperate zones, the summer-green forests go through a cycle—rapid leafing out in spring, fruiting during the summer, intensive coloring of the foliage and shedding of the leaves in the fall—that has spectacular heights at all seasons of the year. In the evergreen rainforests, there is no such coordinating choreography to which all the trees and plants respond more or less uniformly. It is a difference that is understandable if we remember that many rainforest regions lack the clear climatic rhythms of higher latitudes, rhythms that act as timers setting the various reactions in motion.

The fact that rainforests are evergreen does not mean, however, that rainforest trees retain their leaves forever. It is quite common for individual trees to be completely bare of foliage, but they are inconspicuous among the confusion of greenery that surrounds them. Under the unchanging environmental conditions prevailing in rainforests, the shedding of leaves is not associated with any one season. Sometimes single branches react separately and renew their foliage independently of what is

happening in the rest of the tree's crown. Individuals of the same species may also behave differently from each other. Some tree species are never entirely bare, because they do not shed their old leaves until some time after the new ones have emerged, or because the renewal of the foliage occurs in a number of minor, undramatic partial stages. There are no universal, coordinated reactions. The most important life functions take place without reference to the seasons. There are trees with activity phases of about 12 months, but there are also shorter phases of 2 to 4 months and of about 9 months, as well as more extended cycles that take up to 32 months to complete. The rainforest is therefore constantly greening. Because trees differ in their leaf-shedding patterns, there are no dramatic changes in the appearance of the rainforest. In addition, the periods of leaflessness, if they occur at all, are relatively brief, lasting a few weeks, at most, 3 months. The phases of foliage renewal apparently follow an inner rhythm that is only minimally influenced by environmental factors. The same holds true for the growth of wood. Because tropical trees do not grow at an even rate throughout the year, their wood does not show the clear annual growth rings that are so obvious in our woody plants. Growth zones are visible in the wood, but their occurrence is unrelated to the seasons of the year.

The budding twigs of many rainforest trees and shrubs can be identified by the way they look. During the rapid longitudinal growth of the twig and the incredibly fast unfolding of the new leaves, no rigid support tissue is formed. Shoots and leaves are therefore unusually flaccid, hanging down limply. Producing many new leaves at once—a phenomenon called flushing—prevents herbivores from eating any significant amount before the leaves can grow and become tough. Often the young leaves are white,

bluish, or even bright red. It looks as though small pieces of colored cloth had been draped throughout the treetops. After a few days, this strange droopiness disappears. The leaf organs acquire solidity, and the crucial process of photosynthesis suddenly springs into action. Tropical trees do not form protective bud coverings for the developing leaves. The new growth starts in spots that are hidden only by a few scales or hair-like tufts.

One of the striking things about the fully developed leaves is how uniform they are in shape. Only rarely do rainforest plants have deeply lobed, serrate, or palmate leaves. Broad, oval leaves with smooth edges dominate, with a large number of tree species having leaves that terminate in a long, slender "drip tip." The purpose of this elongated tip seems to be to help the precipitation that strikes the leaf run down over the leaf surface as quickly as possible. There are two possible reasons for this: First, a surface that is continually bathed in water reflects much of the available sunlight and thereby reduces the efficiency with which chlorophyll is turned into carbohydrates. In the semidarkness of the canopy's lower tiers, such a loss is surely detrimental. Second, permanently wet leaf surfaces would invite a host of algae, lichens, and mosses. Colonies of such densely growing mini-epiphytes on the leaf surface would block even more light and further interfere with the process of photosynthesis. Such connections between appearance and the biological production processes of plants make the uniformity of leaf shapes more understandable. What still remains a mystery is why the leaves of so many rainforest plants are velvety to the touch and why they either have a metallic sheen or tend to exhibit unusual colors ranging from greenish-black to reddish-black in many fine gradations. These color patterns must reflect some functional principle, for in nature form and color are never

A forest full of strange shapes

In the mist-draped mountain rainforests, tree trunks, limbs, and branches look as though wrapped in an extra layer of vegetation. Thick

layers of lichens, mosses, and other plant forms cover every exposed surface (large picture). The cannonball tree (bottom) exemplifies a widespread phenomenon: fruiting from the trunk. The huge fruits grow right next to the trunk at easy picking height. The monster flower (*Rafflesia*) (top) is a pure parasite living on tree roots. Its flowers imitate dead meat in appearance and grow to almost 1 yard (1 m) in diameter, a record in the plant world.

simply the expression of a playful whim.

Just as the patterns of leafing out obey no seasonal rules, flowering and fruiting conform to no predictable calendar. In the rainforest, there are no waves of exuberant blossoming similar to what we see in our orchards. Exquisitely beautiful and distinctly exotic as most flower creations of the rainforest ecosystem are, they are always an unobtrusive presence. Spectacular optical effects are rare, and when they do occur they always represent a delicate reaction to minimal changes in the plants' environment, changes such as a drop in temperature of a few degrees after a heavy shower. The flowers of rainforest trees often appear in places one would least suspect—not at the end of short twigs in the branches of the crown but much farther down, on the bark of the trunk, for instance. Quite a number of tree species exhibit this feature, which is called cauliflory. A classical example of cauliflory is furnished by the cacao tree, whose pods, filled

with many beans, grow directly on the trunk almost at picking level. Quite a few rainforest trees bear flowers on their trunks all year. Fruits develop at the same time, and, farther up in the crown, branches get ready to leaf out. All growth programs are activated more or less simultaneously, and all the seasons can be observed in an individual tree at the same time. There is no annual cycle in the rainforest; everything is always in season.

Rainforest vegetation is varied in appearance to the point of confusion and characterized by great species diversity. Its luxuriant growth produces records that leave all other terrestrial ecosystems far behind. The annual net production of organic dry material averages about 8 tons per acre and can amount to as much as 15 tons per acre. Even modern agriculture, with all its technological methods and refinements, comes nowhere near rivaling the rainforests. In a mature rainforest, however, about an equal amount of organic mass dies and its nutrients are recycled almost

immediately. Rainforests are immense reservoirs of carbon dioxide, and when they are cut and burned, or even left to rot, they return these vast amounts of carbon dioxide to the atmosphere at a time when the industrial nations are creating a problem by burning fossil fuels. This compounds the greenhouse effect and global warming.

However, the prolific nature of the rainforests is only partially expressed in the quantities of biomass they create. The quality of what they produce must also be taken into account. As long as humans have lived in or near the rainforest, they have derived their sustenance from the forest. The forest always furnished them not only with food, but also with construction materials. For thousands of years, a mutually beneficial balance was maintained between man and nature. The Europeans learned about the rainforests of the Old World and the New and about the riches they contained barely 400 years ago, but they immediately began a systematic exploitation of these new resources. Wondrous natural

You would never guess...

Imitating the appearance of vertebrate creatures' eyes is a highly effective warning pattern adopted by a number of small, defenseless creatures. Often, the overall shape of the body enhances the visual effect. Butterflies' hind wings display patterns that resemble piercing eyes (top left). Some butterfly larvae look like dangerous reptiles (large picture and small pictures, bottom). Meanwhile, a locust relative is taking on the look of a twig to disguise itself (top right).

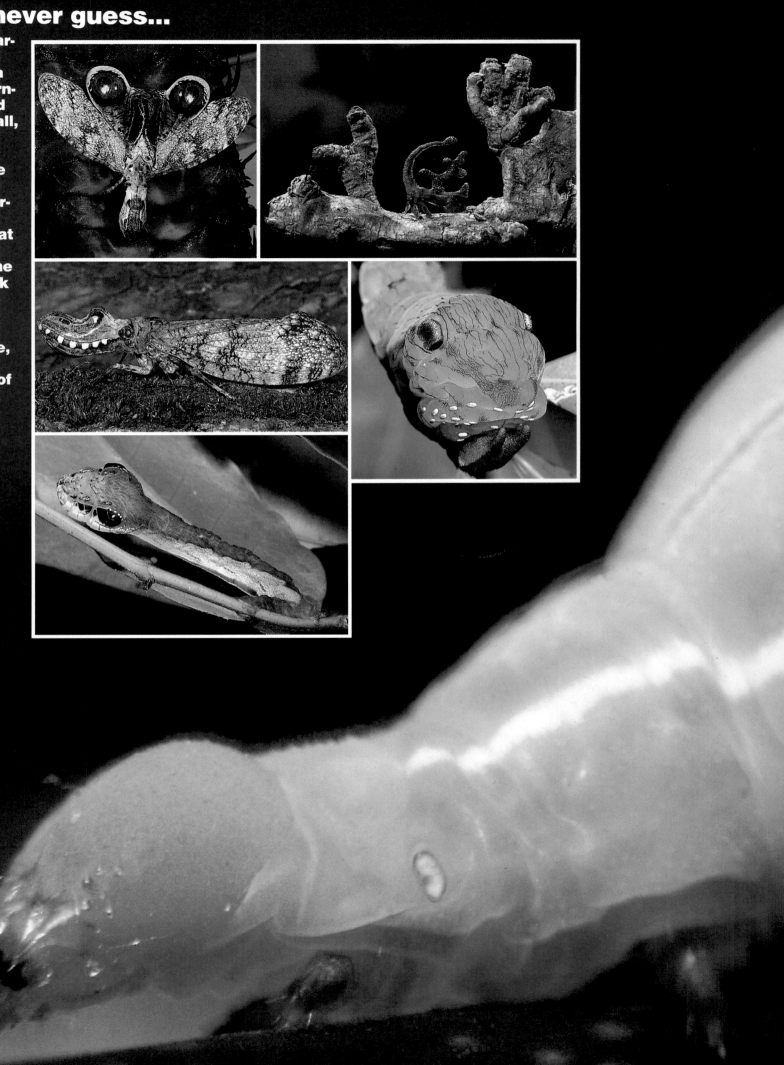

Forbidden fruit and useful diversity

Not all fruits of rainforest plants are salutary for humans. Appearance alone gives no clue to the fruit's edibility (below). Long experience and detailed knowledge are the only way to discover

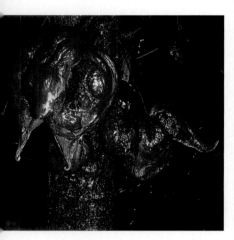

the various gifts the rainforest vegetation can yield. The enormous usefulness of the cacao tree (right-hand page)—a rainforest tree that flowers at the same time that its fruit is maturing—was discovered in this way. There is no specific, well-defined harvest season for cacao fruit.

products were furnished by the tropical forests in the past, ranging from pitch-black ebony through gum or natural rubber to cocoa and cola. In the last few decades, exotic fruits from tropical gardens have reached our markets in greater and greater numbers and variety, all of them from plants that originated in rainforest regions. These tasty new foods range from bananas, the old-time favorite, to less-familiar delicacies like guavas, mangoes, papayas, and durians—the last a foul-smelling fruit with a delicious taste. At least half of the roughly 20,000 plant species that are utilized in some way by people in various parts of the world originated in rainforest regions, and these plants represent only about 5 percent of all known plant species. Looking at these numbers, one suspects that the great majority of rainforest vegetation has not been studied thoroughly enough to make possible an accurate judgment of their potential usefulness to mankind. As was to be expected, closer investigation has led to surprising findings time and again. The greatest successes have come in the area of medicinal plants, which yield many substances that have become indispensable in the production of highly effective medications. Recent pharmaceutical research has confirmed, for instance, that *Adhatoda vascia*, a forest plant from tropical India, is highly effective in treating disorders of the respiratory system. This plant substance, only slightly modified in laboratory processes, is the main ingredient in a leading cough medicine that is sold worldwide. The beneficial, medicinal properties of this plant were extolled long ago in the *Ayurveda*, an ancient Hindu work on medicine written in Sanskrit.

For thousands of years, tropical forests have furnished mankind with amazingly potent plant substances. There is tubocurarine, for instance, a dibenzyl isoquinoline alkaloid derived from South American *Chondodendron* species. It was originally used by the Indians as an arrow poison; today it is used in almost all major surgery to induce controlled relaxation of the muscles, so that the dosage of the actual narcotic can be kept as low as possible. The natural substance that makes the muscles relax is so complicated in its chemical composition that it cannot be produced synthetically in the laboratory. Surgeons all over the world depend on the natural source of this drug. To give another example: In the tropical forests of Madagascar, a plant sometimes called Madagascar periwinkle (*Vinca roseus*), a relative of our periwinkle, but with pink flowers, was discovered. This plant contains over 70 different alkaloids of the indole group. Two of these substances, vincaleucoblastine and leurocristine, have been used for almost 10 years now with considerable success in treating leukemia and some other forms of cancer. Thus a pink-blossomed periwinkle from the tropical rainforests is giving hope to many sick people.

These stories speak for themselves. Can we really afford to continue the senseless devastation of the rainforests, exterminating dozens of unique plants every day in the process, plants that may possess all kinds of properties, medicinal or other, about which we know nothing? Even if we do not need the tropical forests directly as a source of new kinds of food, their genetic potential is crucial for the biosynthesis of specialized drugs, and they represent a resource that is indispensable to mankind.

We live in an age in which new products, the fruits of a technological age, frequently appear. But we tend to underestimate technology's reliance on plant and animal products and on the vast library of genetic diversity that has evolved to date. Today, genetic engineering is rapidly reaching the point at which genes from one species can easily be spliced into another

species to produce a specific material or to confer a particular quality or characteristic. It would be ironic if, at the same time that techniques have become available to extend the array of useful plant and animal products, immense amounts of potentially useful genetic material will have disappeared because of the destruction of the rainforests.

Donald R. Perry

In the Canopy of the Jungle: The World's Most Beautiful Roof

Biologist Donald Perry climbed into the tallest treetops of the rainforest and explored a huge, unknown realm of life there. Using techniques of mountain climbing, this naturalist was able to enter an ecological environment about which even today less is known than about the depths of the oceans.

American biologist Donald Perry ascends to his work station and sleeping platform 130 feet (40 m) above the forest floor by passing through a maze of ferns, bromeliads, and lianas, encountering monkeys and strange-looking lizards along the way.

Curtains of water and clouds

During much of the year, the rainforest is like a steamy kitchen full of boiling pots. Masses of water break from the clouds, burst into fragments upon striking the many layers of foliage, evaporate from the treetops and the ground, and find their way back into the atmosphere within the same region. The rainforest not only depends for life on this circulating system, but also forms an integral part of the cycles of all kinds of other materials.

Food designed only for specialists

The brightly colored flowers of the coral tree (*Erythrina*) are seen from afar and signal to their pollinators that a plentiful supply of nectar awaits them. The flowers clearly appeal to birds, whose eyes are particularly sensitive to shades of red. The shape of the flowers is such that only the long, probing tongue of a hummingbird can reach the sweet nectar in the flower base. The black vultures that have assembled in some numbers in the branches are unimpressed by the flower orgy offered by the tree. Depending on carrion for food, they have specialized in very different tastes.

Death's-heads in the jungle

Making unexpected eye contact is always surprising and heightens alertness. The thing encountered might turn out to be an unrecognized danger or a specialized predator, and instantaneous

flight is therefore the only safe reaction. The pattern on the back of the beetle crawling into a flower (top) is designed to evoke this response. It is unclear who is meant to be impressed by this pale-faced *Angeloa* orchid (bottom) from Colombia; its structure actually represents a specialized adaptation to certain kinds of pollinating insects.

For decades, the study of tropical rainforests was limited almost entirely to what could be reached from the safety of the ground and to whatever fell from the canopy. The resulting picture was bound to be incomplete. The felling of giant trees in the rainforest and the careful investigation of everything that came down in their branches brought a wealth of individual observations, but yielded no reliable insight into the workings of the biological communities in the treetops. Occasionally, rainforest biologists resorted to ladders and movable platforms to get closer to the activities in the upper levels—a rather clumsy and not very productive method because the ecologically most interesting environment, the canopy, often reaches more than 160 feet (50 m) into the air. According to all the bits of information gathered from things that had drifted down from the crowns of rainforest trees, it was clear that a community of life that bordered on the fantastic had to exist up there, and that it had developed an extreme degree of adaptation. The American biologist William Beebe, more famous as a successful deep-sea explorer than as a rainforest ecologist, at the beginning of our century correctly voiced the opinion that no new realm remained to be discovered on the ground we walk on, but that there was an entire unexplored world 100 to 200 feet (30–60 m) above our heads—just the level of rainforest canopies, where we now estimate that almost half of all plant and animal species on earth live. In view of the rapid destruction of rainforests, we will probably never have a complete inventory of the species that exist in this treasure house of flora and fauna, but we are able to investigate accurately some parts of the complex interaction of species that characterizes the ecological system of rainforests, and we are able to do so by direct observation of the canopy region itself.

This important breakthrough in the study of evergreen tropical forests became possible only through the use and adaptation of methods that had been developed for a completely different purpose, which had absolutely nothing to do with rainforests. These methods were designed for highly sophisticated mountain climbing. The rainforest canopy has become accessible to us through rope techniques, borrowed from mountaineering, that occasionally resemble high-wire acrobatics. We are now able to stay in the canopy realm of rainforests for days or weeks at a time, instead of merely casting a few brief glances into it.

A few attempts in this direction had been made earlier: In a report about an expedition published in 1929, R. W. G. Hingston writes of experiments made in the rainforest of Guyana and of trying to shoot a climbing rope into the canopy region with a line-throwing gun. The experiment failed because of the tangle of air roots and lianas, and the explorers finally made do with traditional wooden platforms erected by the natives in individual treetops. Around 1960, H. E. McClure devised similar observation stations in the canopy in the Malaysian rainforest near Kuala Lumpur. The results of all these attempts to penetrate into the higher levels were disappointing, however, because individual canopy regions differ significantly from each other in species composition and because the most interesting things always happen on a neighboring—and often inaccessible—tree. In addition, in many forests few trees are suitable as platforms because many rainforest trees are soft or brittle and cannot support a platform's weight. What was needed was a method that not only enabled explorers to stay safely in the tops of trees for lengthy periods, but also, just as important, allowed greater freedom of movement.

In the summer of 1974, I tested an alternative method for the first time in Finca la Selva, a rainforest preserve of the University of Costa Rica. I shot a heavy arrow over a tree branch with a crossbow; a nylon line attached to the arrow pulled up a thicker cord, which, in turn, pulled after it a solid climbing rope. With this rope I was able to ascend into the higher regions. Indispensable to my enterprise were two Swiss climbing clamps. These devices automatically lock tightly in place when weight is placed on them, but they can easily be released again and slid up or down the rope when the weight is removed. Two other items of climbing gear were of inestimable aid: a pair of stirrups (attached to the lower climbing clamp) and a parachute belt (connected to the upper clamp). By alternately placing weight on the two clamps and removing it, I was able to move up and down the rope with relative ease, and it took me only about a quarter of an hour to ascend the approximately 100 feet (30 m) to the canopy.

Rope and climbing techniques developed for the assault of vertical faces and overhangs proved extremely useful for my purposes, but they could not be applied indiscriminately. The problem lay in the statics of the rainforest trees; in spite of their enormous height, surprisingly few of these giants develop limbs strong enough to safely support a person climbing a rope hanging from a branch. In the race for space and light, rapid growth almost always takes precedence over stress resistance. An example is the balsa tree, whose wood is popular with model builders because it splits apart so easily. Such trees are obviously not good candidates for climbing expeditions, and almost half of all tropical tree species fall into this category.

Even if a tree is solid enough, climbing in its crown is not without danger. This was brought home to me on various occasions and in different ways. Once I almost put my hand on the mottled green head of a fer-de-lance that lay perfectly camouflaged on a moss-covered branch. Another time, a scorpion

The divine bird of the cloud forests

The quetzal, a magnificent rainforest bird, enjoyed great respect among the Aztecs and Mayas, who regarded it as the image of their god Quetzalcoatl and as a symbol of goodness and light. This adoration all too often spelled doom for the birds because their long tail feathers were incorporated as special adornments in cult vestments and ritual decorations.

Scientists discover the canopy

Next to the giant trees of the rainforest, human beings look puny and helpless, even when they are equipped with rope ladders. This is especially obvious when the climber is trying to scale a tree

with a forbidding exterior. Even with the help of observation platforms and towers, little progress was made in the study of the forest's upper stories. Not until rope and climbing techniques borrowed from mountain rock climbing were tried did this ecosystem, which for a long time was known only in its barest outlines, open up and reveal itself to be almost as rich as a new continent (left).

Something to fit any shape of beak

The rainforest offers a plethora of foods, which are enjoyed by a comparable variety of birds, one kind more spectacular than the other. The beak of a bird gives a good indication of its feeding behavior. Cocks-of-the-rock (large picture) are relatively unspecialized omnivores. Hummingbirds (top right and bottom left) hover motionless in front of a flower and drink its nectar. The sunbittern (bottom right) is an adept hunter of fish, while many rainforest birds, such as the South American hoatzin (top left) live on fruits or seeds.

Tiny knights in shining armor

The world of insects is composed of a staggering variety of creatures that account for more than two thirds of all known animal species. Beetles make up by far the largest order. Recent rainforest research

suggests that nature's urge to experiment may have reached an amazing peak here: Scientists think that as many as 20 or 30 million different insect species may live in the rainforest.

Fog, too, keeps the forest fresh

Clouds of fog waft through the mountain forest in Costa Rica. Many plants can make much better use of evenly distributed, microscopic droplets of water in the air than of the brief and violent

downpours typical of the lowland. This beneficial supply of moisture is accompanied by a greater density of epiphytes. Some trees find little room to spread their own leaves among the lush vegetation growing in their crowns.

the size of my hand came shooting out of a crack in the bark with its poisonous stinger raised and ready for use. Bees that discovered my sweating head as a source of moisture and salt in the airy heights drove me almost crazy within moments as they crawled indiscriminately over my eyes, nose, and ears. Once, when I was trying to hack a hole through a curtain of lianas, my knife bounced off some rock-hard wood and hit the rope. It left a minor but obvious notch. There is something else I found out: The amounts of humus that collect on the branches and in the twigs of a rainforest tree add up to many times the weight of dead matter on the ground. The climber who ventures into the suspended world of the treetops inevitably dislodges avalanches of humus and dead plant material and sends them tumbling to the ground. It is almost unimaginable how dirty and foul-smelling a rainforest tree can be.

In 1978, I tested another rope technique for the first time. I had set up my observation platform 110 feet (34 m) above the ground in the crown of a monkey pot tree (*Lecythis ampla*). About 300 feet (100 m) away, two huge almendros (*Dipterys panamensis*), leguminous trees with wood almost as hard as cement, rose up above the surrounding canopy. I had chosen these three trees as supports, and, together with John Williams, an engineer, strung 1,000 feet (350 m) of rope among them in the approximate shape of an equilateral triangle. This rope ran over pulleys, and all of it moved freely. Our platform was connected by another rope to the opposite side of the triangle. This rope, too, was movable. Using a pulley, we could now glide to any point on the rope, attach a climbing rope there, and let ourselves down at almost any spot in the canopy of rainforest trees below us. An area of approximately 1 acre (4,000 sq m) about 100 feet (30 m) in depth was now accessible to us, with almost no obstacles.

At almost every one of the points of observation we had previously selected within this area, we now had access to the upper levels of the rainforest, a layer that comprises almost two thirds of the height of the forest. Almost 95 percent of its entire biomass is produced there, and more plant and animal species are found in even the tiniest area than in any other terrestrial or aquatic ecosystem in the world. The canopy consists not only of a maze of tree branches and lianas, but also of numerous epiphytes—orchids, bromeliads, cacti, and ferns, to name the most prominent. About 16,000 different species have been identified in the rainforests of Central and South America alone. To this are added lichen and moss species in staggering numbers. Like seamless carpets, they cover trunks and branches. The root mass and shoots of epiphytes build up to a thickness of as much as 10 inches (25 cm), and such a matted layer can—especially when it is saturated with rain water—weigh several tons per tree and become too heavy for the branches on which it rests.

Just what belongs to what in this tangle of plants can sometimes be determined only through close examination. A colleague from the University of Washington, using my method of rope climbing, discovered only recently that a number of trees develop auxiliary roots on branches far above the ground, roots that penetrate into the epiphyte layer, where they absorb nutrients released by the humus that accumulates there. The transformation and recycling of dead organic matter thus takes place not only on the rainforest floor but also, to a considerable extent, directly in the treetops.

Epiphytes are a heavy burden on trees in more ways than one. Not only do they weigh heavily on the trees, but they also compete for nutrients and take away much of the available light. It is not surprising that many trees have developed special defense mechanisms in an effort to keep the army of epiphytes at bay. One method is to shed the outer layers of bark frequently, thus dislodging the colonies of plants growing on the tree limbs. Other trees seem to saturate their bark with chemical substances that inhibit germination and act as a brake on the growth of new epiphytes that try to gain a foothold in a tree's crown, yet I have witnessed again and again how quickly epiphytes take over. When I would return to a work station after an absence of a few months, I would find the platform and even the rope network taken over by colonies of small epiphytic plants. There are, however, also rainforest trees that remain consistently free of epiphytes without shedding their bark or resorting to chemical warfare. My observations confirm a theory advanced by D. H. Janzen, according to which certain ants keep trees clear of other vegetation. *Azteca* ants are found on trees belonging to the genus *Cecropia*, and they have a vital interest in keeping the branches in which they nest from breaking under an overload of epiphytes. These highly aggressive ants, like gardeners weeding a flower bed, pluck off epiphytes just starting to grow in the bark of the tree branches. In an experiment, I tied plant parts to the branches with dental floss to simulate epiphyte growth, and columns of clean-up crews immediately appeared on the scene. In this instance, the advantages of my climbing rope proved especially valuable because I had an intimate view of the action, but remained out of the ants' reach. Apparently, an especially close relationship has evolved between *Azteca* ants and *Cecropia* trees over the course of time. These fierce insects act as patrol troops for the tree, not only discouraging epiphytic growth but also driving off other plant-eating—therefore potentially harmful—insects and even small mammals. In return, the ants find accommodations in hollow stems and branches, and they can feed buffet-style on the many small, bulb-like organs, called Müllerian bodies, that

Swooping down after insects from a high perch

The rainforests are alive with insects, and many birds take advantage of this food source. Among the large number of insectivorous birds are the tyrant flycatchers (left),

closely related to our flycatchers. They go after their prey in swift air strikes, then return to their high perch. The multi-colored toucans (above) belong to what is surely one of the most unusual-looking bird families in the rainforests of the New World. Not only does their plumage display the most startling color contrasts, but they also sport dispropor-tionally large, though lightweight, bills.

A beautiful new world

The canopy eco-system is full of surprises. American biologist Donald Perry was one of the first scientists to penetrate more deeply into this un-known and untamed world—an ecological environment that has

been evolving over millions of years, not at our feet, like most of the others, but in the highest treetops. Fascinating encounters with inhabitants of this airy continent are routine events—whether they be with an emerald boa (top) or with one of the numerous tree orchids, such as the lovely vanda (bottom).

Scenes in the tangle of branches

A human observer has to get close enough to touch the interwoven vegetation that makes up the rainforest canopy in order to explore the mysteries of this fascinating and

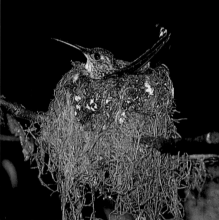

varied habitat. Diurnal as well as nocturnal animals make their permanent home here. An iguana (left) raises its dragon-like head to stare at the intruder. This spotted glass frog (top) and the brooding hummingbird (bottom) are apparently less impressed by his appearance.

Insect hunters stalking prey

Unlike other arboreal lizards (above), chameleons are able to change color quickly in perfect adaptation to their environment. The insect hunter shown making its slow way along a branch (large picture) is hard to detect against the green of its surroundings. The long, curled tail serves as an extra climbing and grasping organ.

Colorful compositions

In all tropical rainforests, birds—attired in multitudinous rainbow shades—represent a particularly colorful group of animals. Blue tanagers (top) wear delicately coordinated hues of blue and gray. The blacknecked red cotinga (center) and the crown pipra (bottom) are showier. In these species, only the males are brightly colored.

grow at the base of *Cecropia*'s leaf stems.

In tropical rainforests, there are no individual plant species that dominate the scene. The number of different species is simply too great to permit the aggregation of many individuals of the same species. But if the distance between representatives of a species is too great, a problem arises. How can pollination from one tree to another be assured? Close cooperation between trees and specific animal species therefore appears indispensable in this important realm of activity, too.

Obvious as it may seem that pollen-bearing insects must play an indispensable role in the genetic reproduction of rainforest trees, it was impossible to prove the existence of animal species capable of pollinating rainforest trees that grow at great distances from each other. In the early days of rainforest research, many ecologists therefore assumed that rainforest trees must be self-pollinating. This theory becomes untenable, however, when one takes into account the fact that a large number of tree species are dioecious—that is, any one tree can produce either male or female flowers, but not both. Under these conditions, evolutionary selection leading to self-pollination is hard to imagine.

No insects that could have been suitable pollinators for the trees were found because naturalists looked for them in the wrong place. As our observations have shown, insects acting as pollinators in the various levels of the canopy are never found near the "basement" of the forest. The bee *Euglossa bemichlora*, which collects nectar in the lower tiers of the forest in vegetation about 30 feet (10 m) above ground, never strays to the higher levels. Other wild bees, like *Eulaema polychroma* in the tier reaching up to about 80 feet (25 meters) and *Epicharis albofasciata* in the next higher tier, up to about 110 feet (35 meters), have clearly assigned work places, to which they keep.

It is therefore easy to understand why no one was aware, for instance, of the bee *Centris fusciventris*, which pollinates flowers in the crowns of the canopy.

In regard to the evolution of individual species, this marked adherence to different tiers or "floors" of the biotic communities—particularly the clear, horizontal delineation between pollination areas—is of great importance. Observation has made clear that no pollen is exchanged between different "floors" of the rainforest. This division into horizontal zones is almost comparable to the geographical isolation caused by mountain ranges or sea passages, and it has no doubt vastly accelerated the formation of new interdependent communities. This stratification of the crown region and the horizontal delineation of different groups of pollinators form a pattern that, on the one hand, encourages diversity and, on the other, reinforces existing spatial structures—a convincing example of how the life communities of the rainforest create the conditions that perpetuate their way of life. Certain norms of bee behavior and of tree florescence further facilitate the transport of pollen over long distances. Many kinds of bees have ways of remembering productive flight routes and travel along them for miles, again and again. It seems highly probable that these bees stop along the way to visit flowering trees of the same species.

In Costa Rica I have seen another strategy. Largish groups of dozens or hundreds of bees belonging to different species fly together in a swarm from tree to tree. These mixed swarms never stop in any place for long and are thus likely to contribute to the long-distance transport of flower pollen simply by their frequent moves. In the almendros among which we strung our rope network, the flowering period lasts almost three months, but each individual tree flowers less long. The blossoms of a rainforest region thus become

available to the nectar-collecting bees in a somewhat staggered way, which is another method by which crossfertilization is made easier. To date, no one has studied in depth what accounts for this slight time shift in the flowering activity of the trees.

On one of my first climbing ventures, I struck my boot against the trunk of a cashew tree while swinging from my rope. A deep thud resounded from the tree, as though from a drum. The trunk was obviously quite hollow. Closer examination revealed an entrance into the hollow trunk in the crown region. This discovery gave rise to a plan to inspect the trunk from the inside, using the climbing techniques I had developed—an adventure of limited appeal to most, no doubt, and one that probably no one had attempted previously.

The ascent to the entry hole was relatively problem-free. This time, no animals were lurking on or behind the bark—at least, I saw none. As complex a phenomenon as a piece of rainforest requires that our senses, especially our eyes, be trained by long practice to discern its structures and peculiarities. I had spent most of my life in the city, where the environment is devoid of stimuli encouraging this kind of sharpening of the senses. Once on the rim of the hole, I aimed the beam of my headlamp down into the cavity. It looked much like a natural smokestack. The rays of my lamp did not penetrate to the bottom—the hollow had to be rather deep.

It was not without some apprehension that I contemplated lowering myself into this shaft, first because the entry hole was really quite narrow and, second, because I had no way of knowing what I would encounter inside and farther down. But my anxieties proved unfounded, and my entry was uneventful. At the top of the shaft, a small colony of *Saccapteryx* bats was dozing away the day. The light of my lamp startled some of them, and for a few moments there was turmoil. I let myself down farther

Danger lurks in the treetops

Tree snakes occasionally go after birds, or at least after their eggs and nestlings. This elegant specimen is winding silently through the branches while drops of water run off its glistening, scaly skin.

Death for one, food for the other

In nature, life and death are never far apart, for life is unthinkable without death. Against this background, the sight of a snub-nosed viper making a meal of an arboreal iguana lacks drama and in fact appears necessary to the functioning of the entire ecosystem.

Its tail inspires many an artist

The almost 3 foot-long (1 m) tail of the quetzal, considered the most splendid bird on earth, looks decorative, as though it were the creation of an artist. This

trailing tail of the bird that was considered divine by early Central American peoples—a tail that surely does not represent a mere whim of nature, but performs a function in intraspecific communication—is depicted in stylized form on various articles, such as wall hangings (small picture on right page, top) and the official seal on Guatemala's paper money and coins (small picture on right page, bottom). The Mayas and Aztecs incorporated the quetzal's tail feathers in cult objects and honored the bird as the god of the air.

The quetzal became associated with the snake god Quetzalcoatl, and its tail feathers became a symbol for the new growth of plants in the spring. The quetzal is the best-known bird of the trogon family, which is represented by various other members in the rain-

forests of both the New World and the Old. Quetzals breed primarily in tree holes where there are ants and wasps. They feed on these insects and on berries, but their favorite food is avocados, which they swallow whole, later regurgitating the huge pit (large pictures, left and right).

Parrots— noisy, clever, and brightly colored

Macaws, birds closely related to parrots, are found throughout the world's tropics. More than 100 different species live in rainforests, with the heaviest concentrations occurring in Australia and South America, followed by Southeast Asia and Africa. They are visually conspicuous as well as highly audible, especially if dozens of them move through the canopy at once. Parrots and macaws are excellent climbers, using their beaks like a third foot. Sometimes they spend hours upside down, swinging among the branches. Many of these birds are very colorful, with shades of green and yellow predominating; red and blue are also common.

into the musty, humid, foul-smelling passage, which, to my surprise, suddenly opened into a sizable wooden grotto. Below me were almost 40 feet (12 m) of empty space—about the height of a five-story building. Looking up, I could see that the cavity extended above the entry hole into the two main limbs of the tree. I shone my lamp into one of these hollow branches, whereupon a loud screeching arose because the light beam had disturbed several hundred leaf-nosed bats. After fluttering around nervously for a few minutes, the bats returned to their relatively safe retreat.

Strange fungi grew on the walls of the cavity, some of them covered in turn with other fungi of a type I had never seen before. I collected a few specimens for closer inspection, but they quickly dissolved into a sticky mass.

Wood-boring beetles and, of course, termites had excavated this arboreal cavity, and some of them were still busily at work. A team of termite soldiers immediately appeared on the scene to protect the workers against me, the intruder. I saw a few crickets about half the length of a finger on the wall, feeling cautiously with their pencil-length antennae for food and aggressors. Just 6 feet (2 m) below the crickets sat a whip scorpion, a grotesque looking member of the order *Amblypygi*, whose long, skinny legs easily could have reached around my hand.

A few feet off the ground, I stopped to inspect the bottom carefully for bushmasters or other dangerous snakes. Luckily none seemed to be there; instead, I discovered a small mammal with blond fur squatting on a wooden shelf directly opposite me. It was a rat opossum, one of those strange marsupials of Central and South America that, unlike most other marsupials, have no pouch. Apparently the hollow tree served as the opossum's safe sleeping quarters, from which the animal ventured out at night in search of edible blossoms and fruits. Just conceivably, it was lying in wait for the bats in the upper part of the shaft; captive rat opossums have been observed to overpower and eat bats. On the ground, finally, I caught sight of a bullfrog almost 8 inches (20 cm) long, *Leptodactylus pentadactylus,* the largest frog found in Central America, an aggressive animal that has been known to eat snakes up to half a yard long without difficulty. Escaping the beam of my lamp, the frog disappeared beneath a ledge and, when I stooped to try and capture it, I discovered that from here, at the bottom of the cavity, a number of small subterranean corridors radiated in all directions, apparently serving small animals as direct passages to the rainforest outside. Here I was sitting inside a tree about level with the forest floor, surrounded by a totally strange world—a world that was a complete contrast to that of the treetops and their mysteries. It was an experience of inestimable value, no doubt, but I was extremely glad that a rope strong enough to support my weight still connected me to the world of civilization.

With the help of colleagues I had constructed an observation station more than 100 feet (30 m) above the ground, in the crown of a monkey pot tree. I spent many days there observing the life all round me and experiencing it as fully as possible.

This day, too, began auspiciously. During my ascent I saw a three-toed sloth resting in the crotch of a *Virola* tree close by. Green algae grow on the long fur of this animal, making it look almost like an especially large epiphyte. Apparently my presence bothered the sloth, for it began to climb upward at a deliberate pace. A dead branch scraped its coat, and half a dozen

Feathers as calling cards

Where numerous members of the same family or closely related species have to coexist in the same habitat, biotopes have to be split up and individual territories well defined, if for no other reason than to make the best use of resources. Recognition of a member of one's own species is as important as the prompt notice of close relatives. The necessary signaling is done by manipulating the plumage in ways typical of the species. Often some specific utterances and behavior patterns assist in conveying the unmistakable character of the species. Difficult as we may find it to tell the many parrot species apart, in nature the biological distinction between species functions well.

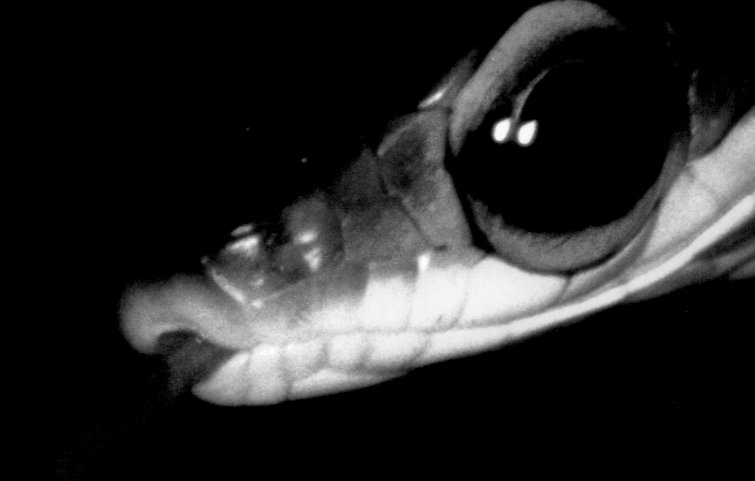

The shape of snakes has no symbolic meaning

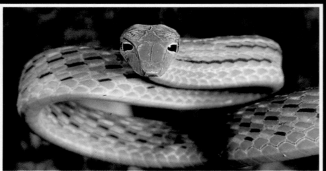

Snakes are no doubt the longest living reptiles. In the Orinoco delta in Venezuela, an anaconda measuring 37.5 feet (11.4 m) was once killed. Snakes are elegant in their smooth and sinuous forward motion, fascinating in their ability to freeze into absolute rigidity, and sometimes dangerous in their use of highly successful hunting techniques. The tree snake (top) and the reticulated python (center right) represent two especially widespread patterns. The coral snake (center left) and the vine snake (bottom left) exemplify other possible colors and shapes.

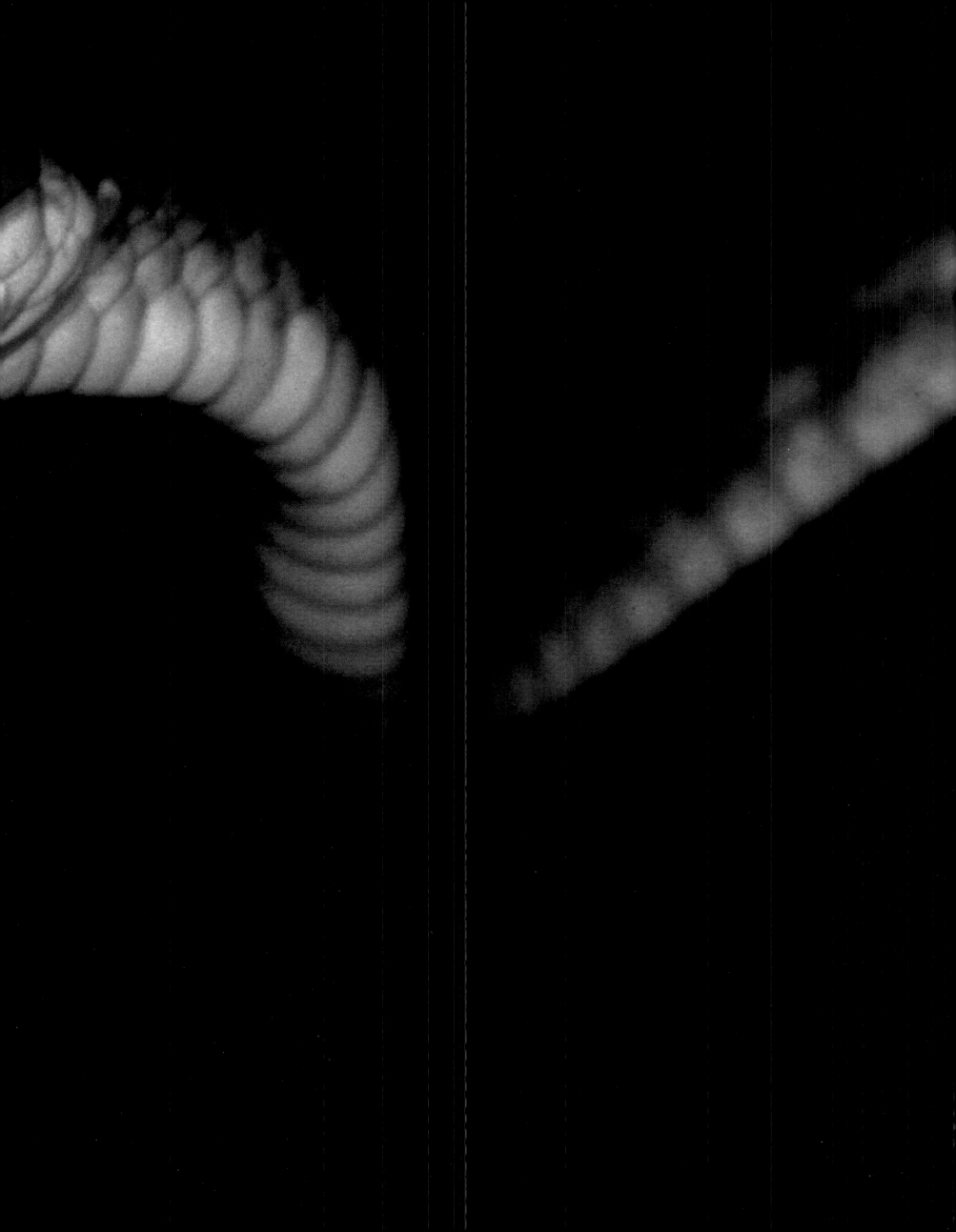

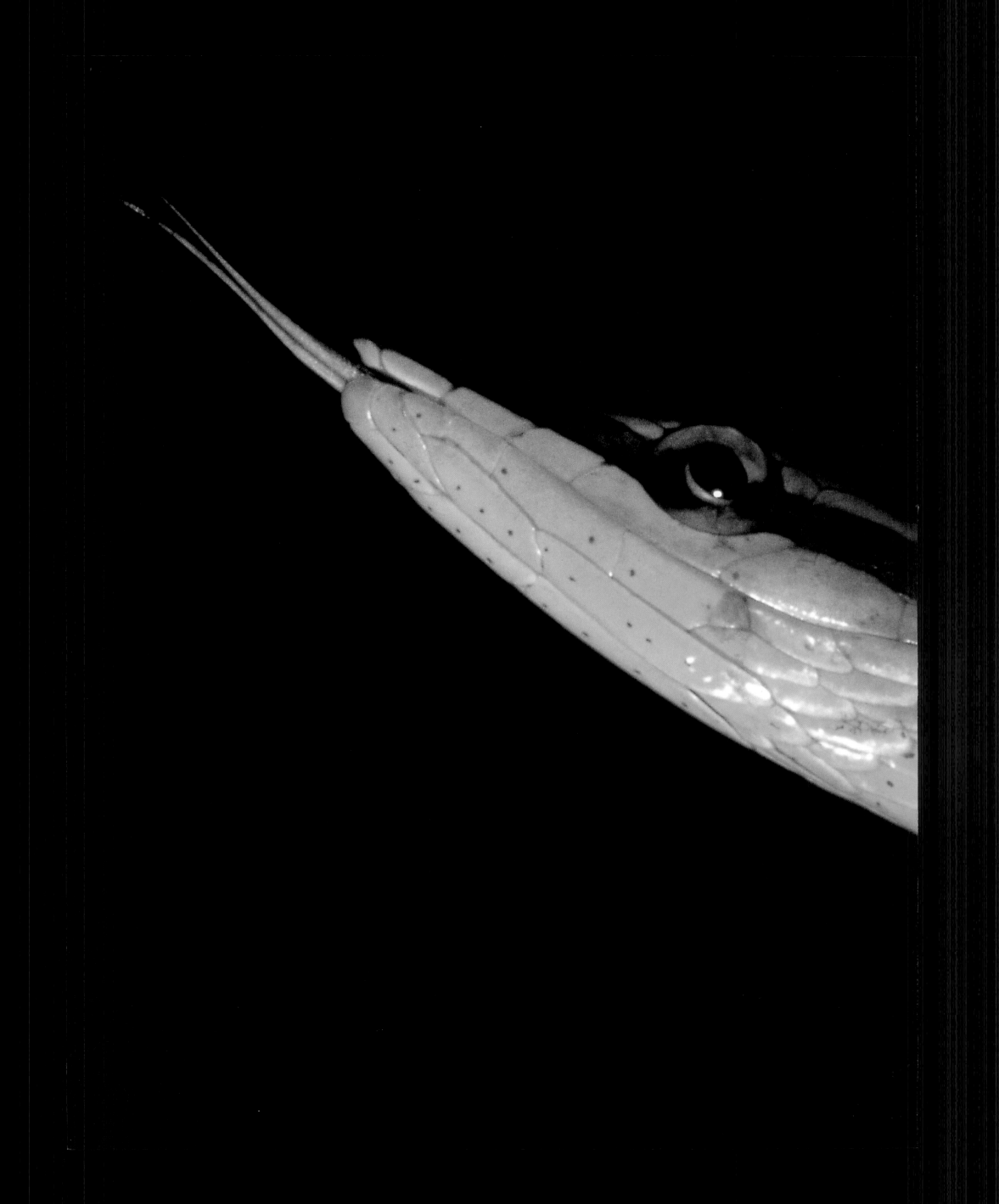

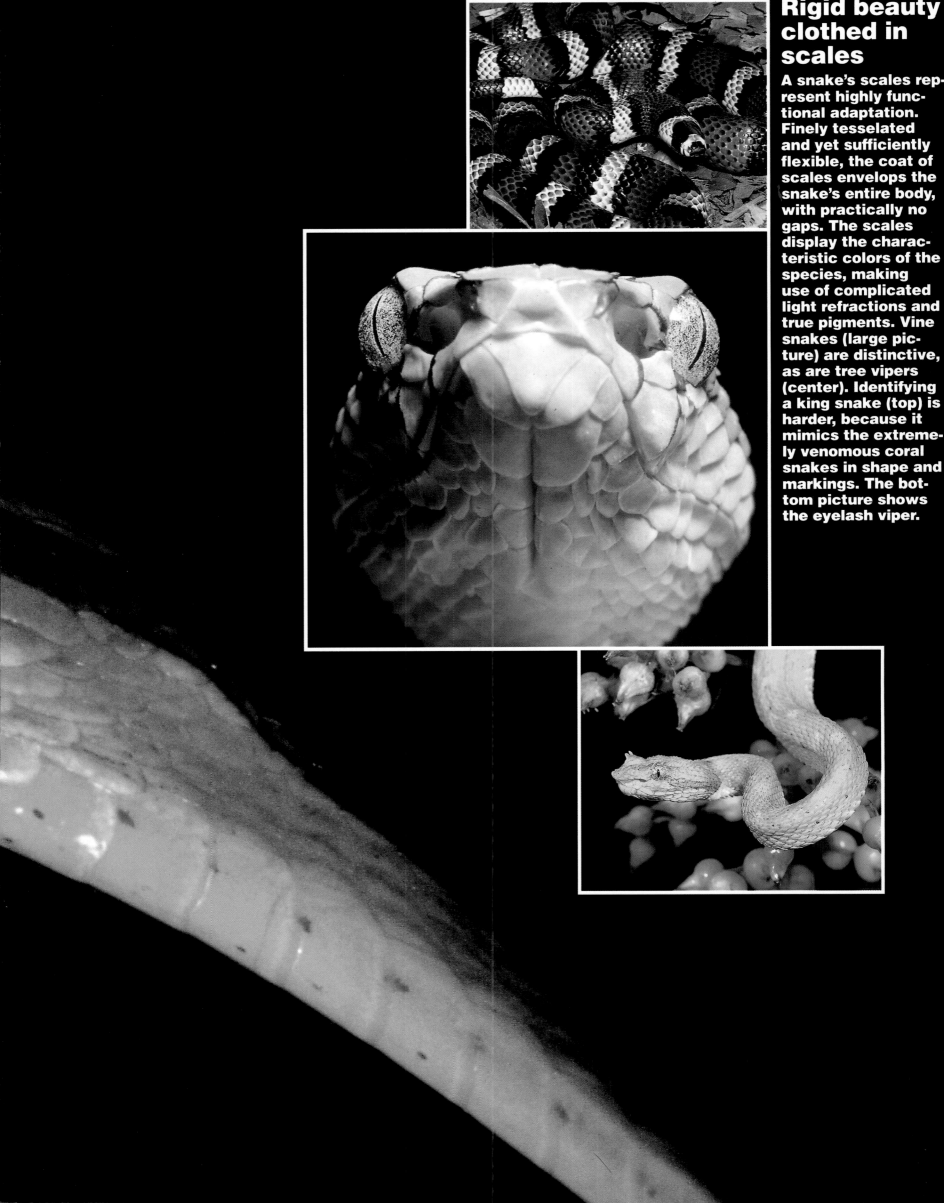

Rigid beauty clothed in scales

A snake's scales represent highly functional adaptation. Finely tesselated and yet sufficiently flexible, the coat of scales envelops the snake's entire body, with practically no gaps. The scales display the characteristic colors of the species, making use of complicated light refractions and true pigments. Vine snakes (large picture) are distinctive, as are tree vipers (center). Identifying a king snake (top) is harder, because it mimics the extremely venomous coral snakes in shape and markings. The bottom picture shows the eyelash viper.

The sun makes the plants grow

Sunlight powers the processes of vegetative growth in the rainforest. When rain clouds darken the sky or low fog sweeps across the landscape, photosynthesis cannot take place at full

efficiency, but even under these conditions there is sufficient light for the plants to sustain themselves. All the animals making up the higher levels of the food pyramid live entirely on what is produced by the plants. Even rainforest birds, like the brightly colored pipra (far right) and the bellbird, with its plumage of contrasting colors (above), are direct or indirect beneficiaries of this plant life.

small moths that had temporarily settled on its fur fled the disturbance. The pelts of these sloths are known to house many insects and mites, and dozens of anthropods also have been found and identified.

On my platform I always feel as though I were inside a huge greenhouse. A casual survey of my surroundings reveals at least 50 different kinds of epiphytes, and a systematic search would no doubt yield twice that number. Through my binoculars I watch bees and other pollinators visit flowers at various canopy levels. Crested hummingbirds hover motionless in the air in front of the sweet-smelling blossoms of a souroubea plant, drawing out the nectar. White-crowned parrots nibble on the fruit of a *Dendropanax* tree. A few moments later, a white-necked puffbird dives down out of some branches, strikes the leaves of my monkey pot tree, and flies away with a wriggling anole lizard in its beak. For a while I watch a single capuchin monkey—it either is being ostracized by a noisy nearby group of its fellows or has not been allowed to join them. Dramatic scenes present themselves at even closer range: Overhead, a jumping spider, or salticid, is scanning the bottom of the transparent plastic roof above my platform, examining each square inch with minute precision, advancing a bit, freezing in place, searching again. Then it makes a sudden, perfectly aimed leap, and lands on the back of a katydid, the deadly fangs closing around the unsuspecting grasshopper's neck.

It is noon and, as usual, a surprising stillness reigns in the forest. A few *Paraponera* ants go about their business on a branch below my platform. (It took only one sting to convince me that it was wise to stay out of their way as much as possible.)

Until I started observing the canopy from the perspective of my observation platform, I had not realized that open corridors run along the top of the tree branches. These corridors are comparable to the animal paths on the forest floor. I have not been able to establish what keeps these highways open, but I have often seen leaves of obstructing plants "cropped" close to the base.

I have seen perhaps 1,000 different animal species in the rainforest canopy—ranging from ants to rainbow toucans, from caterpillars that mimic the head of a snake to howler monkeys a few trees away. In each species are reflected the millions of years of the rainforest's history. Each is part of a large, incredibly complex evolutionary process, a process that undoubtedly will continue if rainforests survive as viable biological environments.

A parrot in a cage, a philodendron in a planter, an anthurium on a window sill—no matter what splendid specimens they may be—are curiosities at best. Isolated, torn out of the context of their ecological community, they have almost lost the meaning of their existence. Today, with the help of new techniques and technology, species can be studied in the context of their environment, not just as museum specimens. Reaching the canopy has opened a whole new world, one almost comparable to the discovery of a new continent, with a gigantic array of species ripe for study in their home territory.

Birds help the dispersal of plants

Trees and plants growing on trees cannot spread far without the help of animals that have a sufficiently large radius of activity. Frugivorous and seed-collecting birds, for instance, add an

important spatial dimension to the reproductive efficiency of plants. The harvesting and collecting habits of animals perform an important function in the rainforest. Through their constant mobility, animals stabilize the mosaic pattern of species distribution that is so typical of rainforests.

Rolf Bökemeier

Holocaust in Paradise: The Genocide of Forest People

Every day, indigenous people are
killed because gold diggers destroy their
homeland through mining or because
ranchers burn down the rainforests to
create more pasture. The relentless advance
of industrial civilization, in combination
with exploding population growth,
threatens the survival of the last
representatives of ancient cultures
in the rainforest.

Before chainsaws and bulldozers, man's effects on the rainforest were minimal. Indians did not battle the wilderness. They carved out small areas in the forest for villages and gardens, then moved to new areas. These clearings were small enough to be reseeded quickly.

Man in harmony with nature

The Yanomami Indians in the Brazilian parts of Amazonia have been living in and off the rainforest for centuries. The forest gives them what they need to live—not in great abundance, but enough to ensure the survival of small populations. Settling permanently in one place is out of the question. The limited food resources force the Indians to lead a nomadic existence.

The diversity of cultures

The rainforest does not feed large human populations. Because of the low population density, forest tribes are isolated from each other; each has developed its own rituals, language, and culture. The destruction of the rainforest deprives these people of their life base. The Amazonian Yanomami and many others are fighting for their cultural survival, sometimes even for their physical survival.

The forest as a home for humans

Primitive peoples live in rainforest regions all over the world. They are biologically similar to the rest of humanity living on the various continents, but they are culturally diverse. The Pygmies in the Central African Congo are a classical example of a unique culture. Are they doomed to disappear?

Responding to the splendor of the forest

The forest Indians of South America respond deeply to the stunning beauty of many of the creatures that live in the rainforest. They incorporate the bright colors of many forest

animals in their own symbols, decorative motifs, and rituals. This Indian girl of the Cofán tribe in Ecuador (above) is feeding her tame tanager. For a dance ritual, the Bororo chieftain from Brazil (right page) has donned a headdress fashioned of gorgeous, brightly colored feathers.

The rainforest. After only a few hours the torment begins. Moving like inchworms, the everpresent blood suckers approach from all directions, as though they had been waiting all their lives just for you. While you swat at mosquitoes, ants, and hornets everywhere you can see, leeches suck your blood on the sly. By the time you bivouac, you pour half a pint of your life's vital juices out of your boots and are thankful that your blood-drenched clothes have not turned into stiff boards.

The rainforest. You wade through an ocean dispersed in the air. Myriads of invisible droplets surround you, but do not quench your thirst. The crystal clear water in the streams that sometimes cross your path doesn't help either, no matter how much of it you drink. The forest has drunk it before you and filtered out every mineral. What is left is distilled sweat.

The rainforest. I have had occasion to curse its cousins along the Amazon, in New Guinea, in Cameroon. But compared with this moss-bearded cyclops on Borneo, this paterfamilias of forests that is over 100 million years old, the others were only poor relations. Sarawak's green inferno spreads in an unbroken cloak of tough lianas and thorny branches across a sea of undulating landscape that extends from horizon to horizon. This rainforest lets you suffer and hunger and thirst. Dry deserts and the inhospitable waters of the sea were its forebears. Their hybrid geological offspring, the jungle, named after the Sanskrit *jangala,* which means desert, is as hostile to man as both forebears together.

How can any human beings, how can the people of the Penan tribe, whom I am on my way to visit, exist in this hell?

After a six-day trek on foot through Sarawak's unpopulated rainforest province of Limbang, my guide, Bruno, and I arrive at the camp of the forest nomads. I do not realize we are there until I am in the middle of it. Five dwellings—simple constructions of sticks resting on stilts and covered with a roof of thatched leaves—fit seamlessly into the surrounding pattern of vegetation. The shelters are perfectly camouflaged.

The Penan live the primitive life of hunting and gathering societies of the Stone Age. They are probably the last true forest nomads left on Borneo, and they are certainly the only people of Sarawak who spend their lives entirely in the rainforest. Sarawak is a Malaysian state located in the northern part of the world's third-largest island, where 26 different aboriginal populations—collectively called Dayaks by the government—persistently resist attempts on the part of the nation's Malayan and Chinese ruling majorities to civilize them. For a decade now, the Penan have been protesting, by necessity militantly, against being robbed of their land. Chain saws and bulldozers have been flattening the forest that has been the Penan's home since ancient times to meet the industrial world's demand for wood and paper, and especially to satisfy Japan's huge appetite for these raw materials.

A male Penan rises from the group before me and approaches me. I expected these people to be of Pygmy stature and am therefore surprised that Buki, the tribe's chief, is practically as tall as I. "So the *ira British rai* wants to spend some time with us, the Penan?" he asks. The Penan initially assume any European to be a representative of Great Britain, the colonial power that ruled eastern Malaysia until 1965.

The first thing a guest needs is a roof over his head. Buki and his men cut the needed materials in the forest with their bush knives, which are as sharp as carving knives, and tie the basic structure together with strips of rattan. A wooden rack supported by four posts and covered with a roof of leaves takes shape, a rack from which I will gratefully rise every morning: Sleeping on such a bed comes close to flogging.

Sun, Buki's wife, immediately starts interrogating me. How old am I? How many children? Where is my wife? *Sitan, pessú, ani-asšo,* the chieftain's wife swears, aghast when she hears that I have a family but am traveling without them. "Devil, pus, and dog shit," Bruno translates with a malicious grin. "A Penan would never leave his family in the forest," he adds. "They do everything together; they share all the game of the hunt with scrupulous fairness, and even the children have chores to do as soon as they are able to walk."

Without this cooperation they could not survive in the rainforest. How much the Penan have adapted to an essentially hostile environment and how dissimilar they are from us settled folk is evident in how much our elementary needs differ. When, at the end of a long and arduous pursuit of a wild pig, I offer my water bottle to Pedeu, the best of the hunters, he watches with amazement as I set the bottle to my lips. The Penan drink no liquids. They need much less water than we do because they hardly sweat, which also means that they have to wash much less than we do. They ingest what fluid their bodies need in their basic staple, sago. This concentrated, starchy food is derived from the pith of the sago palm. The felled trunks of the palm trees, which usually grow as isolated individuals on hillside slopes, often have to be dragged hundreds of yards through dense undergrowth to a stream or river. The Penan depend on the aid of water to obtain their everyday food. Once the men have broken the palm trunk open with their multipurpose tool, the bush knife, and the pink, fibrous pulp has been excavated, the women's work of transforming this raw material into food begins. They stamp the fibrous mass, watering it repeatedly. This is done on bamboo mats that are spread on wooden racks to act as sieves. The yellowish, viscous liquid that drips down makes up the bulk of the daily meal, which

A childhood in Amazonia

To Americans and Europeans, life in the rainforest may appear arduous and frightening, but for the Indians, the forest is what they know and deal with daily. The childhood of the young Indian boy of the Karajá tribe (right page), on whose shoulder two immature king tyrannulets have settled, may be as carefree as that of any other child anywhere else.

is consumed in the evening.

The Penan, like our Stone Age forebears, eat at one sitting everything they have caught, gathered, and prepared in the course of the day. If the day's catch includes a wild pig or a monkey, then, after everyone has eaten the meat, the rendered fat is added to the sago mush in the cooking pan: A feast! Nomads living in the forest cannot store food. Trying to provide for the future would be a burden in the literal sense of the word. Only sago is dried and stored in bamboo canes; it constitutes an emergency ration that is used only if the hunters return to the camp empty-handed three evenings in succession.

But Pedéu, the master marksman, seldom lets things come to such a pass. It is a marvel to see this virtuoso hunter wield his 10-foot hardwood blowgun, sending a foot-long poison dart, with an audible pop from his puffed cheeks, to hit its mark 50 yards away.

The only problem is that the dart poison, which is derived from the bark of the ipoh tree, is not potent enough to paralyze a wild pig instantly. The animal may still be able to run a hundred yards and disappear in the impenetrable brush before collapsing. More game, in fact, is lost this way than through missed shots.

The advance of loggers and bulldozers has brought hard times for the Penan. Of the approximately 3,000 members of the tribe, only a few hundred still live as true forest nomads. The great majority have reluctantly relocated in permanent settlements, even though Penan can really survive well only in the rainforest. On cleared land they have to shun the sunlight, only 1 percent of which reaches the ground in the tribe's native forests. The Penan, moreover, are used to living exclusively on the products of nature. They find enough to eat in the vicinity of their camps for the limited time they stay there. When the resources of an area are exhausted after a maximum of three

months of hunting and gathering and of harvesting sago, the clan moves on to set up a new camp practically overnight, usually on top of a hill, far from the rivers. There are two reasons for this choice of location. Away from the water there are fewer mosquitoes and sand fleas, and unwelcome visitors, who usually approach by way of the rivers, are less likely to turn up. The Penan, unlike the Dayak, are not headhunters, but were for a long time their victims.

In recent times, the circle of nomadic travel has become smaller and smaller because the environment in which the Penan exist has been shrinking. Now, when they return after some years to the site of a previous camp, they often find that chain saws have brought down the lofty roof over their heads.

The same thing is happening to another rainforest people, one living in the Great Sunda Archipelago, where a great variety of nomadic forest tribes used to thrive. West of Sumatra, deep in the interior of the island of Siberut, live the Mentawai, a tribe that could be described as a more elegant version of the Stone Age Penan.

I am lying on my back, gazing into the sky and thinking about nothing in particular, taking a bath. Above the canopy, flying foxes swing along on whistling wing membranes, heading toward the setting sun like lonely vampires. The dark of night is already spreading through the thickets along the water, revealing here and there the glint of a monkey's eyes.

The eyes probably belong to bilous, thought to be the ancestor of all gibbons. Extremely rare animals, they are found only here, on the Mentawai Islands. Because of a different endemic population, a species that belongs to another branch in the family of primates, they have not yet become extinct. This particular group of primates is found only on Siberut and on the neighboring islands of Sipora, Pagai Utara, and Pagai Selatan: These cousins of the bilous walk

upright. They are the tribe of the Mentawai, a proto-Malayan race of humans that until a few years ago had hardly any contact with the rest of the world. "The apes are our brothers," emphatically states Aman Laut-Lau Manai, the highest-ranking elder in the tripartite clan house, the *uma*, a well-hidden structure in the forest that can be spotted only by the smoke rising from the hearth.

"In the beginning there were only the apes," my host tells me. "They lived in the tall trees of the forest. One day all the trees fit to live in were getting overcrowded, and the ape elders came together to hold a council. The result of the deliberation was that half the population was allowed to continue living in the trees, while the other half had to descend to the ground. To restore the balance of justice, the earth dwellers were to be allowed to hold a great feast from time to time. Their arboreal relatives always sacrifice a few of their own as a contribution to the feast."

Aman Laut-Lau is looking at me intently: Has the *sasarèu*, the stranger, understood the meaning?

Aku ma kateibaga katubum mui—I admire you! I could not have told the history of our becoming human, of our relationship to the apes, as clearly and succinctly as you, an illiterate tribesman.

Preparations for the great feast, for which a few apes may be sacrificed, are by this time well under way. Every hand that is not busy with the everyday tasks of food gathering is fashioning festive utensils in the *uma*: fetishes made of goose feathers, gaily embroidered sashes, fringed headbands made of palm fronds, bracelets and necklaces of dried, red-dyed seeds. All this is being readied for the *puliaijat*, the initiation of the shaman, of whom there has to be at least one in every uma.

This time the feast is for Aman Laut-Lau. After three years of instruction in the lore of universal spirits, the 30-year-old head of household is to be

The forest yields all kinds of food

The chore of procuring the daily food is not divided just among the adults. Children and adolescents also help, to the extent of their ability, in providing the basic necessities. The rainforest's

diversity of species guarantees a great variety of different foods—common ones, as well as unusual ones. Proper preparation of the latter, however, sometimes requires experience. The small girl belonging to the Jaguar tribe in Colombia is holding a manioc root (above). Before these roots are eaten, they have to be cooked and specially processed to get rid of certain poisonous substances.

Other cultures—other tastes

Finger-length grubs (below), called *suri* by the Jaguar Indians, are also collected, then roasted and eaten. Such foods, which may appear unusual and possibly unappetizing to us, have

helped people in the rainforest survive for millennia. Insect larvae are especially rich in protein and fat, and they form an essential part of the diet. Primitive peoples have no deficiency diseases resulting from a one-sided diet.

The hunter takes only what he needs

Because humans lack physical specialization, they are inferior to all the larger animals in terms of the speed and agility with which they move

through the forest. Even pygmies would not be able to provide themselves with animal proteins if they lacked effective weapons. The bow and arrow are hunting weapons that have been refined over thousands of years. Yet the bow's ineffectiveness, in comparison with modern weapons, ensured that a breeding population would remain to repopulate the forest and provide a future source of food for the hunter.

initiated as a *se-kerei,* or shaman, by his master Taen Ru-Ru Goo. The shaman—and among the Mentawai, every adult male will someday advance to the state of *se-kerei*—watches over the peace between man and nature.

Peace. Peace is the basic tenor that reigns in Aman Laut-Lau's small jungle realm in the inaccessible center of Siberut. It is not man, however, that is responsible for the peace that exists. Harmony existed before man arrived on the scene. Everything in the natural world exists in a state of balance: animals and plants, water and stones, rain and wind, sun and moon. Everything in nature has a soul: birds as well as worms, apes as well as bananas, the coconut fruit as well as the coconut rat. When one feeds on the other, when the bird eats the worm, the victim's soul first gives up its earthly form and happily joins the community of its ancestors. The soulless worm is released to become food; the world is in order.

This constant balancing act, Aman Laut-Lau believes, is entirely the work of nature. Only man disrupts this order whenever and wherever he interferes.

To keep the harm done to the world around them within proper bounds, the Mentawai shamans simply impose taboos on all kinds of actions. This taboo can be lifted when necessary, but a burden is imposed on the people that is commensurate with the value of the thing taken from nature. The tree that people wish to make into a canoe, the game that is to become human food, the fruits that are to be transformed into dart poison—all these souls have to be reconciled in long and complicated ceremonies, so that people may use the material bodies of the plants and animals without evoking the anger of their ancestral souls.

Liberty, equality, and fraternity—the ideals of bourgeois revolution—are taken literally and rule the daily life of the Mentawai. For Aman Laut-Lau, freedom automatically includes

freedom for his brother. Everybody in the *uma,* old and young, male and female, has the same rights, the same voice in every palaver concerning the welfare of the community. The meat of hunted game is divided into equal portions for everyone, just as it is among the Penan on Borneo. Brotherliness is the natural mode of coexistence because everybody is related to everybody else, either by blood or by marriage. Rivalries between families are thus kept to a minimum, and there are neither chieftains nor warriors, neither lords nor slaves.

Do the Mentawai represent an Arcadian society before the fall of man? Not at all. Here, too, there is conflict, but it does not break out openly. If a quarrel cannot be settled by peaceful means, people try to circumvent it. In a case of serious disagreement, a whole clan may choose to leave the enemy's sphere of influence and move to a new area with all the members of the *uma.* This kind of social behavior is possible only where plenty of forest is available, and soon this will no longer be the case for the aboriginals of Siberut, who number about 2,000.

Already, 20,000 land-hungry settlers are pushing inland from the coast into the forest. They come from Java, whose population is spilling over, and from all the nooks and crannies of Indonesia, the giant mother, ceaselessly producing teeming masses of offspring. These masses, equipped with fire and steel, with water buffaloes and plows, with rice seed and chemical fertilizer, are invading Siberut. Although naturalists and organizations concerned about the environment are doing everything in their power to preserve Siberut as a unique natural laboratory for the study of evolutionary history, it is highly unlikely that the island's tranformation into a western monoculture can be stopped.

A similar fate, though in a different guise, has caught up with the last remnant of another of the few primitive peoples

living in the shrinking rainforest belt of our planet. These people live 1,000 nautical miles northwest of Siberut, on Sri Lanka. The aboriginal inhabitants of this island, the Vedda, sought refuge in the Maduru Oya National Park in the eastern part of the island because they were displaced by a gigantic irrigation project. It was set up to make possible flooded rice cultivation along the Mahaweli Ganga, in a region that was once the home of the Vedda, a people that still puzzles anthropologists.

Some ethnologists estimate that the Vedda have existed on Sri Lanka for 40,000 years, while others think they have been there only about 12,000 years. The earliest mention of the Vedda occurs in a Ceylonese historical chronicle, *Mahavamsa,* where they are referred to as *Yakka,* "wild ghosts," and as *Naga,* "snake people." These forest people have survived for centuries, largely ignored by the world around them, in the eastern jungle of the island, a region that until recently was practically unusable for agriculture.

The villages of the hunters and gatherers seldom consist of more than seven huts of wood, roofed with jungle grass, each one inhabited by a single family. The people living in such a village constitute a clan. They practice slash-and-burn agriculture, moving from place to place and returning to old sites in approximately a 12-year cycle.

Originally, the Vedda were subdivided into 13 clans. Family relationship is defined according to matrilineal descent, but property is bequeathed from father to son. Strict monogamy, mandatory according to tribal law, is enforced by the clan elder, who also serves as the clan's chieftain, priest, and counselor. All the clans are subject to a high chief or "king," who is always selected from the privileged clan of the Bandara.

Such a Bandara chieftain is standing before me in the person of Tissahamy, who enjoys legendary fame among the Vedda.

His ax, the traditional attribute of a Vedda male, rests on his shoulder as though it were an extension of his body. His shoulder-length hair and the beard that flows to his breast are stirred slightly by the wind. He eyes me with childlike curiosity. *"Hondamai*—welcome, all is well," he greets me. We stretch out our hands and clasp each other by the forearms. Our thumbs can feel the other man's heartbeat pulsing through his veins. For a moment we are one, as though his blood and mine were circulating through one and the same body. This double-handed greeting gesture of the Vedda means that we can deal honestly with each other. Deceit is out of the question. I should like, I say, to go hunting with the chieftain's sons. *"Hondamai,"* the old man nods, and only now, after business has been taken care of, does he turn to the presents: tobacco, betel nuts, and honey, in accordance with wishes previously expressed.

We set out at three o'clock in the morning, Wanniya, Gunnabanda, Sitawanniya, and I. I am burdened with and hampered by all the technical gear the white man relies on to keep him safe in the rainforest. The Vedda men are naked except for a loincloth. Their dark skin melts into the surrounding darkness as they nimbly make their silent way through the jungle. Fearing to lose sight of them, I keep the beam of my flashlight aimed on their light-colored heels and curse the water bottle, compass, hunting knife, and binoculars that dangle from various parts of my body and hinder my progress through the dense, thorny underbrush.

A huge granite slab rising above the jungle at an angle is our goal, the lookout from which hunters scan the forest for game. Finally, the morning light touches the land from the east. In this tropically brief moment of dawn, I would be unable to tell a black elephant from a white one. Elephants? Really! But by the time I have blinked my eyes once or twice, the giant gray shapes by the river have dissolved like ink in water. Through my binoculars, I keep scanning all directions for the 4-ton beasts. No luck. Every close-up of forest in my glasses turns out to be a meaningless pattern of broccoli-like shapes. How on earth do the Vedda succeed in spotting their prey in the fleeting half-light of dawn or dusk, the short time of perhaps a quarter of an hour when the animals are on the move?

They do spot animals, of course, but they are not allowed to kill them. The forest is part of Maduru Oya National Park, officially designated a nature reserve. The law forbids the park's human inhabitants—a people attuned to nature, who have lived in and with the forest from time immemorial—to pursue their traditional occupation of hunting. How, then, do the Vedda procure the animal protein that is part of their accustomed diet?

"We set traps secretly," says Wanniya, the oldest of the chieftain's sons. "If we are lucky, we will catch a porcupine, a turtle, or a few forest rats." Can the clan survive on this scant supply? "The government gives us rice and seed," the hunter answers in a low voice, as though ashamed of admitting this. It is probably the government's method of trying to bribe the forest nomads to adopt a settled way of life.

Will the last aboriginal inhabitants of Sri Lanka soon be reduced to living on handouts from the government? If this happens, it spells the end of their ethnic identity as a forest people. They will be subject to ethnocide, like the Papua on New Guinea, who, after a period of intense missionizing, are now dependent on the church.

New Guinea lies in the western Pacific. It is the second-largest island on earth, and as recently as 30 years ago it contained an almost untouched and scarcely explored rainforest biotope of archaic diversity, inhabited by perhaps 500 different tribes. Today this island is the biggest religious battlefield of our century. There is hardly a place to be found on New Guinea where there are not some three dozen Christian missions of all conceivable provenances fiercely competing with each other to save souls. They plunge the aboriginal inhabitants into total confusion. The missionaries, numbering about 1,400 throughout the country, not only are obsessed with converting the natives, but also act as advance guard for civilization of a western stamp. The resulting consumerism fostered by a government influenced by western thinking leads first and foremost to the collapse of the once-viable agrarian structure established by the Papua in the rainforest.

The fact is that the Papua had created a primitive affluent society based on the wealth produced by successful agriculture. This wealth made possible a high degree of cultural and artistic self-realization. Only someone privileged to attend a genuine song festival in the bush can get a sense of these cultural achievements. Such a performance has nothing in common with the tourist spectacles organized in the highland metropolis of Mount Hagen. I will never forget the singing I witnessed in Melpaland, in the forest of Tambul.

It is like a scene from the Age of Discovery, that disastrous period of history when white-skinned explorers, in their ignorance, coined names to describe strange people with different-colored skins, names that are still part of our language, names like heathen, savage, and cannibal. All the same, I have to admit that the figures dancing around me disguised behind martial masks and flashing dangerous weapons, the primordial-sounding singsong, and the deep, rumbling thunder of the drums all send shudders of fear across my white skin.

The athletic bodies keep leaping into the air as though on springs, unrestrainable as jacks-in-the-box. They swing their

Everybody likes bright colors

Almost all primitive people incorporate in their traditional rituals elements of the colorful world that surrounds them. The human body lacks bright colors, which are conse-

quently and understandably regarded as something special and are used to emphasize the unusualness of a given situation. Bird feathers and body painting in contrasting colors serve as decoration.

Indigenous culture under attack

The arrival in the rainforest of modern civilization means exploitation of an ecosystem whose natural structures and life forms cannot withstand such an onslaught. Not only industries, but also droves of adventur-

ers, try to share in the exploitation of ore deposits (as here in the Brazilian state of Rondonia). Wildlife poachers, too, such as the one shown taking a caiman, contribute to the ecological degradation of the entire region.

spears and shields and turn in circles, pirouette-fashion. The yard-high headdresses made from the tails of cassowaries, the feathers of birds of paradise, and pressed human hair nod, whirl, and whip up and down. The grass aprons and leaf skirts rustle as they swing back and forth, and the necklaces and hip bands made of shells and pig's teeth clack in a monotone staccato.

The faces alone remain rigid. They are covered by a layer, as thick as the back of a knife, of painted gesso made out of pork fat, plant sap, ashes, and clay. These masks are works of visual art made up of blackest black, blood red, sun yellow, and ash gray. They are awe-inspiring, minutely executed facial images fashioned to frighten off enemies as well as demons. This singing festival is tough show business, a sudorific Olympic competition in the bush where vanity vies with vanity and finally the better-trained, more lavishly adorned troupe emerges the winner.

The spectacle has a deeper meaning, however. It serves to keep alive the tribe's culture, tradition, artistry, and military capability, for the fashioning of the masks and weapons and the perfecting of the artistic present-ations require a great deal of know-how and commitment to the enterprise. To the govern-ment in Port Moresby, which is intent on the country's becoming part of western civilization, these cultural articles and rituals dating back to the Stone Age are an irritating symbol of backward-ness, and the missionaries are happy to act as pioneers of progress to help get rid, once and for all, of everything heathen. Missionaries performed the same service for centuries in Africa, today a dying continent, where a rich variety of cultures once flourished but had to submit to the leveling force of "becoming civilized" in a process that has reduced the inhabitants of many regions to an impov-erished proletariat.

Africa's last rainforest race, once the classical example of this way of existence, is the Pygmies,

whose name is derived from a Greek term, meaning "humans no larger than fist-size." Theoretically, three groups, adding up to about 150,000 individuals, still survive in the much-thinned central African rainforest. They are the Mbuti in northeastern Zaire, the Bongo in Gabon, and the Mbenga in Cameroon.

I visited the Mbenga in 1982, and already then these artists of survival in the green universe—which to forest nomads is both father and mother, the world both of this life and of the hereafter—were broken physi-cally and spiritually. They had long ago begun hiring them-selves out as field laborers to the socially higher standing Bantus. In the depressing corrugated-tin shacks where the Pygmies now live, leprosy, tuberculosis, malaria, schistosomiasis, and venereal disease were rampant. Hunters went into the forest only in the pay of ivory and wild-animal dealers to kill an elephant or steal the baby of a gorilla mother—or to die. To describe the present state of what were

once the most legendary rainforest people in the history of mankind would result only in a hopelessly depressing requiem.

Where, oh where, is it still possible to find unspoiled examples of that wonderful human species, of that anthropo-logical miracle that somehow came into being in the rainforest of all places, where everything would seem to conspire against human survival? The most likely place is South America. There, in the heart of Brazil, protected by the forest, I met them: Indians of the Yawalapiti, the Mehinaku, and the Txucarramae tribes. If it were not for Orlando Villas Bòas, the father of all Brazilian Indians, these tribes would no longer exist either. Villas Bòas created a sufficiently large reservation on the Rio Xingu in Mato Grosso. This influential co-founder of the Funai, the department for the affairs of indigenous populations, recognized before it was too late that these forest dwellers were in need of, and deserved, protec-tion. "More than any other indigenous people on earth," Villas Bòas believes, "the forest

Indians of South America are condemned to ruin by the advance of civilization. The mere discovery of a tribe by the white man generally spells the beginning of the end."

The Indians have been content to remain simple children of Mother Nature, who is far from merciful; they—unlike the white man—refuse to wage war against the wilderness; and they live in harmony with themselves and the green cosmos that surrounds them. All this is the result of a lesson they learned long ago: If you take more from the forest than you need to live, the forest will kill you, slowly but surely.

Other primitive peoples, from the Eskimos of Greenland to the aborigines of Australia, possess this same unerring feeling of connectedness to their part of the universe, what could be called an archaic sense of responsibility for their world. But the forest Indians, like almost all other rainforest inhabitants, differ from other ethnic groups in one tragic respect: They are not adaptable to new conditions. All their adaptive genius has gone into creating a culture that is in perfect tune with the forest, and this culture, like the ecosystem of the forest, cannot withstand the slightest outside interference.

"It may sound paradoxical," says Orlando Villas Bòas, "but it is their very wholeness that makes these people so vulnerable."

Settlement only in the peripheral regions

European immigrants were reluctant to settle in the huge, wild interior of the South American continent. For a long time, land claims were restricted to regions close to the coast and to major rivers. Depicted here are the descendants of a Pomeranian immigrant family in Brazil (top). Where crops are to be grown, the rainforest has to go. Humans have practiced slash-and-burn agriculture for thousands of years, and all this time the forest could absorb such use because only tiny areas were affected. The vastly increased clearing of forest land in recent times, however, is creating problems of unimagined dimensions. Here, an area in the Congo has been cleared for planting and is being further prepared by burning (center); below, a group is getting ready to set fire to a forest in Brazil.

János Regös

Expeditions into Paradise: A Report from the Rainforest

From the depth of the forest,
the mating call of a jaguar resounds.
Somewhere a night bird is screeching,
and from the riverbank, the metallic
clicking of tiny glass frogs can be heard.
Otherwise, the night belongs not
to the sounds, but to the lights
of the rainforest...

Phosphorescent mushrooms shining in the dark like tiny green lamps are part of the rainforest's nocturnal light show. Chameleons and snakes are a much rarer sight than grasshoppers and other insects.

The tropical forest as a generator of rain

Three quarters of the water that rains down in the Amazon Basin enters the atmosphere from the rainforest itself in the form of evaporation. The water is recycled over and over within the vast forest. The rest of the water is supplied by rain-saturated winds from the southern Atlantic, and only this latter amount is returned to the Atlantic in the mighty Amazon River. Keeping the remaining areas of rainforest intact is of critical importance and an indispensable prerequisite for maintaining the overall water balance in this part of the world.

A bright view from the darkness of the forest

Rain showers and clouds of fog do not always block the view into the distance. Now and then, the tropical sun appears high in the sky, lighting up the rainforest ecosystem and permitting view into the distance that reveals the entire landscape. Even in the most brilliant sunlight, however, the forest's interior remains dark—a realm of half-light between day and night that accommodates only specialists.

Life on a higher plane

The rainforest canopy, a space broken up by a multitude of twigs and branches, is an ideal habitat for those plants that could not possibly survive in the perm- anent gloom of the forest floor and that were therefore forc-

ed to colonize the light-filled upper regions. Choosing this environment re- quires special adap- tation—devices for catching and storing the moisture provid- ed by precipitation, as well as special- ized organs for col- lecting the modest amounts of humus that are available. The basic concept of life in the tree- tops must be quite old because nature has had time to de- velop an incredible variety of species that choose this en- vironment. Brome- liads (right page) and epiphytic orchids are among them.

I am sitting on the trunk of a toppled tree and staring into the green canopy above my head, trying to catch sight of a rubber-cutting bird that has been calling ahead of me on the left at intervals of about 10 seconds. I have been told that this bird starts calling only after it has screened itself from human view. I have just taped the bird's voice on my cassette recorder, but the bird itself is nowhere to be seen. Perhaps I can lure it out of its hiding place by playing back its own lively song, for these birds are said not to tolerate rivals in their territories. I am eager to see the bird, because I have no idea what it is like. The name "rubber-cutting bird" is simply a literal trans- lation from Portuguese and does not convey much information about the bird. I'm sure the scientific name means something completely different, but I don't even know where this bird, said to be about the size of a pigeon, fits into the taxonomy of birds. All my efforts are in vain however; the bird refuses to appear.

For the past few weeks, I have been living here in the Brazilian rainforest, about 100 miles (150 km) northwest of the city of Manaus, in the forests around the Rio Cuieiras. I would be unable to point to my exact geographic position on any map, because the best map I have is on a scale of 1:300,000 and is based on radar pictures taken from an airplane or a satellite. It is virtually useless in trying to orient myself in the forest. I have found lodgings with Pedro, an Indian farmer of the Maku tribe who lives on the Rio Cuieiras, but right now I am several miles away from my new home, having set out early in the morning.

In front of me, the forest is getting less dense, and bright light pours through the foliage of the trees. Because of the in- creased light, the undergrowth is much thicker here than a few yards away in the forest proper, where the unbroken roof of the

canopy characteristic of virgin rainforests allows only 1 percent of the sunlight to filter down to the forest floor. The brook in front of my feet sparkles and shimmers like molten gold, and tiny, silvery fishes flash through the sun-flooded water. The water owes its beautiful golden-brown color to humic acids, the end product of the decomposition of dead vegetable matter.

Every so often, birds fly across the clearing, and now and then, a humming sound can be heard over the soft babble of the water. The sound is produced by hummingbirds, those tiny flying miracles that beat their wings as fast as insects and sometimes are no larger than June bugs. The air is so humid as almost to form water droplets; it is 79° Fahren- heit (26°C), with a relative humidity of 95 percent. I am already fairly well adjusted to this greenhouse climate. I am breath- ing the damp air, scented by the most varied fragrances, and I am trying to get at least a glimpse of a hummingbird now that the rubber-cutting bird has refused to show itself.

All of a sudden, one of these amazing creatures hovers directly in front of my nose. It cannot be more than two steps from me. Because of the speed of the wing beats, the wings are no more than a shadowy outline. This is not one of the smallest species. It may be about the size of a chickadee, but considerably more slender and with a long, forked tail. Shiny turquoise and grayish brown are the dominant colors in the plumage. The hummingbird eyes me curiously, without a trace of fear, turning its head comically from side to side. If only I had my camera at hand, ready to shoot! But the bird has already buzzed out of sight.

Drifting on the surface of the river is an accumulation of branches, leaves, foam, and all kinds of semidecayed as well as still recognizable organic matter, the so-called detritus. Such a floating mass is referred to collectively as surface drift, and many organisms live in it, includ- ing fish and water-dependent

insects. I lift out some of this drifting material with a small net, which I empty onto a cotton sack that I always carry with me for catching largish reptiles. With jerky movements, a semicircular insect measuring about a quarter of a inch (6 mm) escapes from the mass that is beginning to dry out. It is the nymph of an assassin bug. A few slow- moving, worm-like creatures about a quarter to a third of an inch (5–8 mm) long turn out to be mosquito larvae. They cannot belong to the biting, black mosquitoes (*Culex*), because these do not exist in regions with nutrient-deficient black water. Instead, they are white mosquito larvae (*Corethra*), whose bright- red relatives are sometimes sold by pet stores as live fish food. The yellowish-gray version before me feeds on detritus. Suddenly a small water beetle, about 3 millimeters long, emerges.

In the meantime the sky has darkened considerably. A rain- storm is in the making. To avoid being caught by rain, which can be heavy and last as long as half a day, I quickly pack up my gear and photo equipment and head home.

In the darkness that has suddenly descended on the forest, I set out for the path that brought me here. Today's dose of precipitation is already splash- ing down on the treetops in full force. Leaves and branches direct thousands of raindrops down- ward, conducting them into rushing channels and cascades that pour onto my head, my back, and my feet without cease. I am drenched, finding out first- hand what the words "tropical rainforest" mean—a not parti- cularly pleasant learning experience.

Among the most boldly conspicuous creatures of tropical America are the poison dart frogs (*Dendrobatidae*), whose skin exudes a toxic substance. Most of these brightly colored amphi- bians belong to the genera *Dendrobates* and *Phyllobates*. I was lucky to encounter a bright- red *Dendrobates*, or poison dart

Crown jewels in the tropical forest

The fabulous blue in the plumage of the hyacinth macaw is an optical phenomenon that is due less to the chemistry of pigments than to complex manifestations of the physics

of light. Bird feathers, especially on the microscopic level, display such a high degree of order and regularity that only certain waves of the light that strikes them are reflected. Apparently, markings like a yellow cheek spot serve as signals of recognition, allowing birds to identify fellow members of their species at a glance. The powerful beaks of macaws serve not only as a handy tool for breaking open fruits and seeds but also as an aid in climbing. The beak is useful, too, for preparing a nest hole.

frog, on my first expedition into the forest. The poison contained in the skin of these frogs is used, as their English name implies, by many rainforest tribes for dipping the tips of their arrows and blowgun darts. The procedure used to obtain the poison is not something for the squeamish to contemplate. The frogs secrete the potent nerve poison through their skin, but significant amounts are produced only if the creatures find themselves under severe stress or in extreme danger. The Indians consequently spear them on pointed twigs and hold them over a fire. The few drops the poor frogs sweat during this torture are carefully caught as they drip down.

The toxin of poison dart frogs is generally considered the most potent poison derived from an animal. The dose that proves fatal to a mouse is considerably smaller than the amount of the most dangerous snake venom required for the same purpose. Catching the frogs, unlike catching snakes, presents practically no hazard for humans, because the frog poison takes effect only after it enters a victim's bloodstream.

There are several dozen different species of brightly colored frogs in Central and South America. Their range reaches north about as far as Nicaragua. In Costa Rica, about seven species are found. The bright-red, black-dotted *Dendrobates granuliferus* is limited to the small Pacific rainforest area of Costa Rica. Its relative, the strawberry poison dart frog (*D. pumilio*), is bright-red and black and also occurs in Costa Rica. A bold, metallic black and green pattern is found in another species, *D. auratus*. Of the related *Phyllobates* frogs, which inhabit the same region, I encountered only one species, *P. vittatus*, which has two bright-orange stripes down its blackish-blue back. All known species of these two genera live mostly on the shady bottom of the rainforests, although they can climb to a height of several

yards without any difficulty.

Their gaudy colors make poison dart frogs some of the most conspicuous creatures of the forest floor, where many other, nonpoisonous, frogs abound. The latter often have cryptic coloring that makes them practically invisible in their natural surroundings. The bright costume poison dart frogs wear is a warning signal advertising the wearer's unpalatability and toxicity to would-be lovers of frog meat. The combination of being poisonous and of displaying warning colors represents a successful strategy of survival, one that animals that are neither foul-tasting nor poisonous also like to use. This brings us back to the phenomenon of mimicry. We speak of true, or Batesian, mimicry when an innocuous animal resembles in form and color another animal that lives in the same habitat and is inedible or poisonous. Often the imitator belongs to an entirely different class of animal, as in the case of certain flies that assume the guise of wasps and bees. When two animals that are equally poisonous share the same habitat and make use of the same warning signals, we speak of Müllerian mimicry. An example of this is the similarity of marking patterns found in different wasp species. In the case of Batesian mimicry, individuals of the poisonous species that originated the warning signals must always outnumber the nonpoisonous imitators, if the strategy is to retain its effectiveness. After all, predators learn by trial and error which prey is wholesome and which is not.

In tropical forests, many animal species produce toxins themselves or accumulate plant toxins in their bodies, and they advertise this fact by various warning signals. It is therefore not surprising that mimicry is widespread here. Müllerian mimicry is quite common, for instance, among unrelated and similarly insalubrious butterfly species. Examples of Batesian mimicry, too, are found in butterflies, and not infrequently a

"mimicry ring" develops, which involves two poisonous and one nonpoisonous species. Such a threesome linked through mimicry is also found among the colorful frogs. In South America, there are two species of poison dart frogs, *Phyllobates pictus* and *P. femoralis,* that look very similar and are an example of Müllerian mimicry. The resemblance of a third frog, *Lithodytes lineatus,* which is not poisonous but looks much like the other two frogs, represents a case of Batesian mimicry.

For many people, their imagination stimulated by tales of the jungle's horrors, snakes—especially venomous ones—embody the most dreaded danger of the tropics. As a matter of fact, one can spend days and weeks in the rainforest without ever seeing a snake. On one of our expeditions into the Valle de Depressa, Barbara, my wife, suddenly spots a snake that is trying to find cover underneath a fallen log. With the help of some passing workers employed in the construction of a dam, I succeed in moving the log and catching the snake. About 6 feet (2 m) long, it is a beautiful specimen of *Chironius fuscus* of the Colubridae family, dark gray above and whitish-yellow underneath. Trying desperately to get free of my grip, it wraps itself around my arm and voids the contents of its intestines onto my pants. Barbara and my young daughter Erika admire the creature from a safe distance, but soon move farther away because an unpleasant odor is beginning to spread. This mode of self-defense, not uncommon among Colubridae, is also employed by our American garter snakes.

José, one of our volunteer helpers, tells me that this snake, locally known as *sopilota,* is fairly common here near the stream and in the forest. It is possible, of course, that the natives call all large Colubridae that occur here *sopilota.* José goes on to tell that poisonous snakes that are somewhat more colorful as well as thicker and shorter than this one are also not uncommon.

Eagles, monkeys, and adventurers

As predators, raptors have highly specialized food habits. They are usually at the end of a long food chain and therefore cannot occur in great numbers in any

one area. The range of the available food base determines what kind of raptors there are in a given place and acts as a check on population size. The world's rainforest regions nevertheless hold surprisingly many day-active raptors, which have to share the prey animals among themselves. Interestingly, different species occupy similar small ecological niches on the different continents. Thus the Southeast Asian monkey eagle (above) is just as adept at hunting small arboreal monkeys as the South American harpy eagle (right). Catching prey in the tops of trees is, as one would suspect, difficult. The raptors have a chance to get at their prey only where the branches are not too dense.

These can be dangerous if stepped on by someone who is out in the forest at dusk or at night. They are basically shy, of course, and try to get out of the way before they are seen, but some can be quite aggressive, particularly during mating season. To judge by José's description, the venomous snakes most prevalent here must belong to the genus *Bothrops*, the fer-de-lance, of which there are nine species in Costa Rica. Only one rattlesnake, a very dangerous one, is found in Central and South America: *Crotalus durissus*, found in Costa Rica in the dry province of Guanacaste.

Barely 10 percent of all the snakes in Costa Rica are poisonous. To tell venomous snakes from nonvenomous ones, one should be able at least to tell different subfamilies from each other. Anyone planning to travel in a region where snakes are common should also familiarize himself ahead of time with the most important snake genera and species of the area. Thus, someone planning to travel across America needs to know that only one group of the poisonous Elapidae family—which includes the Asiatic cobra and the African mamba—is found on this continent, namely, the conspicuously colored coral snake. Their venom is highly potent, but, because of their secretive ways and docile nature, few incidents of poisoning are known.

There is only one place in South America where the ground is virtually crawling with venomous snakes—the snake farm of the Butantan Institute outside of Sao Paulo in southern Brazil, where antivenom is produced for the treatment of snake bites. Antivenom is an antiserum that contains antibodies, that is, specialized protein substances synthesized in the bodies of all higher vertebrates to counteract snake venom. These antibodies are effective as long as the dose of venom is small enough. At the Butantan Institute, this antidote for snake venom is obtained by injecting horses and other domestic animals with gradually increasing doses of snake venom until the animals are completely immune to the poison and produce large amounts of antibodies. The antivenom used to treat snake bites consists of blood serum from the immunized animals.

It is not surprising that the forests near the Golfo Dulce rank among the most gorgeous rainforests on earth. Made up of huge trees, they dwarf our common notion of forest. The giant trees grow as tall as 100 to 160 feet (30–50 m), and the crowns do not start to branch out until the trees reach 65 to 80 feet (20–25 m). The average diameter of the tree trunks is over 3 feet (1 m). In spite of severely reduced light, some epiphytes of the *Bromeliaceae* family manage to grow on the trunks.

On our wanderings beneath the canopy of these giants, we occasionally come upon columns of small green disks moving along the ground in orderly formation. Concealed underneath these disks are the workers of a leaf-cutting ant colony, each of them carrying back to the nest a round piece of leaf about half an inch (1 cm) across. Along such an ant highway, which may be up to 50 yards (50 m) long, thousands of ants are marching in both directions. These armies are capable of denuding an entire tree in no time at all. The leaves are stashed in a nest several yards underground, where another class of specialized workers masticates them into pulp. This pulp is the substrate on which a certain fungus species is grown, and the mycelia of this fungus are the only food the ants and their larvae eat. The fungus is so essential to the survival of the leaf-cutting ants that swarming females take along fungus hyphae from their old colony when they set out to found a new one. The hyphae serve as an innoculant to start new fungi plantations.

Ants are one of the most important forms of animal life in the rainforest ecosystem, and they have evolved some of the most amazing life patterns. Many highly specialized ants build their nests in certain parts of a plant or use the entire plant. In the Central American forests, there are, for instance, acacias with ants nesting in their long, thick

thorns. These ants, found nowhere else, feed on a secretion of the host plant that contains glucose and proteins. In return, the ants protect the acacias against plant-eating insects and against lianas that might otherwise strangle them. There is reason to think that the ants that colonize *Tillandsia bulbosa,* a member of the pineapple family, live in a similar symbiotic relationship with their host plants. My examination of several shoots of *T. bulbosa* growing from one central trunk revealed that it is always the oldest shoot or trunk, which is already beginning to die, that is inhabited by the ants. The ants do not penetrate into the rest of the shoots, which are generated by asexual reproduction, but merely climb around on them

guarding them from other insects.

On earlier trips to Brazil, I was able to observe symbiotic associations between ants and epiphytes in the forests of the flood plain of the Rio Cuieiras. There one often sees strange-looking shapes hanging in the trees, the so-called ant gardens. These are the nests of arboreal ants (probably members of the *Camponotus* genus). The nest itself is a spherical ball that can grow as large as a child's head. Inside this ball live the ants, and on the outside grow various bromeliads and some viny dicotyledons that are planted there by the ants and that hang down, sometimes as far as several yards.

Ants play a crucial role in cleaning up dead plant and animal matter and preparing it

for further breakdown. Some ant species, though, are true predators, such as the neotropical representatives of the army ants. Of these, the genus *Eciton* is found in Central and South America. Army ants lead nomadic lives. They spread across the forest floor and over low-growing vegetation in broad sheets. Moving along in this way, they can advance as much as 300 feet (100 m) a day. Neotropical army ants on the move feed almost entirely on insects that flee in panic from the advancing

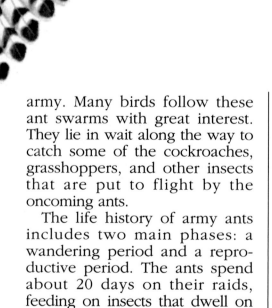

army. Many birds follow these ant swarms with great interest. They lie in wait along the way to catch some of the cockroaches, grasshoppers, and other insects that are put to flight by the oncoming ants.

The life history of army ants includes two main phases: a wandering period and a reproductive period. The ants spend about 20 days on their raids, feeding on insects that dwell on the ground. At night they rest in a "bivouac" formed by their own bodies, in the center of which the ant queen is kept well protected. After two to three weeks of nomadic life, the ants find a hollow tree or some other

Mammals in the aquatic wilderness

Large four-legged animals in the rain-forest seldom venture into the canopy region, but prefer to stay on the ground or, more often, in the water. Capybaras swim among dense colonies of water hyacinths (top). The Brazilian tapir (bottom) is South America's largest mammal. A group of giant otters (large picture) is resting on a fallen log. From here, their hunting ground, the river, is just one dive away.

Graceful hunters with highly perfected techniques

Different fish-eating birds use quite different hunting methods and, because they target different fish species, largely avoid food compe-

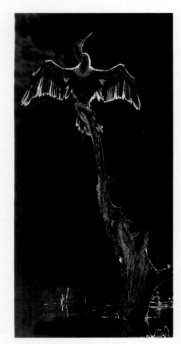

tition. The snakebird (above) dive-bombs its prey; after a hunting sortie, it spreads its wings to dry them. Herons are rather more patient fishermen and only go after prey that is right in front of them.

cavity in which to nest for a longer period. The queen now starts to lay eggs. She is able to produce over 100,000 eggs in a very short time. These eggs are tended and brooded by the worker ants. The larvae and pupae are carried along on the raids.

We see many beautiful butterflies. Usually they fly along the stream, and occasionally they settle on the damp bank to drink. Most often the large blue wings of a *Morpho* butterfly in the branches overhead catch our eye. Gorgeous *Morpho* species are found all over the rainforests of tropical America. In Costa Rica, there are about ten species that belong to this genus.

Stingless bees constitute another interesting group of insects. Most of the bees found in the rainforest are of this variety. Because they have only vestigial stingers, they cannot inflict painful sting wounds, but this does not mean that they are defenseless. The mandibles of the larger species, at least, are strong enough to administer unpleasant bites. The honey these bees produce is truly delicious, and the natives collect it from the bees' nests. Unlike our bees, which store their honey in hexagonal cells, stingless bees keep their honey in wax containers that may be as large as hen's eggs. Earth and other materials are mixed with the wax, and the bees do not condense the nectar as much as our bees do. The natives therefore boil the honey down over a fire for a few minutes. No one has succeeded thus far in domesticating these stingless bees.

The next, and last, stop on our journey through the rainforests of Costa Rica is an area near the small village of Orosi. We are about 3,000 feet (1,000 m) above sea level and plan to reach the higher, damper areas of the region, to explore a different category of rainforest. The valley where the village is located is not very wet. The climate conforms largely to that of the Pacific region, which means that there is a fairly long dry period lasting from December through April. The annual precipitation here barely exceeds 80 inches (2,000 mm).

In the high-lying cloud forests of Central and South America lives a famous bird that figures in many legends and stories: the quetzal, the sacred bird of the ancient Mayas and Aztecs. According to modern scientific classification, the quetzal belongs to the *Trogonidae* family, which includes a number of different species—some extremely colorful ones among them—living in the tropics of the Old as well as the New World. Though most trogons wear beautiful colors, they have normal, short tail feathers. The special feature of the quetzal is its long, iridescent green tail feathers—the basis of the fame it enjoys, but also the reason why the bird is close to extinction in many places. In Guatemala, the country that claims to be the modern descendant of the ancient Maya empire, the quetzal is present everywhere. Its image appears in the escutcheons on school and government buildings and on coins, and the bird itself, stuffed rather than alive, is displayed in the homes of the wealthy and occasionally in museums, as Alexander F. Skutch, a famous American ornithologist specializing in Central American birds, tells in his book. Even in the 1930's, Skutch came upon the live bird only rarely over a five-year period spent in the few mountain forests of Guatemala in existence then.

The quetzal is somewhat less rare in the cool, rainy cloud forests on the northern slopes of the Cordillera Central in Costa Rica. In 1937, during a 13-month stay in that country, Skutch observed six quetzal nests on the north slope of the Poa volcano. He was the first scientist to examine and describe in detail the brooding and brood care of these magnificent birds. Because of the work he did, we know that both parents share in the incubation of the eggs and in the rearing of the young. The female sits on the eggs at night, but the male does most of the brooding during the day. Both parents feed the nestlings with insects, small frogs, and lizards. Toward the end of the rearing period, the mother often begins to neglect the young or even abandons them, so that the male is often left to look after the offspring by himself during the final stage before they achieve complete independence.

On our expeditions into the mountain forests around Orosi, we meet little wildlife. Most of the animals we already know from the time spent in the Golfito area. One exception is a tree frog we have not seen before. Because these amphibians are nocturnal, one rarely catches a glimpse of them during the day, even though there are about 40 species of tree frogs in Costa Rica. Another frog that is new to us is a ranid with bright-yellow legs. It is a representative of the species *Rana warschewitschii*, which is also found in the forests of the Osa peninsula. This amphibian does not live near the water; it is a creature of the forest. We also discover a basilisk species we have not seen before, *Basiliscus plumifrons*. This grass green basilisk is closely related to a similar brown species we had seen in Golfito; the males of both species have very similar crests on the back of the head that look somewhat like a rooster's comb. A similar structure in the females is of more modest proportions.

More impressive than our animal sightings is the world of epiphytes we encounter, especially in the forests around Tapanti, a settlement about 6 miles (10 km) east of Orosi that receives more rain. Epiphytes are not restricted to the tropics, but they are so lush and everpresent in the rainforests that what we find in our own temperate forests pales by comparison. In the southern United States, there are examples of plants growing on trees in the form of Spanish-moss, and in wetter forest areas, mosses and lichens often flourish, but no higher forms of epiphytes grow there. In the

The enemy is probably listening in

With its call, this red-eyed leaf frog unfortunately has attracted a frog-hunting bat rather than a mating partner (large picture). This clever hunter can tell by the frog's voice whether it is poisonous or harm- less (top right). Other species of bats visit flowers (top left) or hunt nocturnal insects (bottom).

Living stars in the roof of a cave.

The young of horse-shoe nose bats. (bottom left) hang from the ceiling of a cave by the thousands (top) while their parents are out hunting at night. Their eyes look like stars in a night sky (large picture). The loud screams of the baby bats (bottom right) help the parents find their offspring again. Parent bats can accurately pick out the voices of their own offspring from among the general noise.

Frogs spied upon by an enemy

It is hard to imagine an animal more conspicuously colored than the Central and South American poison dart frogs. The bright red-and-blue males engage in violent wrestling matches that include body holds and flipping the opponent on his back. Two young strawberry poison dart frogs fight over who gets a seat on a mushroom cap. Among the few predators of these highly toxic frogs are certain tree snakes, one of which is spying on the scene from a distance (large picture).

Creatures that look extraterrestrial

Many of the insects that live in the canopy of the rainforest look completely unreal. Among them are an arboreal grasshopper whose proportions seem all wrong (large picture), a Madagascan giraffe beetle (top left), a leaf grasshopper (top right), a thornbearing hunchback grasshopper (bottom left), and a short-antennaed grasshopper that pretends to be part of a blossom (bottom right).

Wiggling will not save this grasshopper

It will take this toad in its camouflage colors only seconds to down an imprudent long-antennaed grasshopper, but the first gulp did not do the job. The grasshopper's long antennae still stick out of the toad's mouth.

A ride through space

The rainforest monkeys of the New World are amazingly acrobatic climbers. Sometimes, daring leaps are required in the canopy—with the young carried along piggyback (large picture). Only New World monkeys have long, prehensile tails, which they use in climbing like a fifth hand. Old World primates like the imposing gorilla (bottom, left) are more deliberate climbers, but they are no less adept than the agile monkeys with their prehensile tails.

Very distant cousins of *Homo sapiens*

Although the biggest monkeys of the New World rarely exceed 22 pounds (10 kg), a full grown orangutan weighs about 220 pounds (100 kg). In all prob-

ability, this difference indicates that the various primate groups evolved under very different environmental conditions. Apparently, the ancestors of the orangutan family found a much more plentiful food supply in the Southeast Asian rainforests than did the forebears of the New World monkeys, whose present-day representatives subsist mostly on insect proteins. Orangutans, gorillas, and chimpanzees are closely related to humans. The mouse lemur of Madagascar (above) is the smallest Old World primate.

rainforest, on the other hand, not only mosses and lichens but also ferns, bromeliads, *Araceae*, orchids, and other higher plants grow epiphytically. The mountain rainforests and the cloud forests offer especially favorable conditions for this mode of existence. In tropical America, epiphytes, especially orchids, are often called parasites, but this term is misleading because epiphytes use their roots only to hold on to branches and to other surfaces, never to penetrate the live tissue of the host tree, as do true parasites, such as mistletoe plants (*Viscum album*).

As a matter of fact, the roots of many epiphytes—the bromeliads, for instance—have lost their nutrient-absorbing function and now merely support and anchor the plant. In these cases, the plants receive their food exclusively from the air. Dust, dead leaves, pieces of bark, pollen, and dead animals and animal excreta, all of which contain nutrients, slowly accumulate on or near the plant. In spite of abundant rain, epiphytes have to find ways of preserving water because the rain water disappears so fast down the tree branches, and the hot sun that reappears soon after the usually brief showers would quickly dry out epiphytes growing high up in the canopy. Thus, most of these plants have formed water reservoirs. Bromeliads, for example, often have leaves that form watertight tanks, which in some of the larger species can store as much as 1 quart (1l) of rain water. These tanks form small aquatic ecosystems in themselves. Many arboreal frogs, for instance, deposit their eggs in the tanks, where tadpoles hatch and develop. Orchids often have fleshy, tuberous roots that hold water. Because the supply of nutrients is not exactly plentiful and environmental conditions are relatively unfavorable, epiphytes grow slowly. Hardly any animals feed on them, however, and they tend to be extremely hardy and long-lived; thus epiphytes have spread widely throughout the rainforest regions. Orchids are

found all over the world, but they are especially numerous in epiphytic form in the rainforest. Costa Rica alone has over 1,000 species. Unlike orchids, bromeliads are restricted to the New World.

Orchids have evolved complex mechanisms to insure their fertilization. The orchid flower is constructed so that pollen is attached to visiting insects in just the right place to be transferred most efficiently to the next blossom.

Spanish moss, which hangs down from trees in thick, hairy masses, is an unusual-looking representative of the bromeliad family, also called the pineapple family, because the plant that provides us with the fruit of that name is part of it. Spanish moss is the model of an extremely epiphytic mode of life. It does not even develop clinging roots, but grows only loosely connected to the branches that support it. It subsists entirely on sunlight, dust, and rain water, from which the sparse nutrients are drawn and absorbed by the entire plant body.

Tropical rainforests still exist in their overwhelming beauty, and in many places they still resemble a green paradise. This should not blind us to the fact that the politically motivated and programmed advance of civilization is threatening the very survival of the most precious ecosystem found on Earth.

Barbara Veit

The Rainforest Is on Fire: Hell Has Broken Loose in the Jungle

Fire! Fire is raging throughout the entire belt of tropical forests that circles the earth over a length of 13,500 miles (22,000 km), and the pace at which the devastation of nature's most precious gift to mankind is progressing seems to be accelerating. Learning to respect these irreplaceable natural treasures and finding nondestructive methods of dealing with them must be the educational goal of our generation.

About 77,000 square miles (200,000 km²) of tropical rainforest are destroyed annually. What remains is meager pasture land and desert. Once gone, the forests would take centuries to return. Once individual species are gone, they are gone forever.

Apocalypse in Amazonia

In many regions of the Amazon basin, paradise is going up in flames. Satellite pictures show vast clouds of smoke rising from fires like the one in this horrifying photograph made by an eyewitness. Within hours or days, fires set for clearing land destroy what has taken hundreds and thousands of years to grow. What is left is a scene of devastation, with soils that will support crops for only a few years before they collapse into complete sterility.

Billions of victims and a torch of warning

Large-scale burning is used to get rid of the complex and dense web of rainforest vegetation wherever logging would not be profitable or the harvesting of individual trees would prove too arduous. The ashes that are left after the fire represent innumerable generations' worth of biomass production—the end result of the cremation of billions of individual life forms. After this, the landscape will no longer be able to support any permanent use. What is left is ashes from which no phoenix will rise.

The trail of destruction circles the globe

Straight roads run through rainforest (large picture). They provide access for the work of destruction that now operates on a broad front. These roads open up rainforest regions that would otherwise remain inaccessible. Profiteers and exploiters advance along these roads, ruthlessly extending trails of devastation—as in the case of the gold diggers in the Pantanal plateaus bordering the Amazon basin (top). As long as tropical rains continue to pour down on the denuded earth, all the fine soil particles are carried away in muddy streams (left). Left behind are landscapes of bare, crusty earth deprived of nutrients. These regions will have difficulty giving rise to forests again, and they are lost to all future agricultural use (bottom).

Last stop: burnt earth

An intact rainforest ecosystem automatically regulates its own use and availability of water. Rain water collects and runs down in rivulets and cascades from the foliage and complex branchwork of the

canopy. Much of it stops along the way in innumerable small holding tanks and eventually returns into the atmosphere in the form of vapor. Dead, burned earth, however, is exposed to the full attack of the elements without benefit of any cover. Wind and water inflict further destruction and deeper wounds (above). It is almost impossible for life to gain a foothold here. Even cultivated plants can get a start on life only if they are painstakingly watered (right page). The natural circulatory system has been reduced to a one-way street.

Anyone flying over the Amazon region today is exposed to a strange experience: The rainforest seems to be on fire everywhere. Big plumes of smoke hang in the air, hiding the ground from sight. When the traveler gets off the plane, the air smells of smoke, and the odor may be so strong that he or she will think twice before opening the window of the hotel room at night.

The forests are on fire! This is literally true. As this millennium draws to a close, the rainforests are being destroyed at breakneck speed, not only in Brazil, but in Asia and Africa as well.

At the beginning of the colonial era, there were approximately 6 million square miles (16 million km²) of evergreen rainforests in the world, covering 12 percent of the earth's surface. By the early 1890s, half of these forests were irretrievably lost, but it was not until after World War II that the deforestation of the tropics took on alarming proportions. The reasons are manifold. They range from general economic growth, increasing consumption of wood for fuel, and the constant search for new resources on the one hand, to lack of land reforms, explosive population growth, and huge, unscrupulously conceived development projects in the Third World on the other. This complex of economic, political, and social motives is responsible for the fact that today the survival of the last remnants of tropical rainforests is severely threatened.

At present, about 75,000 square miles (200,000 km²)—that is, 50 million acres (20 million ha)—of evergreen rainforest are destroyed annually. Approximately 6,000 mammoth rainforest trees are felled daily, and every day between 50 and 100 plant and animal species are exterminated. Huge logs of fine wood from trees that took at least 100 years to grow are being shipped to Japan, the United States, and Europe. The rainforests furnish 2.3 billion cubic feet (66 million m³) of commercial timber a year. The giant logs are turned into furniture, windows, doors, bridges, coffins, plywood, packing crates, and even into toilet paper.

Meanwhile, the plight of the tropical rainforests has met the same reception that we have afforded most of the environmental problems of our world. A concerned few started expressing alarm long ago about the threat to this unique form of vegetation, but it took decades before the severity of the danger began to penetrate the public consciousness.

Evergreen rainforests are not the same in any two places on earth. They vary from continent to continent, and different landscapes lying right next to each other can be home to vastly different fauna and flora. The German naturalist Alexander von Humboldt (1769–1859), who traveled extensively in South America, was awed and delighted by the vast diversity of species he encountered there. "Without having to leave their native land," he wrote enthusiastically, "people living in the hot regions of the world could enjoy the privilege of seeing all the plant forms found on earth." What seemed to Humboldt of such obvious value, we modern human beings have yet to learn to appreciate. Learning to respect nature and finding ways to treat it with consideration are the most pressing tasks of our time. They represent a kind of delayed cultural development, and they are fast turning into an urgent question of survival.

Until quite recently, nature—and rainforests along with it—was regarded primarily from a utilitarian point of view. This attitude is expressed in the question: What earthly good is a huge forest that is uninhabitable for civilized man? Since colonial times, the term rainforest has signified a "green hell," a sinister, impenetrable place where fierce animals and giant snakes abound and "savages" lie in wait, ready to greet explorers and scientists with poison darts from their blowguns, for even the explorers of colonial times realized that the jungle was not completely uninhabited by humans. Travelers kept running into villages of indigenous peoples, whose image in the minds of the white men who saw and heard about them continue to shift throughout history. Often these representatives of the human race were despised as barbarians and heathens; sometimes they were idealized in the figure of "the noble savage" envied by Europeans for a natural way of life. Jean Jacques Rousseau's call for a "return to nature" grew in part out of the impression made on him by tales about how the Indians of Latin America lived. Today, one view sees aboriginal peoples all over the world as standing in the way of progress because they are asserting claims to land that must be developed at all costs. At the same time, a notion of a forest "paradise" prevails that is diametrically opposed to the concept of a "green hell." This idealization, too, is a distortion of the real nature of the people who live in the rainforest. From the earliest contacts with Europeans to this day, indigenous populations have been in jeopardy whenever economic interests were at stake, because civilization has always regarded them as inferior and has not shied away even from mass murder.

Thus, Amazonian Indians are killed almost daily as gold diggers invade their territory or cattle ranchers cut down the forest to create more pasture. In Africa, the survival of the Pygmy tribes is threatened because the forests where they live keep shrinking and they, as a hunting and gathering people, cannot survive in small enclaves. The Punan of Borneo are being pushed farther and farther back by loggers, and the Papuas on New Guinea are suffering a similar fate.

The advance of civilization spells disaster for primitive peoples because the civilized world forces them to abandon their traditional way of life. They

When forests are turned into pastures

The dead trunks of burned rainforest trees stick up like memorial posts. In places where last year or the year before a lush eco-system still flour-ished, the degraded forest floor is cover-ed with grass and herbs. This new vegetation extend-ing from horizon to horizon is used as pasture for cattle ranches.

All of creation is in danger

Plantations are not biotopes. Monocultures created by man are unsuited to this climate and these soils; the larger their dimensions grow, the more potentially disastrous they are. No

natural life communities can exist here, and there is no room for species diversity. Ecologically specialized life forms or species that depend on at least a partially intact environment—creatures like the red-cheeked parrot—cannot survive in such a uniformly desolate environment. The disappearance of the forests not only causes the extinction of individual species, but also endangers the largest and richest segment of all of creation.

are decimated by diseases to which they had not been exposed previously, and finally they are condemned to a miserable existence on the fringes of modern societies, crowded into reservations and dependent on outside sources for the essentials of survival.

The annihilation of the rainforests, therefore, does not destroy nature alone; it also can destroy autonomous cultures and a vast store of knowledge that could be of great significance to humanity—the knowledge of how to live with nature, using its powers without destroying it. Knowing enough not to decimate any natural species is basic to most indigenous peoples of the rainforests. They have always had a sense of the density of the various populations, and if certain kinds of animals or plants became scarce, a taboo was placed on them. These plants or animals were then protected, and no one was allowed to hunt or harvest them.

The life of people in the rainforest is not idyllic, by any stretch of the imagination; it is a hard life shaped by adaptation to extremely difficult environmental conditions. Living in the rainforest means rarely seeing the sun, being immersed in a permanent green semidarkness. Cultivating the ground is arduous; fruits have to be gathered painstakingly; game is extremely scarce. Life expectancy is not high in the rainforest, but it is an authentic life, rooted in surrounding nature and in the spirit world through which nature manifests itself.

Previously unknown Indian tribes are still being discovered in Amazonia—in October 1989, for instance, when loggers illegally moved into a forest region that had been isolated from the rest of the world. These primitive people are now confronted with the daunting problem of facing modern civilization while trying to preserve their authenticity and avoid being swallowed up and destroyed by modern life. They cannot survive, however, if civilization continues to deal with them the way it has up to now. In Latin America alone, the number of Indians living in the forest plummeted from 10 million in the early days of colonization to a mere 20,000 or so by 1989. It is true that Brazil, for instance, has enacted laudable legislation to protect its Indian populations and has set aside reservations for many tribes, but all too often these laws exist on paper only, with no attempt made to enforce them. Yet, whenever economic priorities are cited, the Indians are forced to yield. The world-renowned Brazilian ecologist José Lutzenberger has expressed the problem in a nutshell: "If human rights alone were considered, Amazonia would still be intact." Let us look at one example. The government of Brazil has embarked on a gigantic project for energy generation, "Plano 2010." Several dozen artificial lakes are to be constructed by that date to supply hydroelectric power plants that are expected to deliver a total of 50 megawatts of electricity. These hydroelectric projects are to be built in the rainforest of Amazonia, and some of them are already completed. Their construction has been financed in part by the World Bank's first energy-sector loan and by bilateral loans.

The result thus far is ecological and human disaster: The Balbina reservoir, north of Manaus, covers an area of roughly 1,000 square miles (2,500 km^2); the Tucurui reservoir, 800 square miles (2,000 km^2); and the Itaipu reservoir, 550 square miles (1,400 km^2). In none of the three locations was the rainforest cut before the sluices of the dams were closed. Cutting the wood would not be economical, it was argued. Thus, thousands of square miles of rainforest were slowly inundated. Before the flooding, the Indians of the region were forced to relocate. In the case of the Balbina project, it was the Waimiri-Atroari—a tribe already reduced to 374 people (in 1905 there were about 6,000)—who had to move. These Indians lost not only their villages but also the river Uatumá, which had been rich in fish but was turned into a huge, foul-smelling, flat lake in the course of 1988. Silently and relentlessly, the water rose to the right and left of the river's original banks. Amazonia's terrain is flat, and consequently the dammed water covers vast areas. Indeed, the size to which such an artificial lake may ultimately grow is often unpredictable.

When the water rises, animals and plants perish. Only a few animals manage to get away; most of them drown when the water first catches up with them, or they seek temporary refuge on islands that eventually are also overtaken by the rising water. The leaves and wood of the dying trees and shrubbery decompose quickly, rapidly depleting the oxygen in the water. As the enormous amounts of biomass decay further, sulfur dioxide forms. This toxic and pungent gas threatens any organisms that are still alive and also endangers the health of people anywhere near the artificial lakes and even downstream along the rivers that flow from the lakes. In Surinam, for example, workers employed in the Borokopondo hydroproject were forced to wear gas masks for two years. The result is complete ecological disaster.

Sulfur dioxide, however, is not the only gas released as the dead trees decay; methane and hydrogen are also released. A further consequence of these processes is the acidification of the water, which is likely to cause rapid corrosion of the power plants' metal parts.

Once a reservoir has filled, a thick carpet of aquatic plants begins to spread across the water's surface. At the Borokopondo site, an area of 50 square miles (130 km^2) was taken over by such vegetation within one year. The vegetation prevents sunlight from reaching the water, and this, in turn, inhibits the formation of oxygen. In Surinam, the water was sprayed with defoliants to counteract the

New agricultural land for only short-term use

Clearing land by burning, as was done here in the Brazilian state of Para, destroys the rainforest and creates space for nomadic agriculture or cattle grazing. However, after a few years—usually no more than three years after burning—the soil is completely depleted. The natural potential for production, which supported a complex and self-supporting community of life forms for millennia, has become a dead-end. Recently cleared land has to be abandoned quickly and a new piece of rainforest falls victim to devastation in a development that is deadly because it is no longer part of a self-rejuvenating system.

problem. Nothing has been heard about the effects of these highly toxic chemicals on humans or animals (2,4,5-T was sprayed, among other defoliants), but many stories from the Vietnam war attest to the harmfulness of these compounds.

This is not the end of the woes associated with the hydroelectric projects in Amazonia. The stagnant, plant-covered surfaces of these huge artificial lakes also make ideal breeding grounds for mosquitoes, the carriers of malaria. Scientists have found that freshwater snails that carry the worm which causes schistosomiasis are especially plentiful in water reservoirs—a finding that confirms what had been observed in connection with the Aswan High Dam project in Egypt. Schistosomiasis, also known as bilharzia, is a terrible chronic disease prevalent in many parts of the Third World.

The electricity generated by the Balbina dam is earmarked for the free-trade zone in Manaus. In addition, industrial plants established there by companies from Japan, the Federal Republic of Germany, and other European countries qualify for a reduced rate for the power they use.

The hydropower projects, with their effects on ecology and human beings, are only one part of the economic developments that are taking shape in Amazonia. There are many other huge projects. There is Carajas, for example, where the nations of the European Economic Community are financing the mining of iron ore, and there are the huge cattle ranches—established with the aid of state subsidies—that have inflicted deep wounds on the rainforest.

The belt of devastation extending across the earth is as extensive as the rainforests themselves. To convey a sense of the speed with which this devastation is progressing, we need first to quote some statistics:

Latin America possesses the greatest portion of earth's evergreen rainforests. These forests, distributed over 23 Central and South American countries, cover an area of 2,212 million acres (895.7 million ha), 1,676.4 million (678.7 million ha) of which are closed forests. Ten million acres (4.12 million ha)—that is, .6 percent—disappear annually. The major causes of destruction are ambitious development projects such as the ones mentioned, the infrastructure needed for their realization, industrial development, tax breaks granted for clearing land, and landless farmers who burn forest to plant crops.

The argument that the enormous growth of Brazil's population is the primary cause of the destruction of Amazonia is not a convincing one. The population density of Brazil is 42 people per square mile (16 per km²); for comparison's sake, the number for the United States is over 66 per square mile (30 per km²). The reason for the relocation of landless farmers in Amazonia is the lack of land reform, for almost 90 percent of the fertile land in southern Brazil is held by

The dead forest is no longer a home

Destruction of the natural productivity of a rainforest site offers only temporary benefits because the soils will become exhausted after a few years. Settlement projects have only a slim chance of success because the supportive context of intact nature is gone.

They all need their ecological habitat

The pillaging of the rainforests represents a wave of destruction of apocalyptic magnitude. The rainforest cannot be understood as a sum total of

potential raw materials to be measured in tonnage or volume. It is instead a highly dynamic and carefully integrated community of species that has evolved over millions of years. The web of mutual associations and dependencies reaches down to the most minute partners of complex life communities. This incredibly wonderful world is in serious jeopardy.

a few major landowners and by multinational companies. On this land, soybeans and sugar cane, rather than food for the country's population, are grown. The soybeans are exported to Europe to provide protein-rich feed for beef animals, and the sugar is turned into fuel for cars.

In Asia, in the 16 countries that lie in the tropical rainforest zone, 837 million acres (336.5 million ha) of rainforest still exist, but deforestation proceeds at a rate of 4.5 million acres (1.82 million ha) per year—that is, .54 percent. The primary motive for deforestation there is commercial logging, followed by resettlement of landless farmers and, as in Amazonia, huge development projects including hydroelectric dams.

On the African continent, the rainforests are divided among 37 nations and cover an area of 1,737 million acres (703.1 million ha), though only 535 million acres (216.6 million ha) consist of closed forests. Annually, 3.3 million acres (1.3 million ha), or .6 percent, are burnt or cut. In Africa, too, the main cause of deforestation is commercial logging. The opening up of the forests to logging, which necessitates the construction of roads and is accompanied by the building of human settlements, inevitably attracts nomadic farmers who practice slash-and-burn agriculture. In Africa, the procurement of firewood has also become a major threat to the forests.

The devastation of the tropical rainforests is affected by several factors, all of which are interconnected. International timber companies play a pioneering role in this catastrophic process. Tropical timber, especially hardwood, is in great demand and is almost always cheaper than homegrown wood. It is of superior quality and especially long-lasting. The forests of Southeast Asia and of West and Central Africa, rather than Amazonia, are the prime suppliers of this commodity. The World Bank estimates that roughly 12 million acres (5 million ha) of

tropical rainforest are logged annually. In almost all cases, the tropical forests are pillaged in the process.

The scenario follows a similar pattern everywhere: First, a company receives a concession to log a certain region. Roads are built in virgin forests and big yards cleared for collecting the logs. Then heavy machinery penetrates the forest and causes a dangerous compacting of the ground. In Africa, the cutting is done selectively, that is, only certain commercially valuable trees are felled, but even this practice has grave environmental consequences. When one of these mammoth trees topples to the ground, it always pulls down other trees with it. By the time the trunk is moved out, 70 percent of the surrounding trees have been heavily damaged or completely destroyed.

In most situations, however, a timber concession means that the wooded land is clearcut. Huge machines crush all the brush to the ground. What is left when they get through is only deeply furrowed, naked earth, where erosion then takes a heavy toll. Depending on the terrain, what develops is either desert or treeless grassland.

Let us look at Papua New Guinea as an example. In 1969, a Japanese company entered into a contract with Australia to "develop the Gogol area." This tropical country was still under Australian administration, but the realization of the project went forward as planned, even after Papua New Guinea became independent in 1975. The "development" of the region consisted mostly of the construction of roads to provide access to the area's 168,000 acres (68,000 ha) of forest. Then began the clearcutting, the technical term for the practice of—as the word implies—cutting and removing everything, so that nothing is left of the forest vegetation. Logging began in 1973; since then 124,000 acres (50,000 ha) have been cut. The forest dwellers were bribed with promises that were not kept. The

clauses in the contract calling for reforestation are being treated as an unimportant side issue. Between 250 and 500 acres (100–200 ha) per year are being replanted with fast growing eucalyptus trees, which are harvested again after a few years. This is a mere drop in the bucket when compared to the 10,000 acres (4,000 ha) that are being denuded annually. The people living in the area around the Gogol River are reduced to subsisting in part on canned food, since hardly any fish are left in the river and the game has disappeared along with the forest. Meanwhile, in Madang, the capital of the province, the wood from the rainforest trees is chipped and later used in Japan as packing material for such products as VCRs and stereo sets.

Rainforests might withstand selective and strictly limited logging, but many scientists have come to doubt that sustainable forestry can be practiced in most rainforests. Until now, the arrival of loggers has always set in motion a devilish sequence of events. Everywhere on earth, loggers are followed by people in search of arable land. This second wave of people burns down what is left of the forest and tries to grow agricultural crops.

In West Africa alone, 2,700 square miles (7,000 km²) of forest are destroyed by fire every year. In western Africa, the advance of the Sahara is driving people into the forest; but the more forest is lost, the faster the desert advances, and the more severe and devastating are the droughts.

In Indonesia a large relocation project called *transmigrasi* has been in progress for several years. Farmers from the overcrowded island of Java are being resettled on neighboring rainforest islands. However, this project looks more and more like a failure. The soils of cleared rainforest areas are of marginal fertility to start with, and they become completely exhausted in just a few years. The new settlers find no lasting security; the forest, meanwhile, is gone for good.

The world's largest importer of tropical wood is Japan, which uses about 26 million cubic yards (20 million m³) annually. More than all the countries of the European Common Market combined import, this figure represents about 40 percent of the world total. The Common Market, importing 20.5 million cubic yards (15.7 million m³) per year, is a close second.

Japan controls almost all the timber industry of Southeast Asia, as a result of the enormous growth of the Japanese economy in recent decades. This rise of productivity was accompanied by an increasing demand for lumber, packing materials, and paper. Japan imports a total of 123 million cubic yards (94 million m³) of wood. Two thirds of this amount is supplied by North America and the Soviet Union; the rest is tropical wood.

Until recently, Japanese importers dominated the timber markets of Southeast Asia, but more competition has sprung up. China and the Middle East have also begun to compete for the raw material wood. Added pressure is exerted because several countries of the area are no longer in a position to export wood. The Philippines, for instance, lost 55 percent of their forests between 1960 and 1985 and now themselves depend on wood imports. For these reasons, Japan in recent years has turned more and more to Africa and Amazonia to satisfy its demand for wood. Japan is not the only large consumer of wood from the rainforests; Germany, Italy, France, and the rest of the Common Market countries, the United States, and Australia also are heavily involved in the business of harvesting wood from the rainforests.

In West Africa, 85 percent of the tropical rainforests have succumbed to the sawmills. In the Republic of the Ivory Coast, for instance, fewer than 7.5 million acres (3 million ha) are left of the original 30 million acres (12 million ha) of rainforest. Because wood has grown scarce in the Ivory Coast,

West German logging companies have moved on into the Congo Basin, which had remained quite undeveloped.

In very recent times, people all over the world began to realize that the tropical rainforests are not only a source of cheap wood, but also a gift of nature to humanity that cannot be restored once it is destroyed. Moreover, countries where the rainforests have been almost completely destroyed have suffered bitter consequences. Catastrophic floods are devastating parts of India, Bangladesh, Thailand, and many other countries every year. In those places, the rainforests that once absorbed the violent rain storms are gone. Only 15 percent of Thailand's once luxuriant rainforests remain. The felling of trees and the clearing of land are now forbidden there by law. In the meantime, Thailand is importing wood from Burma—thus the problem is passed on. Indonesia has at least forbidden the export of raw timber in order to start domestic wood-based industries and reduce the rate of tree cutting. Other countries are increasing the areas allotted for parks.

There are many such individual attempts to contain the damage, but they will not be enough to save the situation. According to many scientists, leaving a piece of rainforest standing here and there—as nature refuges, so to speak—will do little good. If the tropical rainforest belt is to go on serving as a moiture reservoir and generator of warmth, and as home to an unimaginable wealth of life forms, then it has to be preserved on a large scale, in whatever totality still exists.

The governments of many countries in Latin America, as well as in Asia and Africa, still vehemently resist the idea of outside interference in their affairs. When accused of facilitating the destruction of rainforests, they respond angrily that it is the industrial nations that poison the earth's atmosphere by emitting vast quantities of carbon dioxide, and that they are caus-

ing catastrophic changes of climate. The industrial nations themselves are destroying more and more of nature, spokesmen for poor countries say, and now these nations want to act the part of nature's protector in the Third World. It is understandable that former colonial countries should react with heightened sensitivity to outside tutelage. It seems nothing less than hypocritical if the countries that originally poured huge amounts of money into the exploitation of rainforest in the form of direct investment and loans now suddenly seem to have changed course to pursue different goals.

The policy followed during the last few decades of making excessive credit available for economic development has resulted in catastrophic burdens of foreign debt in the entire Third World. The pressure of these debts forces agriculture almost everywhere to concentrate on so-called cash crops; that is only those agricultural products that bring in foreign money are grown. One of these cash crops is soybeans, used to feed our beef cattle. Coffee, bananas, sugar, and cocoa also are sold on the foreign market—as is tropical wood. All these goods, however, are traded at prices below their real value. Tropical wood is much cheaper to buy than our locally grown varieties, even though it has to be transported halfway across the world. It is the economic dependency of Third World countries on the developed world that forces them, among other things, to produce export goods instead of growing food for their own populations.

Small beginnings are being made in the right direction. Innumerable large and small environmental organizations have sprung up around the world and are actively trying to exert moral and political pressure to preserve the rainforests. In addition, most of the governments of industrial nations promised at recent meetings and summit conferences to do everything in their power to keep the tropical rainforest alive.

Sustainable use

The tea plantations interspersed in the rainforest regions of Malaysia are one example of how the natural potential inherent in the forest can be tapped productively while the ecosystem is treated with respect and

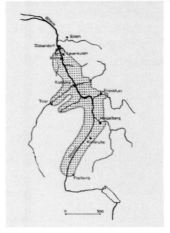

consideration. Here nature and economic interests coexist without conflict.

280

For millions of years, bearers of hope

Cycads are ancient gymnosperms that in some ways are reminiscent of palms, as well as of ferns. There are stands of them in northern Australia and some other tropical places. For the few species that occur as living fossils in the ecosystems of the tropics, an evolution that spanned millions of years will end if their environment is destroyed. These plants have survived huge geological catastrophes. Will they also survive our modern world?

The governments of tropical countries have not even begun to consider the sources of potential economic return that the rainforest can offer if it is not cut down. According to recent projections, collecting rainforest fruits and plants with medicinal properties, carefully tapping rubber trees, and even harvesting certain tree species while adhering to ecologically sound methods could bring much greater financial rewards that have been obtained by treating the rainforests as we have been. There are already concrete examples of such projects.

On the Mexican peninsula of Yucatán, several village communities have been managing 740,000 acres (300,000 ha) of forest land. The villagers sell mahogany wood, but make sure that the amount of wood taken does not exceed the new growth. Almost 3,000 families are making a living this way and protecting the forest against intruders.

Most of the time, however, economic forces—which consist, of course, of individual persons— seek short-term gains at the expense of the rainforests. There are some absurd examples of this. In the north of the Brazilian state of Mato Grosso, for instance, one person bought up thousands of acres of rainforest to create a large-scale settlement project for Dutch and German farmers. This kind of thing is still possible today because we lack a global concept for saving the rainforests. The idea that human beings have only one world to live in has not yet sunk into our heads. There are still the few who try to dictate to the rest what they must and must not do. That is one of the reasons why the large projects conceived by organizations such as the World Bank so often do more harm than good. The World Bank, meanwhile, has devised a rainforest action program, which is, however, not very effective and actually is largely detrimental to the cause.

Native scientists were not consulted in the drawing up of the various plans, and the populations that will be directly affected had no say whatsoever. Some action plans, perversely enough, call for an increase in commercial logging. This is the case in Ghana, for instance. Other plans suggest a program of quick reforestation, using fast-growing commercial species, trees that are in no way suited to restore the ecological balance.

The most recent inspiration to save the rainforest goes by the name of "debt for nature swaps" and takes as its point of departure the huge debts of Third World countries. The "swaps" are financial maneuvers by which debt is turned into money that is available for the protection of nature. However, dependencies are again created and outsiders meddle in internal affairs.

As long as people worldwide are unwilling to reduce drastically their use of tropical wood, as long as no land reforms are enforced, no plans made to forgive foreign debt, no nutrition projects for impoverished populations instituted, chances for the tropical rainforest to survive are dim. Not until we stop viewing the rainforest regions as investment opportunites that take the form of huge industrial developments, not until we recognize these forests as an ecological resource belonging to all mankind and as the rightful home of the people living there, can there be any hope of saving the rainforests.

REPORTS,
DATA,
BACKGROUND

Between 1970 and 1990 the annihilation of species has taken on a magnitude never before imagined. Whereas in the previous 200 million years an average of one species vanished per year, scientists now estimate that since the mid-1980s species have become extinct at a rate of at least one every hour.

This picture by C. W. Röhrig shows that the tropical forests are now very much under human control.

The Last Chance:
A Global Starting Point for Saving the Rainforest

The tropical rainforests are a legacy from the prehistory of mankind. They contain the essence of evolution on our planet. They influence global and regional climates. They may play a key role in feeding humanity in the future as well as in medical research. They are the only place where indigenous societies and certain ethnic minorities may survive. And they are an important factor in the world economy. Thus, the countries lying within tropical forest regions and the industrialized nations not only share a

responsibility and obligation to preserve these forests; they also have a common interest in doing so.

In 1990 approximately 79,000 square miles (200,000 km²) of tropical forest were destroyed—that is, more than 200 square miles (500 km²) a day of forest that contains an unimaginable diversity of trees, other plants, and animals. A large portion of this valuable ecosystem, which has played an essential part in our evolutionary history, has already been irretrievably lost, and

more is dying daily—much of it unknown, never scientifically studied, now never able to be studied. The tropical forests still standing amount to a total of seven million square miles (18 million km²); in another ten years there may only be six million square miles (15 million km²) left.

If we are to succeed in diverting disaster in time, we have to mobilize quickly all the forces that will help save this unique environment, an environment that may act as a crucial reservoir for further genetic development on earth.

Ed. Note—In 1987, the German Parliament, the Bundestag, charged a special committee on "Measures for the Protection of Earth's Atmosphere" with exploring the causes and effects of climate change as well as with drawing up measures for the protection of the atmosphere. This group viewed the rainforest as a major player in their scenario, and their report contained a number of far-reaching measures to ensure the protection of the tropical rainforests. The proposals put forth by this group in a 1990 report (which included plans for a multistep global

action plan), in conjunction with salient recommendations of programs within the United Nations such as the United Nations Development Programme and the United Nations Environment Programme, the Food and Agriculture Organization, and the United States Environmental Protection Agency, among others, could well serve as a global starting point for saving the rainforest. The following text is a compilation of material drawn from the most pertinent points of the Bundestag committee's proposed action plan as well as from the general concepts and theories underlying the policies and directions of the other organizations noted above. (See page 302 for a complete list of the sources used.)

The destruction of tropical forests should be viewed in the context of the growing greenhouse effect, which, together with the ozone loss in the stratosphere, represents a major threat to life on earth as we now know it. Until recently, environmental damage and pollution were regarded as problems that could be contained and to a large extent redressed, but it is now becoming increasingly apparent that the consequences of global warming, ozone reduction, and deforestation amount to a global danger to all humanity. The potential extent of the danger is already apparent, although no one can as yet predict in detail what the regional and local consequences will be because of the extremely complex interaction among the various forces. Nevertheless, even though there are gaps in our knowledge and even though computer models cannot yet calculate with absolute certainty how much the climate will be affected, the atmospheric changes that have already taken place and that are predicted are convincing more and more scientists as well as political leaders that the protection of earth's atmosphere is the biggest environmental challenge facing us today. It is a challenge to the nations of the world to mobilize action against these threats as quickly as possible.

The Extinction of the Species

The tropical forests are of special importance because they harbor such a large proportion of the world's animal and plant species. The ten so-called "hot spots" in the tropical forests alone—areas that have an unusually rich diversity of species and are in acute danger of destruction are called "hot spots"—contain some 17,000 plant and at least 350,000 animal species, although they account for only 3.5 percent of the tropical forests worldwide and a mere .2 percent of the earth's land surface. The forests of these ten areas—located in western Ecuador, on Madagascar, in the Atlantic rainforests of Brazil, on Borneo, and on the Malaysian peninsula—are in danger of being severely damaged, de-

stroyed, or completely eliminated in the course of the next decade, thus also eliminating any opportunity for the many forms of plant and animal life within them to be studied or for their potential importance to be explored.

Between 1970 and 1990 the annihilation of species has taken on a magnitude never before imagined. In the previous 200 million years, an average of one species vanished per year. Scientists now estimate that, since the mid-1980s, species have become extinct at a rate of at least one every hour. If this trend continues, between 20 and 50 percent of all plant and animal species worldwide will be gone by the end of this century. The devastation of even small forest areas can mean the end of a species that has a very limited range.

In Colombia alone are found 10 percent of all presently known plant species worldwide. At La Selva, a research station in Costa Rica that covers an area of only 2.9 square miles (7.3 km²), there are more mammal, bird, and amphibian species than in all of New England. According to our present state of knowledge, Colombia has the richest flora of all the countries in

the world. Twenty-five thousand of the 250,000 plant species known worldwide are native to Colombia's 118,000 square miles (300,000 km²) of rainforest, which make up a third of the country's total land area of 430,000 square miles (1.1 million km²). In the Choco region alone, which lies on Colombia's western coast, 208 different tree species were counted in an area of 6,500 square feet (600 m²). By comparison, larger areas of forest in temperate zones, as in North America, for example, only contain between one and two dozen tree species in total. Altogether the forests of the temperate and northern latitudes are only made up of about 160 tree species, even though they account for half the forest area on earth.

Thus far the world record for diversity of tree species is held by an area near Iquitos, Peru, where about 120 different tree species per acre (300 per ha) were discovered. In the Amazon Basin more than 2,500 species (according to some sources, as many as 8,000) have been identified, and in the tropical forests of the Indo-Malaysian Archipelago over 3,500—and probably as many as 10,000—tree species are

found, as well as over 30,000 plant species.

In Costa Rica there are 8,000 plant species, five times as many as in Great Britain, which is about five times the size of Costa Rica. Another example of extreme species diversity is the biological research station Rio Palenque in the Pacific rainforest region of Ecuador, where 1,033 plant species were identified on .67 square miles (1.7 km²).

Species diversity and species composition of individual areas in tropical moist forests depend on local factors such as climate, soil characteristics, and frequency of disrupting events. The optimum is reached where all these factors show average values. There is still some controversy about just how the abundance of species in tropical moist forests is to be explained as a whole. Although one school of thought tries to account for this diversity by pointing to the 760 million years of constant ecological conditions, other scientists see the key to an increased development of new species in recurrent periods during which tropical moist forests receded and formed isolated islands.

Three hundred and ninety-four different kinds of birds thrive in the 2.9

Many processes going on in tropical rainforests are still not fully understood and present us with many puzzles. The scientific study of the forests' complex interaction of systems and of their species diversity has only just begun. Even though our knowledge is still limited, there are some things that are beginning to emerge. The U.S. National Cancer Research Institute has noted that about 3,000 plant species to which cancer healing properties are attributed are now known. Seventy percent of these grow in the rainforests. The Indians of Amazonia know more than a thousand medicinal plants that have not yet been studied by scientists.

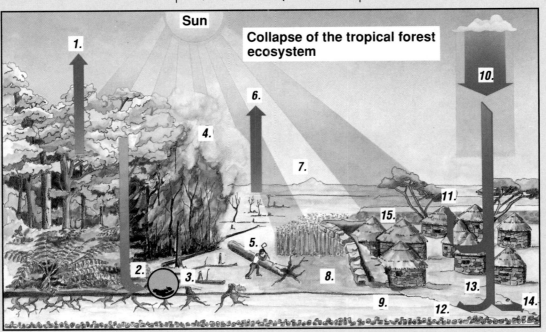

Sun

Collapse of the tropical forest ecosystem

1. Decline of species diversity 2. less dead biomass 3. dead microorganisms 4. fire 5. clearing land 6. decrease in transpiration 7. the sun's rays strike the ground directly 8. shortened fallow period 9. thin layer of top soil 10. less precipitation 11. increased evaporation of the precipitation 12. decrease of water storage capacity 13. soil erosion 14. increased surface runoff 15. spreading of settled areas.

REPORTS, DATA, BACKGROUND

Species diversity and species composition of individual areas in tropical moist forests depend on local factors such as climate, soil characteristics, and frequency of disrupting events. The optimum is reached where all these factors show average values.

square miles (7.3 km²) of rainforest of La Selva in Costa Rica—more than twice as many as are found in the entire state of Pennsylvania, which has an area of over 45,000 square miles (116,550 km²). Three out of every ten species of birds—or about 2,600 species worldwide— depend on the rainforest for survival. Half of these, or 1,300 species, occur in the tropical forests of Latin America, 900 in the forests of Asia, and 400 in the forests of Africa. In some areas the percentages are even higher: Over 78 percent of the bird species of New Guinea and the Sunda region (Malaysia, Singapore, and parts of Indonesia) depend in some way on the presence of closed forests.

The larger the number of different species in an ecosystem, the greater the number of possible interrelationships among them. This is shown particularly clearly in the extremely diverse plant and animal life found in tropical forests.

Various forms of symbiosis, a relationship that brings advantages to both parties, are especially common here. One example is the association between ants and Cecropia trees, the latter being pioneers that very often invade clearings. Hollow trunk sections of these brittle trees offer the ants a home, and in return the ants defend the trees against harmful insects and plant-eating mammals.

Complicated defense mechanisms developed by various plants and animals constitute another area of complex interrelationships. Plants threatened by insects produce a variety of toxic substances, and in reaction to the toxins new insect species evolve. This constitutes a kind of ecological and chemical interplay, a phenomenon that is of special interest for two reasons: First of all, detailed investigations can give us clues for the development of biological pest control; second, this

interplay explains why tropical organisms so rapidly develop resistance to pesticides. Insects or plants that are, so to speak, used to "chemical warfare" have extremely rapid adaptive mechanisms. Chemical pest control is therefore not very effective in the tropics.

The abundance of different species and of different habitats in the tropical moist forests requires mechanisms to regulate population densities and sharp delineation of species ranges on the one hand and, on the other, highly specialized life strategies on the part of individual species. The competition between species and the cooperation between animal and plant species resulting in mutual benefits—cooperation that takes the form of offering protection, food, pollination, or dispersal of seeds—play an especially important role in maintaining the equilibrium of the many-leveled tropical forest ecosystems.

Losses—Known and Unpredictable

Many processes going on in tropical rainforests are still not fully understood and present many puzzles. The scientific study of the forests' complex interaction of systems and of their species diversity has only just begun. The National Cancer Research Institute of the United States has noted that about 3,000 plant species to which cancer healing properties are attributed are known. Seventy percent of these grow in the rainforests. The Indians of Amazonia know more than a thousand medicinal plants that have not yet been studied by scientists.

The tropical plant and animal world also represents an important potential source of food for mankind. The tropical forests provide between 200 and 300 million people with a rich variety of nuts, wild game, fish, honey, fruits, and other foods. The great

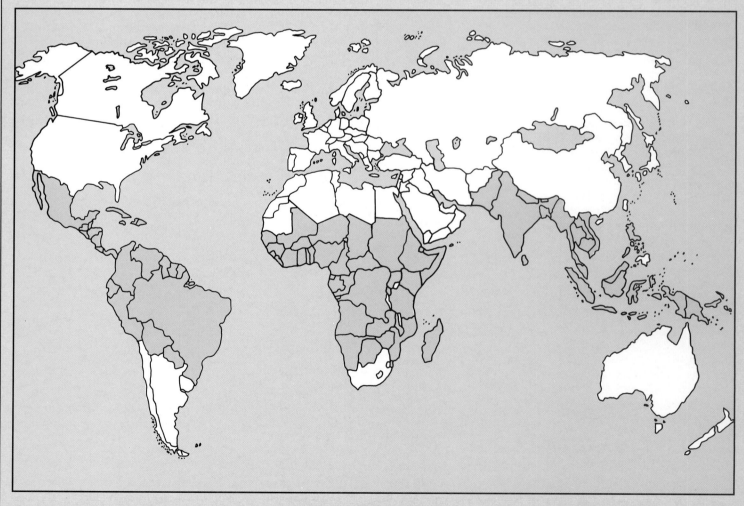

The total 1987 wood harvest of the 76 countries lying in the tropics is estimated by the FAO to have been around 2,200 million cubic yards (1,700 million m³). Of the wood included in this statistic, 84 percent was used for fuel and 14 percent for other purposes.

majority of humanity depends for food on barely more than a dozen plant species, some of which are highly bred cultivated varieties that are extremely susceptible to disease. Making use of the edible plants in the tropical forests or crossing them with those we presently depend on would mean an invaluable enlargement as well as protection of our entire nutritional base.

The Accelerating Pace of Devastation

About 10,000 years ago, about 24 million square miles (62 million km²) of the earth's surface were covered with forests. Today about 14 million square miles (36 million km²) of forest remain. The rest gave way, particularly in North America, Europe, the European part of the Soviet Union, India, and China, to cultivated land. Today, essentially untouched forests are left only in parts of the tropics, in Scandinavia, and in small areas of the northwestern part of North America.

In 1980, the total forest area in the tropics still amounted to about half of its original dimensions. Of these 7.6 million square miles (19.4 million km²), about 4.7 million square miles (12 million km²) were closed and about 2.9 million square miles (7.4 million km²) were open forests. From 1981 to 1985 the annual rate of deforestation was estimated at 45,000 square miles (114,000 km²), but this estimate is now considered to be much too low. At present, it is assumed that in 1990 about 77,000 square miles (200,000 km²) of tropical forests were destroyed. That is the equivalent of the entire state of Nebraska.

If adequate countermeasures are not taken, the magnitude of the destruction will continue to increase rapidly. By the year 2000, about 6 million square miles (15 million km²) of rainforest may

Nutrient and water cycles in the intact tropical forest ecosystem

Sun

1. Evaporation *2.* thin humus layer *3.* dead biomass *4.* recycling of nutrients through microorganisms *5.* root network with mycorrhiza *6.* return of nutrients to vegetation *7.* nutrients available in the air (C, N) *8.* evaporation *9.* runoff *10.* layer of sand *11.* layer of clay.

Because the consequences of deforestation in the tropics extend beyond individual countries and regions, the international community must immediately initiate coordinated action to save the forests. This is not meant as an interference in the internal affairs of the countries involved; rather, the intent is to support these countries in preserving their forests through economic and financial cooperation.

remain; by the year 2050, the forest will have shrunk to perhaps 3.5 million (9 million km²), that is, barely half of the rainforest area still existing today. Many countries lying in the tropical forest belt will, no doubt, have no forests left at all. Even today the timber reserves of the Ivory Coast and of Sabah (a state of the Federation of Malaysia) are almost completely depleted. Complete devastation of the tropical forests is expected in Nigeria by the year 2000. By that time, it is estimated, Thailand will have lost 60 percent, Honduras, Nicaragua, and Ecuador over 50 percent, Guyana, Guatemala, and Colombia about 33 percent, Madagascar 30 percent, Ghana 26 percent, and Brazil 8 percent of the tropical forest areas they still had in 1981.

The Need for Food and Fuel

If we want to find the ways and means to protect the last remaining tropical forests, we have to understand the many and varied causes of their destruction. These not only differ from country to country and from region to region, but they also change over time, depending on economic,

political, and social factors.

Burning forests to clear land is one form of destruction. It is done to create arable land, so that food for local populations can be produced, crops can be grown to bring hard currency into the country, or cattle can be raised on a large scale for export. The use of wood for fuel and commercial logging result in overharvesting or clearcutting, which, in turn, often leads to further burning of forests. Finally, the building of roads and industrial projects contributes to the destruction of the tropical forests.

All these factors play a role in the tropical forest regions of South and Central America, as well as in those of Africa, Asia, and the Pacific region, but their relative importance in individual countries and regions varies a great deal. Thus, although commercial logging has been relatively insignificant in Latin America so far, the clearing of land for agribusiness and for industrial development has played a far greater role there than in Africa and Asia.

The worldwide need for new crop land by the year 2000 is estimated at about 350,000 square miles (almost 1 million km²), and

it will be filled for the most part at the expense of the tropical forests. In Latin America especially, state-subsidized cattle ranching, mostly oriented toward export, has led to the transformation of vast areas from forest to pastureland. It is estimated that about 8,700 square miles (22,000 km²) of forest are turned into cattle ranches per year. In addition, the creation of extensive agricultural monocultures of crops such as soybeans, wheat, and sugarcane—whose production tends to be highly mechanized—leads to the displacement of small farmers and to the loss of jobs in smaller agricultural enterprises. Because there are generally few other job sources, the displaced workers move to less desirable sites in the tropical forest.

Large tracts of forest are also destroyed by state-organized relocation programs undertaken to ease overpopulation in densely settled areas. These programs are a substitute for needed land reforms, are part of the state infrastructure, or grow out of policies designed to advance industrialization. The need for firewood and the logging of commercial timber are also

REPORTS,
DATA,
BACKGROUND

The tropical forests are part of humanity's collective heritage. They are in danger of being lost forever. Only international cooperation that bridges individual systems can ensure their preservation. Together we have a chance to save the tropical forests that are still in existence and to preserve them as part of the foundation of human life not just for ourselves but also for future generations.

factors leading to the destruction of forests and/or to overexploitation of wood resources. Since 1987, worldwide logging has added up to 4.45 billion cubic yards (3.4 billion m³). Of this total, 2.1 billion cubic yards (1.6 billion m³) were cut in the industrialized countries and 2.35 billion cubic yards (1.8 billion m³) in developing countries. Forty-six percent of the wood was used for industrial purposes, and 54 percent was burnt as fuel.

According to estimates made by the Food and Agriculture Organization (FAO), in 1987 the total wood harvest in the 76 tropical countries with rainforests was about 2,200 million cubic yards (1,700 m³). Of the harvested wood included in the statistics, 86 percent was used for firewood and 14 percent were used as commercial timber. Twenty-eight percent of the commercial timber was exported (88 million cubic yards, or 67 million m³).

Apart from the fossil fuels of oil, coal, and natural gas, wood is the most important source of energy. Although only 1 percent of the energy needs in industrialized countries is met by wood, developing countries rely on wood for 21 percent of their energy needs. The cutting and gathering of firewood is a problem primarily in the dry tropics, but it also poses a threat to tropical raingreen forests and to trees and other woody plants in the savannahs. In the moist tropics the destruction of forests due to cutting for firewood affects primarily areas surrounding large cities. Because of the high birth rates and the continual migration of people to the cities, the need for firewood keeps increasing. Because of the lack of alternative energy sources, forest resources near the cities dwindle and the price of firewood rises. If present trends continue, many tropical forest countries will be unable in the near future to fill even their own needs

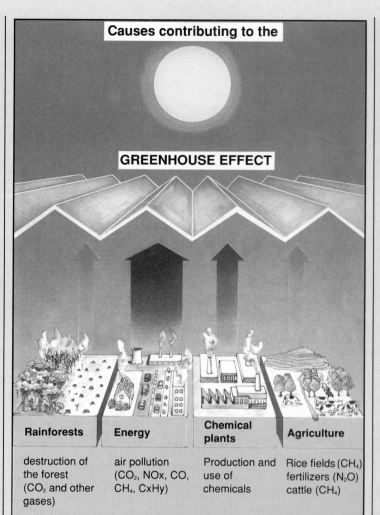

Causes contributing to the

GREENHOUSE EFFECT

Rainforests	Energy	Chemical plants	Agriculture
destruction of the forest (CO₂ and other gases)	air pollution (CO₂, NOx, CO, CH₄, CxHy)	Production and use of chemicals	Rice fields (CH₄) fertilizers (N₂O) cattle (CH₄)

for wood and wood products.

The Pressure of Population Growth

Slash-and-burn clearing, logging, and the other activities mentioned above contribute to the devastation of the tropical forests, but they are not the real causes of it. The real reasons have to do with social, economic, and political matters. First among the immediate causes is the population growth that is rapidly accelerating in all the tropical forest countries. In 1950, there were approximately 2.5 billion people on this planet; in 1990, the world population was over 5 billion. By the year 2000, it is estimated, the world population will be between 6.1 and 6.5 billion. Much of this growth is concentrated in regions of Asia, Africa, and Latin America that were poor to start with. The average growth rate lies between 2.2 and 2.8 percent, with Surinam and Kenya showing what are probably the highest rates,

4.3 and 4.2 percent respectively. By contrast, the United States' growth rate has been going down; it was 1.1 percent in 1990 and, by 2035, the country is projected to have a negative growth rate. Western Europe and Japan now also have very low population growth rates, and Germany, with a birth rate of −.2, has the lowest worldwide.

Population growth is one of the most serious issues affecting the rainforests. Most of the developed countries of the world have or will have in the near future stable or only slowly growing populations, but this is not the case in the developing world. Although the pattern of population growth has been fairly consistent around the world, modern public health practices and medicine continues to reduce the death rate—particularly for infants and young children, which leads to a rapid growth in population. Eventually, as families have more children live to adulthood, the birth rate will

also go down, but this does not happen immediately and a number of factors influence its decline. The lag between the decline of the death rate and the reduction of the birth rate is called the demographic transition.

The most notable and consistent factor speeding up the demographic transition has been economic development. When national economies reach a certain level, and particularly if women become players in the economic structure, birth rates tend to drop. For many, however, trading a fast-growing population for a more affluent one seems like a double-edged sword. The traditional view is that the richer and more developed nations are more environmentally destructive, that they use more energy per person and that the technology that accompanies development introduces more—and more potent—toxins and pollutants into the environment. Yet, several recent energy price increases and the success of industrial development in Japan show that the level of production and energy consumption is not inextricably linked. Many of the more advanced technologies, such as computer chips and biotechnology, have very low energy-to-product ratios. In regard to toxic waste and general industrial pollution, the high levels of pollution in what was East Germany and in Poland, both countries with very low productivity, versus the lower levels of pollution in the Federal Republic of Germany, which has a high level of productivity, show that pollution and industrial productivity are not always linked in any simple linear fashion.

There are uncertainties about the future and the effect that more affluent populations will have on the earth and on the rainforests in particular. One thing is certain, however, and that is that the 5 billion people presently on earth are only

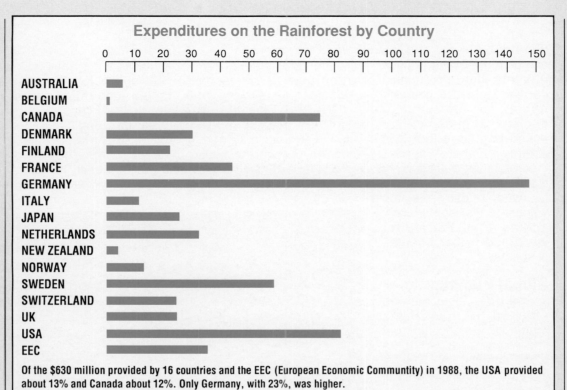

Expenditures on the Rainforest by Country

Country	0	10	20	30	40	50	60	70	80	90	100	110	120	130	140	150
AUSTRALIA																
BELGIUM																
CANADA																
DENMARK																
FINLAND																
FRANCE																
GERMANY																
ITALY																
JAPAN																
NETHERLANDS																
NEW ZEALAND																
NORWAY																
SWEDEN																
SWITZERLAND																
UK																
USA																
EEC																

Of the $630 million provided by 16 countries and the EEC (European Economic Communtity) in 1988, the USA provided about 13% and Canada about 12%. Only Germany, with 23%, was higher.

REPORTS,
DATA,
BACKGROUND

Our earth
is at stake:

Protecting the environment is a matter of human survival. The goal, in its most basic terms, is to preserve life on earth. Only if we protect nature for its own sake will it allow human life to continue.

The tropical rainforests are the most crucial ecosystems on earth. They play an irreplaceable role as a regulator of world climate, as a water reservoir, and as a natural filter of the atmosphere. Their destruction could have consequences beyond our imagination on patterns of water distribution, climate, and temperature. What we neglect to do today will affect us all tomorrow. We do not control nature; rather, we are a part of an ongoing living cycle.

---

the harbingers of the stress that an increasing population will have on the world. The earth's population will double by the year 2020 or even earlier, which is, after all, only one generation away (even at what seems to be a modest growth rate of 2 percent a year—and the present rate is higher—the population doubles in about thirty-five years). The bulk of this increase will be in the developing world, and much of it in countries with rainforests. The stress that will be created by 10 billion people is almost unimaginable, and the next doubling, which would bring the earth's population to a staggering 20 billion, is even less so. The hope is that this growth rate will be tempered and that simultaneously a more energy- and material-efficient economy will develop along with an ethic for the preservation of biodiversity and the complexity of the world's ecosystems. Many of us are still puzzled—in fact, transfixed—by a schizoid vision of a simpler, more basic world on the one hand and the promise of a technological fix on the other. Whichever future prevails, the earth's ecosystem is likely to be more stable with a total population closer to the 5 billion figure than the 10 billion one.

Civilization as a Destroyer of Ethnic Culture

The tropical forests are not only a major library of evolutionary history, a regulator of climate, and an economic factor, but they are also the home of and an essential part of the cultural identity of many primitive peoples and ethnic minorities. Among these are the Pygmies of Central Africa, the Penan of Sarawak in Southeast Asia, and a great variety of Indian groups in South America. As little as 50 years ago 300,000 Pygmies still lived in Central Africa, primarily in Gabon, the

Congo, Zaire, Cameroon, and Rwanda. Today only 100,000 are left. The Nambiquara Indians numbered about 20,000 at the beginning of this century; now there are only about 550.

For the indigenous populations, economic development of tropical forests is a process that spells relocation, exile, and, for many, extinction. In Amazonia, for instance, 40 Indian territories were dissected by large highways. With the devastation of the tropical forests the life basis is withdrawn from populations that have adapted their way of life to the forest, people like the nut gatherers and the rubber tappers in Brazil. Contact with the white man has also had disastrous consequences for the health of primitive peoples. Measles and mere colds can be fatal for Indians because their immune systems have no defenses against these sicknesses that were never before part of their health history. Contact with modern civilization usually also results in demoralization, loss of economic independence, and ultimately, loss of cultural identity. As a consequence, native techniques developed over centuries of utilizing the

forest in socially and ecologically beneficial ways, site-specific agricultural technologies, and traditional methods of healing are in danger of being lost forever, along with the forest's indigenous inhabitants.

The goal of using the natural resources offered by the tropical forests heightens the conflict of interests of competing social groups. A peaceful coexistence of Indians, small-scale farmers, and large land owners, each group with its specific economic goals, is unlikely. Conflicts over land are increasing and often even claim lives. In past years, when tens of thousands of gold diggers invaded the traditional territories of the Yanomani Indians in Brazil and Venezuela, attacks on the indigenous Indian population were not uncommon. Although the rights of ethnic minorities are legally guaranteed in many states, in reality they are often ignored.

Because the consequences of deforestation in the tropics extend beyond individual countries and regions, the international community must immediately initiate coordinated action to save the forests. This is in no way meant as

an interference in the interior affairs of the countries involved; the intent is to support these countries in preserving their forests through economic and financial cooperation. The immediate goal to be targeted by the tropical forest countries as well as by the international community is to reverse immediately the rapid acceleration of deforestation in the tropics. After that, the need is to try to prevent devastation altogether and to begin to reforest—as much as is feasible—the decimated regions.

REPORTS, DATA, BACKGROUND

Preserving tropical forests and reforestation should be regarded as complementary strategies. It is true that reforestation cannot recreate primary forests nor replace their ecological, climatic, and social functions, but it is already an urgently needed method in large sections of the tropics as a safeguard for watersheds, protection against further soil erosion, and as a reserve of fire-wood and timber in areas of scarcity.

Global Planning

This goal could best be reached by following a multistep action plan that involves all members of the global community. A summary of the salient points of this plan follow:

• Starting immediately and continuing until the year 2000, the efforts of tropical forest countries and other members of the international community must concentrate on lowering the rate of destruction as much as possible, at least far enough for the annual rate of deforestation in every tropical forest country to fall below the rate of 1980 by the year 2000. In this first phase, an immediate program for the protection of the tropical forests should be enacted and contain measures to prevent the destruction of especially threatened areas of primal forest. Primary targets should be the "hot spots" of especially high species diversity.

• By the year 2010 at the latest the destruction of tropical forests has to be forbidden everywhere in order to maintain the total area of tropical forests still in existence.

• Between the years 2010 and 2030 the focus must be on increasing forested areas in the tropical forest countries until they once again reach the level of 1990. A return to the amounts still extant in 1980 seems unrealizable because parts of the areas that were once forest have been converted to other land uses or because the

soil quality has deteriorated so much that reforestation is no longer an option.

• The timetable of the action plan is not to be understood as allowing for a period of time during which the destruction of tropical forests may continue. Anyone who keeps in mind the difficulties involved in realizing the

If half of all the plant and animal species of this planet are lost, we will also lose a genetic potential of inestimable value.

proposed measures—difficulties of a political, social, cultural, and economic nature—will understand that meeting the plan's goals will necessitate immediate translation into action of all the measures on all fronts. The immediate program in particular is meant to accelerate all possible action.

• The immediate program would provide for the seven nations (Italy, France, Germany, Great Britain, the United States, Canada, and Japan) that participated in

the 1990 Houston economic summit to, until such time as a trust fund for the protection of tropical forests is set up, make available monies amounting to an annual total of approximately $450 million. This amount would be independent of nationally raised monies and used for coordinated projects and

programs worked out in cooperation with the tropical forest countries. The money would go, for instance, toward planned or already existing measures to protect highly threatened primary forests in accordance with the aims of international agreements. Compensation payments would also be made to tropical forest countries that voluntarily agree not to harvest their forests and that demonstrate that they are in the process of creating protected areas.

• In addition, extensive agro-forestry projects should be promoted in Asia, Africa, and Latin America, especially in localities where population pressure leads to the destruction of forests through slash-and-burn clearing and nomadic agriculture. More intensive utilization of areas already devoted to agriculture is to be supported, so that rising harvests will prevent the need for new crop land.

• Tree plantations would be set up to supply firewood and timber, and plans made for developing non-polluting energy sources, so that the Third World will be guaranteed a sufficient supply of energy and enough wood for the countries' own use, as well as to take pressure off the tropical forests.

• Tree planting would be done in already deforested areas, and regions that are turning into steppes would be reclaimed for agriculture.

• Finally, integrated regional development would be supported with a special emphasis on increasing trade and industry and on the creation of jobs in areas lying outside the tropical forests.

Trust fund for tropical forests

The most important medium-range to long-range measure to help realize this plan would be the creation of an "International Convention for the Protection of Tropical Forests." Such an agreement would have to include internationally binding commitments on the part of

A great many countries are already financing sensible protection measures spelled out in national Tropical Forest Action Plans. Sixty-six tropical-forest countries ranging from Indonesia to Mauritania are taking part in these efforts.

the signatory countries. Countries that do not have tropical forests would be urged to sign the agreement to show that they share in the responsibility for protecting tropical forests, as they still benefit from them in tangible and intangible ways.

Support for the tropical forest countries should take several forms:

• Access to money for designated programs, preferably in the form of subsidies that do not have to be repaid;

• Extensive research programs that involve cooperation between industrialized and tropical forest countries, and also an ongoing exchange of the results of research;

• Transfer of ecologically and socially beneficial technologies in the fields of forestry and agriculture, as well as in the fields of environmental protection and energy technology;

• Improved provision of goods to meet the basic needs of the populations living in tropical forest countries with the aim of ensuring a minimum standard of living;

• Access to specialized know-how in the fields of agriculture, forestry, and

regional planning.

At the same time, industrialized nations must commit themselves in a parallel agreement to initiate immediately measures of their own designed to counteract the danger of global changes in climate. The sincerity and credibility of the industrialized nations' international environmental policies will be measured by the success of these efforts.

Within the frame of the "Convention for the Protection of Tropical Forests," signatory countries that have tropical forests should declare their willingness:

• to keep intact as much of their primary forest as possible and, with this goal in mind, create more forest preserves;

• to manage the rest of their forests naturally and in a sustainable manner;

• to initiate reforestation and regeneration measures so that over time new secondary forests will grow; and

• to protect the environment of the indigenous inhabitants and thus help preserve their cultural identity.

In addition to specifying these general commitments, the convention

should set up a protocol on how these measures will be realized. Not only do the rights and obligations of the signatory countries have to be defined, but the implementation of financing, sanctions, and checking on the fulfillment of obligations must be established.

One possible financing mechanism would be the creation of a project- and program-oriented international "Trust Fund for the Protection of Tropical Forests," to be administered by the United Nations Environment Programme (UNEP) with technical advice from FAO and the World Bank. Experts calculate that in order to take the necessary steps to implement the programs an average of $6 billion would have to be made available per year.

In the establishment of more protected areas as part of national plans to protect tropical forests, the setting up of biosphere reserves as called for by the UNESCO program "Man and the Biosphere" is to be especially encouraged, as is the creation of protected areas as suggested by the "International Convention for the Protection of our Global Cultural

and Natural Heritage." In the course of this, tropical forest countries will initially sustain short-term economic losses, but adequate compensation could be given by the trust fund already mentioned.

New criteria for awarding financial aid

Within the framework of the UN, too, activities aimed at protecting tropical forests should be stepped up. Above all, the following goals should be pursued:

• Coordination of actions already in progress to protect tropical forests should be improved, and it should be determined what funds individual UN organizations can afford to invest in working out the mandates of the "International Convention for the Protection of Tropical Forests."

• New criteria need to be developed to determine where money is to be channeled by financing and project realization organizations of the UN. These criteria should heavily emphasize ecological and social concerns.

• Existing gaps in the UN's fields of activity should be closed.

• The activities of institutions under the aegis of the UN and of all the member states should be checked to make sure they have no negative impact on tropical forests. This demand is directed particularly to project execution organizations such as the World Bank, the UNDP, and FAO.

• UN project-execution organizations should also develop and institute programs and aid projects that place an increased emphasis on agriculture, on the provision of firewood and timber for local populations, and on population policies. The measures of these organizations should culminate in integrated development aid projects.

• In addition, international government organizations under the auspices of the UN should improve and check the guidelines for employing innovative technologies in developing countries. Of special importance would be the transfer of environmentally beneficial technologies to Third World countries and removal of trade barriers, as well as easier access to and participation in research and further development of environmentally beneficial technologies.

Canceling debt in exchange for forest protection

Crushing debt burdens have inhibited development in many tropical forest countries. Apart from contributing to general efforts aimed at solving the debt problem of the Third World, the developed countries should continue and expand present efforts in the area of forgiving debt, especially toward tropical forest countries—in what has come to be known as the "debt-for-nature" program.

Forgiving debt can be linked, among other things, to the condition that the country in question clearly demonstrate by its actions that the protection of its forests is of high priority.

For the indigenous populations, economic development of tropical forests is a process that spells relocation, exile and, for many extinction.

The sincerity of this attitude can be shown in administrative, legislative, or social measures taken by the country or by the country's taking part in establishing or ratifying an "International Convention for the Protection of Tropical Forests."

The countries in question must also embrace measures of their own to overcome their economic problems and to ensure lasting economic development. There must be support for measures that will counteract the causes of poverty. This will provide dual benefits of enormous significance. In the first place, it will raise the standard of living and improve the quality of life for millions of people. Secondly, it will help to relieve the pressure exerted on the forests in certain heavily populated regions and ultimately contribute to resource protection. Saving the rainforest will thus provide direct economic benefits to the tropical countries involved and indirect benefits to the entire world.

Joining together for the future of the rainforest

The tropical forests are part of humanity's collective heritage. They are in danger of being lost forever. Only international cooperation that bridges individual systems can ensure their preservation, and past mistakes must be corrected through immediate and effective measures now.

The United Nations can take central responsibility for the coordination, execution, and supervision of the necessary programs. It is then up to the members of the international community of states to demonstrate their solidarity by participation in these programs.

By working together, we have a chance to save the tropical forests that are still in existence and to preserve them as part of the foundation of human life not just for ourselves but also for future generations.

The preservation of primary (virgin) rainforests has to be given a much higher priority within the framework of an improved Tropical Forest Action Plan than it has had in the past.

Viewed from the air, in many places the endangered lands still appear intact.

Seen from the air, the rain-forest looks like a sea of watercress (large picture). But below the canopy, nature's laboratories have created an incomparable wealth of genetic and chemical products. Tropical biologist Norman Myers estimates that the value of medications alone derived from the rainforests amounts to about 40 billion dollars per year.

A Look at the U.S. Position on the Rainforest

In the 1980s, the governments of the Western industrialized democracies became increasingly alarmed by the growing loss of Third World tropical rainforest acreage to slash-and-burn agriculture, strip mining, and other forms of development. As a result, these governments began to play a more and more active role in attempts to save these endangered areas and draw a halt to the ever-expanding devastation. In part, their motivation was simple altruism— an unselfish desire to protect the long-term economic and environmental well-being of tropical peoples, both in the rainforests and in urban areas; to preserve endangered species and all facets of the biological diversity that the rainforests have long fostered; and to save the threatened rainforest habitats of migratory birds.

A self-motivated interest also played a part in the growing interest of the developed world. The danger of a global warming trend heightened the awareness of the importance of the rainforests in the environmental chain, as experts pointed out that these forests serve as vital storehouses of carbon dioxide from the atmosphere, thus offering a potential "sink" for the absorption of the vast quantities of carbon dioxide emitted by vehicles and factories in the developed areas of the temperate zones. It was becoming evident, however, that this "sink" function was becoming threatened as the forests inexorably disappeared. It is currently estimated, for example, that 10 to 30 percent of the carbon dioxide released from all human sources to the atmosphere each year is due to the adverse effects of tropical deforestation. The resulting carbon dioxide build-up hastens global warming, a widely predicted but still controversial atmospheric trend that is of growing concern to the United

Ed. note—This overview of programs initiated and positions adopted by the

United States government is based upon materials supplied by the U.S. Environmental Protection Agency. It also reflects data provided by the U.S. Forest Service, as well as statements made by President George Bush.

REPORTS, DATA, BACKGROUND

An etching from the travel journals of Prince Maximilian zu Wied from his expedition to Brazil in 1815–1817 (above). What no one could have imagined then has in the meantime been established as scientific fact: Every tree that is felled pushes the world climate further toward catastrophe. Only ecologically sound, sustainable-yield forest management can correct this situation, and the ecologically most valuable virgin forests at the centers of working forests must remain untouched and under the strictest protection.

States and many other national governments. And, it should not be forgotten that rainforest destruction is also of concern to many industrial nations because of the threatened loss of important products of the tropical forest such as pharmaceuticals, crops, wood products, gums, resins, and many plants and animals, on many of which we have come to depend.

The U.S. government has made a number of strenuous efforts in recent years to help save the tropical rainforests, and, in the process, taken a new look at the status of its own forests. This latter review has resulted in a variety of initiatives designed to improve their present and future well-being, and it is hoped that these internal measures will prove to the tropical nations the sincerity of the U.S. commitment to global forest preservation and recognition of the importance of biodiversity both at home and abroad.

International Initiatives

According to one preliminary study, in fiscal year 1991 the United States is spending approximately $160 million a year for the conservation and management of tropical rainforests located in foreign countries. This figure, which includes both direct and indirect expenditures, is largely accounted for by projects sponsored by the U.S. Agency for International Development (USAID). (Indirect expenditures are U.S. contributions to multilateral development banks such as the World Bank, UN programs, and agencies that have tropical forest programs.) Funding goes toward social forestry for community benefit—fuel wood plantations and forestry projects that provide food, and animal fodder for local communities, and so forth as opposed to industrial forestry, which is aimed at

Forests are the economic lifeline of many countries. Over thirty countries export tropical woods and wood products valued at about 9 billion dollars annually.

maximizing commercial timber yields); conservation and forest management; forestry research; and global warming research. At the present time, USAID has about 150 forest projects in more than 40 tropical countries, with another 25 projects being planned. Reforestation of tropical rainforests is only one part of the USAID program and accounts for less than a fifth of the USAID funds worldwide.

The government (most notably USAID) has also formed partnerships with private-sector conservation organizations for the specific purpose of preserving the tropical rainforests. In 1989, USAID signed a new agreement with a consortium of conservation organizations, including the World Wildlife Fund, the World Resources Institute, and the Nature Conservancy. These privately funded organizations are now collaborating with local institutions in USAID-assisted countries on projects designed to protect rainforests and biological diversity.

The U.S. policy is currently evolving along several different fronts, including debt-for-nature swaps, trade in tropical hardwoods and support for the Tropical Forestry Action Plan, and promotion of the Global Forest Agreement.

Debt-for-nature swaps

On June 27, 1990, President Bush proposed his Enterprise for the Americas Initiative, a component of which is to renegotiate the public debt owed to the United States by Latin American coun-

tries and to apply the interest on the new debt to environmental protection and conservation projects. Prior to Bush's initiative, the United States had encouraged debt-for-nature swaps in order to reduce the Latin American debt owed to commercial banks. The new program, however, for the first time in history permits official debt—that is, debt owed to the national government—to be purchased at a discount for environmental purposes. Congress is now at work implementing the legislation required to permit the selling of the official debt at a discount, and Latin American debtor countries are in the process of establishing environmental trust funds to process their new income. It will still be a few years before official debt is actually converted into local currency ear-marked for specific environmental goals, with rainforest protection among them, but the basic direction and mechanisms have been established.

Given the often-extraordinary burden of commercial and official debt that many underdeveloped Latin American countries bear, it is hardly surprising that these nations are sometimes tempted to neglect environmental protection or to look to the wealthier members of the international community for assistance. Altogether, Latin American countries owe the United States alone some $12 billion in public debt, $7 billion of which was borrowed to promote development and the remainder to assist trade. These nations additionally owe about $38 billion to the governments of European countries and Japan, and the United States has been urging these allies to institute debt-for-nature swaps of their own to further enhance the budgets of national parks and pollution control and forestry agencies in the nations of the tropical regions.

In Shinzu harbor on the Japanese island of Honshu (above), we see where trees cut in the rainforests of Southeast Asia end up.

A specific example of debt-for-nature is one recently instituted with Madagascar, in conjunction with the World Wildlife Fund:

Madagascar, an island nation that has often been called "a living laboratory of evolution," has become the focus of intensive conservation activities in recent years. The island's nearly 4,000 square miles (10,000 km²) of tropical rainforest face severe threats from fires, slash-and-burn cultivation, poaching, wetlands drainage, and uncontrolled livestock grazing. Since 1988, USAID, in collaboration with the World Bank, has developed a multifaceted environmental action plan for Madagascar that includes rainforest protection for forest reserves and national parks, creation of newly protected forest areas, environmentally sound rural development programs, rational utilization of natural environ-

ments outside protected areas, and thorough review of existing native forest cover using satellite imagery and aerial photography. A new national park has been established on the Masaola Peninsula, one of the island's largest intact blocks of tropical rainforest, in the northeast of Madagascar. The project includes development activities for the local population that are aimed at providing food self-sufficiency, income generation, basic health care, and various kinds of education. In addition, USAID announced in 1989 a $1 million grant to the World Wildlife Fund to support a major debt-for-nature swap in the island nation. When all the finance mechanisms are in place, this commitment will enable the World Wildlife Fund to acquire up to $2.1 million of Madagascar's commercial debt that it will then convert into local currency ear-

marked for conservation activities.

Although there are some vociferous opponents of the debt-for-nature swap concept, this process can allow underdeveloped countries with heavy financial liabilities some relief from this burden while, at the same time, encouraging the development and structure of more positive environmental plans.

Free trade in tropical woods

The United States has consistently opposed efforts to restrict free trade in tropical hardwoods through taxes, bans, or other trade disincentives. The position of the United States is that these efforts are more likely to increase tropical deforestation than to encourage it to decline. For example, it makes little sense for a country to sell very valuable wood for which there is little demand on the local market as cheap construc-

tion material at home, but this is precisely what a boycott of tropical woods by industrialized countries would bring about. By contrast, the national economy is served if these valuable woods, for which there is no local demand, are exported. Cheaper woods can then be imported to serve local needs. The export of woods with the highest value and, if possible, of value-added wood products plays a major role in meeting the local population's rising need for wood and in realizing the potential of the forests through utilization compatible with nature. It would be indefensible for a wealthy industrialized nation to refuse to buy highly valuable products from a poor but forest-rich country and thus force that country to market valuable veneer woods as construction wood locally and significantly below its export value.

The extent of global deforestation has reached dangerous levels today. Over a hundred and fifty years ago—at the time when Alexander von Humboldt recognized the tropical rainforests of South America to be a new wonder of the world—twelve percent of the earth's surface was covered by rainforests. Since then, mankind has irrevocably destroyed half of those forests. Barely twenty percent of Africa's original rainforests still exist today.

REPORTS, DATA, BACKGROUND

The rainforests are a treasure chest for all humanity. Their plants represent a wealth beyond measure. Used properly, they could do much to alleviate poverty and hunger, particularly in the Third World. Fruits, medicinal plants, oils, rattan, and many other products could be harvested by the inhabitants of the forest without damaging the natural environment. But efforts to stop the encroaching devastation have remained ineffective thus far.

About 2 billion cubic yards (1.5 billion m³) of wood are used annually in the tropics. About 85 percent of the total is used as firewood, 10 percent for construction, and 5 percent for export. It would seem that the most important task on an international and national level is to establish sustainable forestry practices in the tropical forests that will thus insure the continuing harvest of forest products, of which wood is only one. This is the only possible protective measure that is likely to prevent slash-and-burn practices and the conversion of of forests into agricultural lands. Sustainable harvesting of the forests means development, jobs, income, and a higher standard of living.

Measures for preserving forests and developing sound management practices and necessary restrictions on harvest practices and on exports have to come from the producing countries themselves and must be accepted by the industrialized nations. The industrialized nations cannot impose unilateral import prohibitions on the products of the Third World. Rather, unilateral export prohibitions—provided they are necessary for preserving the forest and thus protecting a nation's economy—belong among the measures spelled out in the Tropical Forestry Action Plan (see below) for the preservation of rainforests.

If tropical countries and industrialized countries want to utilize renewable resources from tropical forests as profitably as possible, then both the national and international markets for these products have to be developed. The International Tropical Timber Organization (ITTO), which acts as an outreach organ of the FAO, can work toward this end. In fact, wood export and the import of tropical woods actually contribute little to the destruction of rainforests, as the following figures show:

Latin America leads the world in destruction of rainforests (77 percent of the world's total), yet it holds only 6 percent of the international market in tropical wood export. Southeast Asia accounts for more than 80 percent of tropical wood exports, but only 7 percent of the tropical forest destruction. A country like Gambia has practically no timber economy worthy of mention and has never exported wood, yet its rate of tropical forest destruction exceeds that of every wood-exporting country in Africa.

The great importance of firewood to people in the tropics is often underestimated, and the use of wood as a relatively economical material in construction and housing is becoming increasingly significant in developing tropical countries. It can easily be forgotten in this regard that the demand for wood in heavily populated countries poor in forests can be met only by the exports of neighboring countries rich in forestland.

Along with the export component there is a great and constantly growing domestic demand. Some tropical countries that were wood exporters have actually put a stop to exports and become wood importers (e.g., Thailand and Nigeria). Domestic use of wood in tropical countries is estimated at 260 million cubic yards (200 million m³), and the total export of wood amounts to only 65 million cubic yards (50 million m³). It is necessary to examine the great differences in supply and demand from country to country to understand the problems of each individual country.

Support for the Tropical Forestry Action Plan (TFAP)

The TFAP is an international program sponsored by the UN Food and Agriculture Organization (FAO), the UN Development Programme (UNDP),

President George Bush proposed debt-for-nature swaps in his 1990 Enterprise for the Americas initiative.

the World Resources Institute, and the World Bank. Since 1985 the TFAP has been the best means of raising public, private, and governmental awareness of tropical deforestation, mobilizing donor support and coordination, and developing national forest sector plans. Efforts are now underway to reform the TFAP process so that better quality control, more attention to the environment, and greater participation by the local people may be ensured.

President Bush's 1991 budget includes a first-time request of $500,000 for the TFAP. This plan is supported by many OECD countries, along with 66 tropical forest countries. Although the proposed United States participation in the TFAP is commendable, the requested contribution is minimal when compared to, for example, that of Germany, which provides an annual contribution to the Plan of $150 million.

Support for a global forest agreement

A long-term strategy for securing the international cooperation needed to stop forest destruction in all areas—be they tropical, temperate, or boreal forests—is the Global Forest Agreement, or GFA. The GFA was the result of a series of international meetings, including the so-called "G-7" economic summit that took place in Houston, Texas, in July 1990. The seven participants at that meeting were

Italy, Germany, France, the United Kingdom, Canada, the United States, and Japan, and all endorsed the concept of a GFA.

Principal elements of the GFA would include: targets for conservation and reforestation, for biodiversity, and for sustainable forest management and agricultural practices; controls on development schemes as well as on fiscal policies and incentives that promote forest loss; forest monitoring through remote-sensing; trade issues; research; and debt swaps. These guiding principles and the general commitments inherent in the agreement could subsequently be developed into individual country-specific protocols that would deal with the pertinent problems and functions of various forests around the world.

Full adherence to and implementation of the GFA has, however, been delayed, in large part by the United States, which does not wish the GFA to be linked to a proposed global climate change convention (to be sponsored by the Intergovernmental Panel on Climate Change). This link is favored by many developing countries as well as by some of the "G-7" summit allies, most notably Germany.

At the present time, support for a forest agreement separate from a climate change convention is growing, and most countries favor a non-binding statement of principles, at least initially. Developing countries, however, do not wish to be rushed by the developed countries on the issue of preserving the tropical rainforests, and many developing countries are still suspicious of the U.S. motives in promoting a GFA separate from a climate convention; consequently, these countries may need to be coaxed to the negotiating table. Moreover, there seems to be a sense on the part of those nations critical of the U.S. position that it would be possible to use the

United States' interest in the forest agreement as a means of forcing this country to negotiate reductions in its emissions of greenhouse gases (particularly carbon dioxide) through such a climate convention.

Domestic Initiatives

Scientific theories (as well as the position taken by some developing countries as noted above) about the importance of the tropical rainforests as carbon dioxide "sinks" have led to a significant change in the way federal officials view forests within the boundaries of the United States. It is now realized that America's temperate forests, like the tropical rainforests, are valuable sinks for carbon-containing gases—not to mention their long-recognized value as wildlife habitats and sources of usable timber. Thus, U.S. forests have recently become prime candidates for reforestation and conservation programs such as the one President Bush unveiled in 1989—the "America the Beautiful" initiative.

This plan seeks to plant, improve, and maintain a billion trees a year within the United States. The Administration requested $175

million to launch the program, but in the 1990 Farm Bill, Congress allocated only $75 million for the program in the 1991 fiscal year. Although less than

Funding for U.S. forest and rainforest programs require Congressional approval.

hoped for, this funding has proved to be adequate to start the program, and regulations are being written and sites selected for target tree-planting locations. The bulk of the projected plantings will be on marginal farmland throughout the United States, with the purpose of preventing soil erosion; but urban, community, and wilderness forests are being targeted for increased reforestation as well. The federal government will subsidize participating farmers and others who agree to take on some

of the total cost of the program.

By the year 2030, assuming full Congressional funding for this program in the interim, it is projected that four to five percent of the U.S. carbon dioxide emissions will be absorbed by the billions of trees that will have been planted and grown to maturity as a result of the program. In addition, there will have been a marked increase—approximately 500,000 acres (200,000 ha) annually—in the U.S. forest acreage available for wildlife habitats, recreational activities, and other purposes.

In a parallel development, major revisions in the Clean Air Act designed to counteract the tree-blighting effects of acid rain were also made. Emissions of sulfur dioxide and nitrous oxide, gases considered key precursors of acid rain, are to be cut 10 million tons and 2 million tons respectively by the year 2000. Similar efforts by other developed countries around the world could add significantly to a positive environmental effect for the world's forests.

All Is Not Lost

In 1991 remote-sensing detected a slight decrease in the rate of destruction of

the rainforests. Only time will tell whether the decrease was a statistical or historical anomaly, or whether a new direction is being plotted. Yet even if this trend proves to be positive, it does not mean that our vigilance should be relaxed; the magnitude of the problem and the amount of destruction yet to come should not be minimized. There is some justification for optimism, however. World awareness of the problem of rainforest destruction is being constantly enhanced, national and international organizations are being developed, and a growing scientific understanding of the complex world of the rainforest is emerging. While raw materials are still important, the world economy is being transformed from material-based to information- and service-based, which will ultimately be less stressful on the world's resources.

One of the factors that is driving change is the continuing globalization of what were once national economies. With education—and some luck—a global ethic can be developed that will be more respectful of the earth.

Population growth remains a difficult problem, as does the unequal distribution of wealth as divided by historic political boundaries. The race has started between the rapid pace of destruction and a growing awareness of the earth's vulnerability and how little time we have to change course.

It has been less than a generation since we were first able to look back on the earth from space. This view of the green planet, our home, at once both smaller and more complex than we once saw it and yet without visible boundaries, has been forever changed in our conciousness. It is for all of us to transform this new vision into policies that protect the whole earth from the detrimental effects of technology power and our evergrowing numbers.

Rainforests are a treasure trove for botanists. Left alone, they are practically self-sustaining. As their plant diversity has become richer in the course of evolution, their nutrient cycles have become increasingly immune to losses.

One hectare of rainforest contains up to 800 tons of biomass. By contrast, the mixed forests of the eastern United States produce at most 150 tons.

Afterword

As the foregoing chapters have made clear, the rainforests of the world are extraordinary in many respects. Their lush and brilliant (though often hidden) beauty can delight the senses, and our sense of wonder is heightened by their complexity and mystery, as well as by the worldwide ecological role that they play. They make up only 7 percent of the land area of the world, yet they provide the only known natural home to over half of the plant and animal species on the earth.

The majority of people in the industrialized world understand that the rainforests are being systematically destroyed and that their destruction is a loss to the planet as a whole, not only to a single country or continent. Yet, for most of us, the rainforests are only a vague and perhaps somewhat romanticized image formed by scenes from old jungle movies, unsupported by first-hand experiences or precise written materials—and for good reason, for the rainforest is hard to know.

Although the number of people who live in or near the rainforests is sizeable, it is but a small fraction of the world's total population. The rainforests, after all, do not form one of the primary habitats of humans, and certainly not of those used to more industrialized settings. The vast numbers of different species of animals and plants—each in itself often relatively rare—and the complex ecology of this environment also adds to the difficulty of knowing and understanding the rainforests.

The superb photographs and detailed text presented here help to overcome some of the difficulties and begin to open at least a few of the hidden secrets of the rainforests to our view. The grand views and the intimate close-ups captured in this dramatic visual presentation provide a powerful introduction to this world that is so vital and yet so distant from most of us and leaves us, perhaps, with a better vision and greater understanding of its needs and its future.

Each chapter of the text is written by a different author. Although the chapters occasionally overlap in information and perspective and sometimes present conflicting points of view, they ultimately provide a diversity of ideas and material that, in combination, touch on all crucial facets of the rainforest.

Although steps for action must be taken now to save the valuable world resource that is the rainforest, it is too early to close off debate on the issues when creative and thoughtful solutions are still needed. It is hoped that this book can contribute to our general awareness of the rainforests, of the threat to them, and of their importance to life on earth. Our knowledge is constantly increasing, and through knowledgeable action we may yet be able to help save what remains of this glorious Garden of Eden.

Edward G. Atkins

ORGANIZATIONS CONCERNED WITH SAVING THE TROPICAL RAINFOREST

Artists United for Nature
Kunigundenstrasser 48
8000 Munich
Germany

Canadian Environmental
Network
P.O. Box 1289, Station B
Ottawa, Ontario K1P 543

Canadian Parks and
Wilderness Society
160 Bloor Street East
Toronto, Ontario M4W 1B9

Earthwatch
680 Mt. Auburn Street
Box 403B
Watertown, Massachusetts
02272

Environmental Defense Fund
257 Park Avenue South
New York, New York 10010

Friends of the Earth (USA)
218 D Street, SE
Washington, D.C. 20003

Global Tomorrow Coalition
1325 G Street, NW, Suite 915
Washington, D.C. 20005

Greenpeace
1436 U Street, NW
Washington, D.C. 20009

National Audubon Society
801 Pennsylvania Avenue, SE
Washington, D.C. 20003

National Geographic Society
17 & M Streets, NW
Washington, D.C. 20036

National Museum of
Natural History
Smithsonian Institution
Washington, D.C. 20008

National Wildlife Federation
1400 16th Street, NW
Washington, D.C. 20036

National Resources
Defense Council
40 West 20th Street
New York, New York 10011

The Nature Conservancy
1800 North Kent Street
Arlington, Virginia 22209

Probe International
225 Brunswick Avenue
Toronto, Ontario M53 2M6

Rainforest Action Information
Network
Box 75, University Center
University of Manitoba
Winnipeg, Manitoba R3T 2N2

Rainforest Action Network
301 Broadway, Suite A
San Francisco, California
94133

Rainforest Action Society
2150 Maple Street
Vancouver, British Columbia
V6J 3T3

Rainforest Alliance
270 Lafayette Street, Suite 12
New York, New York 10012

The Rainforest
Foundation, Inc.
1776 Broadway, 14th Floor
New York, New York 10019

Sierra Club
730 Polk Street
San Francisco, California
94109

Smithsonian Tropical
Research Institute
APO
Miami, Florida 34002

Survival International USA
2121 Decatur Place, NW
Washington, D.C. 20008

World Resources Institute
1735 New York Avenue, NW
Washington, D.C. 20037

World Wildlife Fund (Canada)
60 St. Clair Avenue East,
Suite 201
Toronto, Ontario M4T 1N5

World Wildlife Fund (USA)
The Conservation Foundation
1250 24th Street, NW
Washington, D.C. 20037

United Nations Environment
Programme
Room DC 2 - 0803
United Nations, New York
New York 10017

The Authors

Dr. Thomas Wassmann

Born 1945, studied botany and ecology at the universities of Münster and Kiel. He has made research trips to many tropical countries, conducting studies in taxonomy and biogeography. He has published numerous contributions in books and journals, and he is now working as a consultant to major environmental organizations.

Prof. Dr. Hans Joachim Fröhlich

studied forestry at the University of Göttingen and, later, biology. He completed his habilitation in the social science division of the University of Munich in 1967 and was also appointed to teach forestry. He developed the Institute for the Cultivation of Forest Plants. From 1968 to 1988 he directed the state forestry administration of Hessen, with responsibility for fisheries, wildlife, and nature protection. In this same period, he worked on many development projects in South America, Africa, and Asia, and on numerous research trips he became acquainted with the tropical zones of the Amazon, Central and East Africa, Australia, New Guinea, South Sea islands, and the Philippines.

Prof. Dr. Ernst Josef Fittkau

Born 1927, chair of the German Society for Tropical Ecology. After studying biology in Göttingen, Freiburg, and Kiel, he worked at the Max Planck Institute in Plön from 1954 to 1976. Since 1976 he has been the director of the zoological collection in Munich and a member of the faculty at the University of Munich. His special fields are aquatic entomology and the ecology of flowing water in the tropics. During his tenure at the Max Planck Institute, he conducted research in the Amazon region of Brazil.

Prof. Dr. Josef H. Reichholf

Born 1945, studied science with a major in zoology at the University of Munich. Since 1974 he has been a staff scientist at the state zoological collection in Munich, serving as director of the ornithology section and of the department for fauna and ecology. He teaches at both universities in Munich. He is the chair of the scientific advisory committee and a member of the executive committee and the board of the German chapter of the World Wildlife Fund, a member of the Commission on Ecology of the International Union for the Conservation of Nature (IUCN), a fellow of the Linnean Society in London and of the Royal Entomological Society of London as well as a Scientific Fellow of the Zoological Society of London. He has conducted research in the tropics of South America and Africa, especially in Brazil, and is the author of many books, among them *The Tropical Rain Forest, The Irreplaceable Jungle,* and *The Riddle of Human Evolution,* as well as of numerous scientific publications on tropical ecology.

Dr. Bruno P. Kremer

Born 1946, studied biology and chemistry at the University of Bonn. Many years of research on questions of ecological adaptation took him to many scientific institutions throughout the world. Since 1979 he has been teaching at the University of Cologne in the fields of organismic biology and nature preservation. He is the author of numerous books on natural history, writes serial broadcasts for the radio, and publishes contributions in scientific journals.

Dr. Bruno P. Kremer

B. Schmidbauer

Prof. J.H. Reichholf

Prof. E.J. Fittkau

Barbara Veit

Dr. Donald R. Perry

Olivia Newton-John

Prof. Fröhlich

Dr. Edward G. Atkins

Dr. Donald R. Perry

is a biologist, researcher, writer, and photographer. He spends a great deal of his time satisfying his insatiable curiosity about the hidden biological riches of the jungles and forests of the world. Perry has worked on many films about the wilderness and has published often in both scientific and popular journals. He is an environmental biologist with a special interest in the biological communities found in tropical rainforest canopies. In his book *Life above the Jungle Floor* he describes his experiences and discoveries in the crowns of rainforest trees.

Rolf Bökemeier

Born 1940, studied political science, spent three years in the Merchant Marine, studied to be a printer, and has been a journalist since 1968. He has worked for the magazines *Merian* and *stern* and has been an editor and reporter for *Geo* since 1976.

Prof. Dr. János Regös

Born 1940, studied biology at the University of Budapest. Now in Switzerland as a professor for tropical ecology, he took his doctorate in biochemistry and genetics and has devoted increasing amounts of his time since 1973 to ecology. Numerous research trips have taken him to Costa Rica, Brazil, and Peru, where he has written descriptions of the plant and animal worlds of this threatened paradise—the forest primeval.

Barbara Veit

Born in 1947, she studied political science and journalism, worked as an editor for the *Süddeutsche Zeitung,* and has been a freelance writer since 1977. Her main interests are the environment and the Third World. Her books *The Gentle Revolution: On the Necessity of Living Differently, The Environmental Book for Children, The Third World Book, The Book of Animal Protection,* and the mystery-book series *Scene of the Crime: Environment* have received considerable acclaim.

Bernd Schmidbauer

Retired school administrator, born 1939 in Pforzheim, studied physics, chemistry, and biology in Karlsruhe and Heidelburg. He has been a member of the German Bundestag since 1983; he is chair of the Bundestag's committee of inquiry on the protection of the earth's atmosphere and author of the committee's report on the rainforest (which was utilized in compiling "The Last Chance: A Global Starting Point for Saving the Rainforest").

Olivia Newton-John

in addition to her well-known career as singer and actress, is U.N. Goodwill Ambassador to the United Nations Environment Programme.

Dr. Edward G. Atkins

holds a PhD in Biological Sciences and a BS in Anthropology from Columbia University; he is a former member of the Columbia faculty, the author of several scientific journal articles, and editor of a number of popular science books. He is now executive editor for Children's Television Workshop in New York City, where he also served as director of content for the popular science show, 3-2-1 CONTACT, and as executive editor for award-winning specials on the rainforest, AIDS, garbage, water, and oil. Dr. Atkins's most recent publication, *Antarctica,* was produced by CTW for the National Science Foundation's Polar Institute.

The Master Photographers: The World's Green Conscience

by Ulrike Kaechelen

"We know more about the back side of the moon than we do about tropical rainforests," said famed U.S. tropical biologist Norman Myers recently. If the gaps in our knowledge are beginning to close at least bit by bit, the credit should go primarily to a handful of individualists who are as committed as they are courageous. In spite of many dangers and hardships, they have used their cameras to give us significant and also stunning insights into the complicated ecosystem of the earth.

On daring expeditions, surprised by jungle thunderstorms of elemental power and by poisonous snakes, hanging like circus trapeze

The stars among the international nature photographers travel hither and yon through the "green hell"....here, the French photographer Raphael Gaillarde uses a dirigible with its own landing platform.

A small group of nature photographers are constantly in search of interesting and exciting stories. They travel widely through the "green hell," using modes of transportation as exotic and adventuresome as the places where they work: With helicopters and mules, with Land Rovers and motorboats, with "cable cars" and dirigibles that have their own landing platforms they penetrate the as yet unexplored jungle wilderness.

Despite many dangers, Dieter and Mary Plage give us stunning insights into the jungle world.

Wolfgang Bayer...

on the lookout for exciting stories everywhere

In the forest canopy: Donald R. Perry

Bringing us staggering insights: Carsten Peter

On a high perch: Gertrud Neumann-Denzau

Uwe George, rainforest expert at *Geo*

Always ready to shoot: Hans D. Dossenbach

Hans Gerold Laukel on expedition

artists from thick lianas, diving with snorkles and wet suits in the swampy waters of mangrove forests that rise above the water like armies on stilts, squatting in tiny camouflage tents pitched high as church steeples in the crowns of jungle giants, and always motivated by an inexhaustibly curious spirit, they explore for us the last blank spots on the map of this planet we call home, much like those scientists and aristocratic adventurers of past centuries who set out to find the source of the Nile or explore the secret reaches of the Amazon. Between the leather bindings of Victorian books we can still admire their pictures today: In defiant poses, these heroes of their time look at us with sharp-eyed glances. There is no doubt that a journey into the unimaginably huge Amazon wilderness was the equivalent, in Darwin's or Alexander von Humboldt's time, to a modern astronaut's setting out for a distant planet without benefit of a protective space suit or radio contact with earth.

Helpful as the equipment and safety precautions of our modern photographers and filmmakers may be to an expedition into the unpeopled wilderness, there is still much that even the most refined technology cannot supply: a talent for improvisation, adaptability, patience, endurance, and knowledge of biology. And last but not least, a dash of luck is essential if we homebodies are to be delighted and astonished by photographic sensations from the depths of the jungle.

The best jungle reporters of the world have offered their photographic pearls for this volume, creating a monu-

We owe a good part of our knowledge of the life and behavior of animals in the tropical rainforests to committed nature photographers. Flash attachments, telescopic lenses, and sophisticated camera technology, along with endless patience and persistence, enable them to give us pictures from their rapidly disappearing Garden of Eden that are as intriguing as they are exciting.

Andre and Cornelia Bartschi—two experts with a passion for their calling

Rolf Bokemeier with rainforest Indians

A multitude of fantastic creatures lives in the tropical jungle. Honey-sweet nectar rains down from the blossoming treetops. Birds pollinate blossoms with their feet, and the forest echoes with their calls. Native hunters prepare the poison they use on their arrows from the skins of garishly colored frogs.

Michael Herzog and Sara Meyer

Endless patience: Konrad Wothe

Helmut Denzau on patrol

Daring and dangerous situations...

...are routine for Martin Wendler.

mental painting of this green cosmos. They convey to us at the same time the comforting assurance that untouched, magical, and exciting wilderness is still a living part of our earth. Their pictures reveal to us the unsolved riddles of the tropical rainforest, its fascinating mysteries and the dramas that play in its largely unexplored canopy, most of which are acted out unseen and unheard. They show us bizarre creatures from strange worlds, instruct us about the manifold, interlocking survival strategies of plants and animals, surprise us with scary yet fascinating encounters in the hot, steamy jungle labyrinth, introduce us to the shy nomadic peoples of an endangered paradise, and stir in us inklings of the age-old mysteries of a picture-book wilderness that is at risk today.

They have photographed for us cat-sized chameleons, the airy dance of hummingbirds, a crocodile's death in the embrace of a giant snake, flowers as huge as wagon wheels, carnivals of butterflies on the banks of the Rio Negro, a forest on stilts, fruits like cannon balls, metallic and

D. R. Perry climbs to the roof of the jungle

S. Dalton: high-speed photography

Loren A. McIntyre knows the Amazon basin well

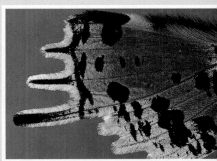

Skjell B. Sandved, photographer, filmmaker, and author, all rolled into one

Michael and Patricia Fogden live in their own rainforest.

The green of the tropical rainforest as seen from the air reveals itself, on closer inspection, to be a festival of color. The red macaws could well have taken flight from the palette of a Gauguin. The iridescent wings of this moth could be the inspiration of Tiffany's famous opalescent glass lamps.

Hans Werner Scheller, a gentle lyricist

Frans Lanting, a sharp observer

Gunter Ziesler, a close friend of the wilderness

iridescent beetles as large as clothing brushes, winged lizards reminiscent of prehistoric dragons, the green vampires of the plant world, colorful parrots whose feathers shimmer like the opalescent glass of Tiffany lamps, lizard-like iguanas that shoot up above the water, and the bromeliads that live, as it were, on a higher plane and have, in the truest sense of the word, lost touch with the ground.

The eyes of these star photographers see differently. They perceive light, shadow, and nuances of color where most people see only an object. Among them, there are hard-nosed reporters, lyricists who draw with soft lines, critics of our times, perfectionists who bring us microscopically clear photos even from cloud forests.

These are all gifted photographers. Thanks to their indefatigable and often risky commitment to their metier the fate of the tropical rainforests is now in the spotlight on the stage of world politics. These nature photographers are the green conscience of the world.

Photo Credits

Archive for Art and History, Berlin: 17 photos. Eric Bach, Superbild: 2. Andre and Cornelia Bartschi: 31. Karlheinz Baumann: 8. Wolfgang Bayer: 9. Bavarian State Library, Munich: 1. Helmut Bechtel: 3. Collection of Dr. Bezzel: 3. Bert Berkenstrater: 4. Pictorial Archives of the Prussian Cultural Collection: 5. Jonathan Blair, Woodfin Camp, Focus: 2. Frieder Blickle, Bilderberg: 1. Rolf Bokemeier: 3. Klaus Bossemeyer, Bilderberg: 1 Thomas Brodmann: 1. Hans Jurgen Burkard, Bilderberg: 5. James Carmichael, Jr., NHPA: 1. Bob and Clara Calhoun, Bruce Coleman, Inc.: 1. Alan Compost, Bruce Coleman, Inc.: 1. Alan Compost, Survival Anglia: 1. Stephen Dalton, NHPA: 5. Stephen Dalton, OSF, Okapia: 1. Kenneth A. Deitcher: 3. Hans D. Dossenbach: 23. From *Durin's Kafer*, Schirmer und Mosel Verlag, Munich: 2. Klaus E. Fiedler: 7. Focus: 2. Michael and Patricia Fogden: 44. P. M. L. Fogden, Okapia: 2. P. M. L. Fogden, Bruce Coleman, Inc.: 2. Reinhold Frech: 1. Peter Frey, The Image Bank: 7. Roger Gaillarde, Gamma: 2. Karl Geigl: 1. Uwe George: 8. Gerstenberg Archives: 2. Georg Gerster: 1. Sven Halling: 1. Robert Harding: 5. From Jakob Heckel, *Art Forms of Nature:* 1. Günther Helm: 2. Herzog and Meyer: 20. Carol Hughes, Bruce Coleman, Inc.: 1. Werner Kalthoff: 1. Erika Kanne: 1. Dmitri Kessel: 1. Anton Klein: 3. Rudolf König: 21. Stephen J. Krasemann, DRK Photo: 1. Harald Lange: 1. Frans Lanting, Minden Pictures: 10. Hans Gerold Laukel: 8. Jürgen Liepe: 8. From *Jungles*, Marshall Editions, Ltd., London: 3. Shinzo Maeda, The Image Bank: 1. Loren A. McIntyre: 11. Loren A. McIntyre, Woodfin Camp, Focus: 1. Ted Mead, Okapia: 1. Horst Munzig, Anne Hamann Agency: 1. Hans Peter Neuner: 1. New York Convention and Visitor's Bureau: 282. Gertrud and Helmut Denzau: 3. M. K. Nichols, Magnum, Focus: 4. Okapia: 1. Onyx: 2. Jurgen Partenscky: 2. Donald Perry, Camera Press: 2. Carsten Peter: 11. Manfred Pforr: 6. Oliver Piehl: 3. Fritz Poelking: 1. A. P. Price, Bruce Coleman, Inc.: 1. Pro Regenwald e. V., Munich: 1. Benoit Renevey: 2. Walter Rohdich: 1. Carl-W. Rohrig, Hamburg: 4 illustrations. Carmen Rohrbach: 1. E. S. Ross, California Academy of Sciences: 7. Kjell B. Sandved: 43. Frieder Sauer: 7. Frieder Sauer, Okapia: 1. Hans-Werner Scheller: 4. Günther Schumann: 2. Florian Siegert: 3. Achim Sperber: 2. Hans Sylvester, Focus: 4. Merlin D. Tuttle, Bat Conservation International: 3. David Unger: 5. The U.S. Capitol: 295. Alan Weaving, Ardea London: 1. Martin Wendler: 9. Weyerhaeuser: 288. The White House: 291, 294. Konrad Wothe: 9. Veronika Zanker: 11. Gunter Ziesler: 24. Library of the State Zoological Collection, Munich: 19 All the drawings at the ends of chapters are by Eckard Kruse, Munich. The illustrations on the title page, dust jacket, and in the book are by Carl-W. Röhrig.

As curiosity has been motivating more and more researchers to undertake journeys into the rain forests, graphic artists, too, have been falling under the spell of the tropical forest. The Hamburg artist Carl-W. Rohrig is among them, and one of the best among them. When the major magazines of the world (*National Geographic, stern,* or *Geo,* for example) or industrial firms whose works is scientifically related want to show nature in its purest form, they often call on this Munich-born artist. For this volume, too, "Pablo," as he is affectionately known to his friends, has demonstrated his remarkable talents once again. The illustrations on the front and back of the dust jacket and the picture on

these pages, showing a cloud-forest branch covered with moss, lichens, and bromeliads, are impressive examples of his much sought-after talent.

Much of what you see in this volume, on which a staff of authors and photographers, text and picture editors, graphic artists and lithographers, worked for almost a year before the best printers and bookbinders put it into its final form, required an extensive process of drafting and redrafting. The entire editorial staff found itself faced again and again almost every week with a new task when with an almost overwhelming array of choices, even more fascinating and sensational photographs arrived week after week. Sometimes we felt

The Pro Terra staff at work

we could almost smell the dankness of the cloud forests, so fresh were the photos these world-class photographers were delivering. The images we unearthed in libraries in order to publish, particularly in

the historical section of this book, some pictures with patina were also witnesses from another world (and we are particularly grateful for the assistance we received in this work from the State Zoological

Publication Data

English Translation © Copyright 1991
by Barron's Educational Series, Inc.
Published originally under the title *Der Garten Eden darf nicht sterben* by Pro Terra Bücher, Munich

Idea, conception, and overall production:
Kurt G. Blüchel
Editor in Chief: Dr. Bruno P. Kremer
Editor: Sonnhild Bischoff
Picture Editor: Ulrike Kaechelen
Graphics: Michael Bauer, Harald Britschgi
The article by Professor János Regös was taken from the book *The Green Hell—A Threatened Paradise*, with the kind permission of the publisher, Paul Parey Verlag, Hamburg.

The article "The Last Chance" and the accompanying illustrations are based on Bernd Schmidbauer's report for the Bundestag's committee on "Measures for the Protection of Earth's Atmosphere" and also on articles by Prof. Dr. Lutz Wicke, Dr. Hinrich L. Stoll, and Hans-P Repnik.

Translated from the German by Rita and Robert Kimber

All inquiries should be addressed to :
Barron's Educational Series, Inc.
250 Wireless Boulevard
Hauppauge, NY 11788

Library of Congress Catalog Card
No. 91-14919

International Standard Book
No. 0-8120-6246-9

Library of Congress Cataloging-in-Publication Data

Der Garten Eden darf nicht sterben.
  English Vanishing Eden: the plight of the tropical rainforest / Thomas Wassmann, et al; [translated from the German by Rita and Robert Kimber].
    p. cm.
  Translation of : Der Garten Eden darf nicht sterben.
  ISBN 0-8120-6246-9
  1. Rainforest ecology. 2. Rainforests.
3. Rainforest conservation.
4. Deforestation—Tropics. I. Kimber, Rita.
II. Kimber, Robert. III. Title
QH541.5.R27G3717 1991
333.75'137'0913—dc20
                                   91-14919
                                         CIP
Printed and Bound in Hong Kong

1234 2300 0987654321

Carl-W. Rohrig

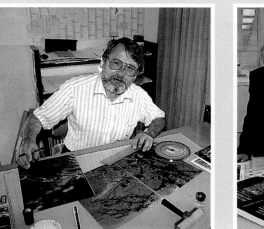

Graphics Designer Michael Bauer

Lithographers at work on *Vanishing Eden*

Collection in Munich under the direction of Professor Fittkau).
  For the North American edition, Edward G. Atkins, PhD, corrected the common and scientific nomenclature to reflect the most up-to-date usage in the United States and Canada. Dr. Atkins also amplified or replaced allusions based on distinctively European experience with comparable material that would be familiar to a North American audience. Thus, discussions of European forests were replaced by similar American examples. The graph on page 287 was also redone to show the American and Canadian financial contributions to the tropical forests. However, all of the other magnificent photographs and illustrations appear precisely as they did in the original Pro Terra edition.

Index

Boldface indicates illustrations